THE PROPERTY TAX
REVOLT

CENTER FOR REAL ESTATE AND URBAN ECONOMICS
University of California, Berkeley
Kenneth T. Rosen, Chairman

The Center for Real Estate and Urban Economics of the University of California at Berkeley was re-established in January 1979. Its research is directed toward improving understanding and encouraging innovation in the housing and mortgage finance systems, and providing detailed analysis of the urban and regional economy of California, as well as issues related to the real estate development process. An additional goal is the communication of research findings to both the public and private sectors, particularly those concerned with the allocation of urban land resources.

The Center sponsors both public lectures and professional conferences. Research findings are made available in books, working papers, and reprints from scholarly journals.

The research program is supported by contributions from the private and public sectors, and by the Real Estate Education and Research Fund, administered by the California Department of Real Estate.

THE PROPERTY TAX REVOLT
The Case of Proposition 13

edited by
GEORGE G. KAUFMAN
KENNETH T. ROSEN

BALLINGER PUBLISHING COMPANY
Cambridge, Massachusetts
A Subsidiary of Harper & Row, Publishers, Inc.

International Standard Book Number: 0-88410-693-4

Library of Congress Catalog Card Number: 81-1338

Printed in the United States of America

Library of Congress Cataloging in Publication Data

Main entry under title:

The property tax revolt.

  Includes index.
    1. Real property tax — California — Addresses, essays, lectures.
2. Local finance — California — Addresses, essays, lectures. I. Kaufman, George G. II. Rosen, Kenneth T. III. Title: Proposition 13.
HJ4191.P76   336.22'09794   81-1338
ISBN 0-88410-693-4   AACR2

CONTENTS

LIST OF FIGURES

LIST OF TABLES

PREFACE

A statewide property tax limitation initiative, known as Proposition 13 or the Jarvis–Gann initiative, was approved by California voters on June 7, 1978. The initative, which took effect on July 1, 1978, had the following key provisions. First, the maximum amount of any *ad valorem* tax on real property could not exceed 1 percent of the full cash value of the property. The one exception to this rule concerned any taxes used to pay the interest and redemption charges on any indebtedness approved by the voters prior to the passage of Proposition 13.

Second, in addition to limiting the rate of taxation on real property, the initiative defined the full cash value of the property in a quite restrictive way. Full cash value was defined as the county assessor's evaluation of real property as shown on the 1975–76 tax bill. If the property had been transferred since 1975, then the full cash value was defined as the market value at change in ownership.

Third, changes in the full cash value over time were limited to annual increases of 2 percent, with the exception, of course, of properties that were sold, in which case the full cash value became the market price.

Finally, Proposition 13 prohibited both state and local governments from imposing any additional *ad valorem* taxes on real property. It also prohibited the state from imposing *any* additional taxes without a two-thirds majority vote of the legislature and prohibited the cities, counties, and special districts from imposing additional taxes without a two-thirds majority vote of the electorate.

Quite clearly Proposition 13 encompassed a broad and fundamental change in the property tax system in California. It led the first year to an average cut in property tax receipts of over 50 percent, raising a number of interesting research issues for the astute political economist. First, one might ask why Proposition 13 occurred. Were there any systematic relations between votes for Proposition 13 and prior increases in property taxes and property values? Were there differential voting patterns based on households' economic and political characteristics?

Besides the political economy question, one can study the economic impacts of Proposition 13. Much of the preproposition debate centered on the potential overall impact on the California economy. Massive layoffs and a collapse of the local public sector were predicted. Proponents of the proposition predicted a construction boom and at the same time a slowdown in the transfer of existing properties. Also predicted were effects related to changes in California's municipal and state bond rating and future state and municipal spending patterns.

Because of the complexity of issues surrounding Proposition 13, this change in California's property tax system can be viewed on many different levels. The representative articles selected for this book attempt to address the social, political, and most importantly the economic aspects of this amendment. The purpose of this book, however, is not to espouse one argument over another nor to plead any causes or effects, but rather to present a sample of materials about the history and ramifications of Proposition 13 and provide a readily accessible source for those interested in studying the subject. This should be especially important in that the tax revolt in California has now spread to over a dozen states.

In Chapter 1, Jack Citrin and Frank Levy explain how, after a decade of failure, the antitax forces in California met with the sudden success of Proposition 13's passage. They analyze the intentions of the voters who passed both Proposition 13 and Proposition 4 and describe recent trends in public attitudes and government policies that bear on taxing and spending issues.

William H. Oakland's chapter describes the general fiscal climate that precipitated the formulation of Proposition 13. He addresses its implications by showing how much it has reduced the size and growth of public expenditure in California, and he speculates upon its future impact not only on public expenditure but on the overall revenue structure of California government.

A microeconomic analysis of Proposition 13 is presented in Chapter 3, by Frederick E. Balderston, I. Michael Heyman, and Wallace F. Smith, who explore the meaning of this legislation in respect to property turnover rates and its effect on the homeowner and rental markets as well as on nonresidential real estate. They discuss the effects the new market conditions will have on California households, business enterprises, and both governmental and public organizations.

The next four chapters are more detailed analyses of implications of Proposition 13. In Chapter 4, Ann R. Thomas examines the effects of fiscal limitations on municipal credit theoretically. She does this within a framework built upon previous empirical studies of municipal bond risk and financial theory. Summarizing her findings, she then extends them to the policy issues regarding access of California local governments to the credit market.

Ronald Forbes, Alan Frankle, and Philip Fischer elaborate on the relation of Proposition 13 and the municipal bond market in the next chapter. They empirically analyze interest rates on new issues of tax-supported bonds after Proposition 13 as compared to those preceding the amendment, then utilize this information to examine the efficiency of the municipal bond market.

Jack H. Beebe's contribution examines new-issue interest costs for different categories of California municipal bonds from 1977, when Proposition 13 was placed on the ballot, through March 31, 1979. The interest cost for new issues is used to provide estimates of the effects of Proposition 13 on the value of outstanding debt using an econometric model that explains statistically the interest cost of new issues. The model also estimates the overall effect of Proposition 13 as well as the individual effects of changes in bond ratings and the effects on the value of outstanding California municipal debt.

John E. Petersen analyzes the potential impact of Proposition 13 on big city finances in Chapter 7. Calculating various financial gaps caused by differential rates of growth in revenues and expenditures, he examines ways in which such gaps may be financed or in other ways closed. He thus provides insight into how the financial condition and operations of the governments of major cities might be influenced by the application of tax and expenditure constraints.

Robert Edelstein analyzes the tax-cutting measure in a small, general equilibrium model. His model produces some counterintuitive results concerning the capitalization and other economic consequences of Proposition 13.

In the final chapter, George Kaufman summarizes the scenario that led to the instigation of Proposition 13, ponders its long-term social and economic consequences, and postulates alternate solutions to the problems that precipitated its enactment as law.

These studies, undertaken at the early phase of Proposition 13's institution and focusing mainly on California should provide crucial insights to states as diverse as Idaho and Massachusetts that are considering or have enacted similar legislation to reduce the tax burden fundamentally. The most recent such limitation approved by voters is Massachusetts's Proposition 2½, which limits property taxes to 2½ percent of real property value (a cut of 26 percent).

Adverse consequences of similar measures in other states must be considered, for they might be quite severe because the large state monetary surplus, which made for a relatively smooth transition in California, is not available in most other states. This state surplus was, to some degree, the cause of the tax revolt in California, as well as the cushion that prevented the disaster predicted by many opponents of Proposition 13. The consequences of the California initiative should be of much value to analysts in those states considering or having recently enacted similar initiatives.

Kenneth T. Rosen

1 FROM 13 TO 4 AND BEYOND
The Political Meaning of the Ongoing Tax Revolt in California

Jack Citrin and Frank Levy

After failing at the polls in 1968, 1972, and 1973, the movement to cut taxes and limit public spending in California achieved notable successes in 1978 and 1979. In June 1978 the electorate passed Proposition 13, the Jarvis–Gann initiative. This measure contained the following elements:

1. The full cash value of each property is set equal to the property's cash value in 1975 or at the time of the property's last sale, whichever comes later.

2. As long as a property is retained by the same owner, its full value can increase by no more than 2 percent per year. At time of sale, the property can be revalued based on actual market price.

3. The combined property taxes of all jurisdictions must be limited to 1 percent of a property's full cash value. (In 1977, California property taxes averaged about 2.6 percent of market valuation.)

Portions of this paper are drawn from F. Levy's "On Understanding Proposition 13," *Public Interest* 56 (Summer 1979) and J. Citrin's "Do People Want Something for Nothing?" *National Tax Journal* 32, no. 2 (June 1979). The California Poll surveys analyzed in this paper were conducted by the Field Institute and made available through the State Data Program, University of California, Berkeley. The authors gratefully acknowledge the valuable assistance provided by Eric Smith and Lyn Richards in the preparation of this paper.

4. Any general tax increase requires a two-thirds vote in the state legislature (rather than the majority vote previously required). Local governments may not increase *ad valorem* taxes and may increase other taxes only with the approval of a two-thirds majority of the relevant electorate.

The implementation of Proposition 13 reduced property tax revenues by an estimated $7 billion in a single year. Property taxes in California fell from a level more than 50 percent above the national norm in fiscal 1977–78 to a level 35 percent *below* the national average in 1978–79 (California Roundtable 1979).

In November 1979, the voters turned from reducing taxes to limiting spending. By a majority of 74 percent to 26 percent the electorate passed Proposition 4, an amendment to the state constitution drafted by Paul Gann. This measure limits the allowable growth in appropriations made by state and local governments from fiscal year 1980–81 on, to the percentage increase in the cost of living and the percentage increase in either the state's or localities' population. Proposition 4 defines the initial base for allowable public expenditures as the sum of all appropriations initially available for expenditure during fiscal year 1978–79 that were financed from the "proceeds of taxes." It also requires that the revenues in excess of the annual appropriation limit be returned to taxpayers within two fiscal years of collection. Another popular initiative proposed by Howard Jarvis threatened to restrict further the state's fiscal powers. This proposal to cut the state's individual income tax rates by one-half was defeated by a wide margin, however. The passage of Propositions 13 and 4 signifies a major shift in the locus of authority over the budgetary process. Lacking trust in the willingness or capacity of their elected representatives to limit the growth of taxes and spending, voters in California, as in Michigan and several other states, seem prepared to place government in a fiscal straitjacket, if not a noose. Both government and business are in the early stages of adjusting to life in the era of plebiscitary budgeting, so it would be premature to speculate much about the long-run consequences of Propositions 13 and 4. Instead, the purposes of this study are (1) to explain the sudden success of the antitax forces in California after a decade of failure; (2) to analyze the intentions of voters in passing Propositions 13 and 4; and (3) to describe recent trends recent trends in public attitudes and government policies bearing on the taxing and spending issues.

Our argument is that strong resentment over high taxes and disenchantment with government in general coexists with continued public support for the maintenance or expansion of specific government services. The ability of California to provide substantial tax relief to property owners without significantly reducing government expenditures or public employment has rested on the existence of a massive surplus in the state treasury. Should the surplus shrink substantially due to the combined effects of fiscal relief to local governments, a slowdown in the state's economy, and changes in the tax code, the public will no longer be able to postpone the trade-off between taxes and services.

THE CAUSES OF PROPOSITION 13

The story behind the recent tax revolt in California and the success of Proposition 13 is by now familiar (Levy 1979, Oakland 1979), so we shall confine ourselves to a brief summary of the highlights. The main protagonists are Reform, Inflation, Public Cynicism, and Political Ambition. Reform in the name of good government is responsible for the system of property tax assessment that prevailed in California before the passage of Proposition 13. In 1965 it was revealed that elected tax assessors, most notably Russell Wolden of San Francisco, were receiving "campaign contributions" to "review and adjust" assessments on business properties. Spurred by the outcry over this scandal, the legislature passed a bill (AB 80) in 1967 that required communities to reassess all property at 25 percent of market value (the single roll) within three years and then to conduct subsequent reassessments with sufficient frequency to keep the ratio intact. The immediate result of these reforms, neither anticipated nor intended by voters, was to *increase* the assessment for homeowners. For despite the special treatment of some commercial properties, business as a whole had usually been assessed at a higher ratio of market value than single-family housing (Paul 1979). The application of the uniform ratio of 25 percent to all property therefore meant that homeowners had to assume a greater share of the burden if the overall level of property tax revenues was to be maintained. And, because residental property tends to be resold more quickly and assessors employ sales prices to establish the market value of "similar" properties, shortening the reassessment cycle added to the relative burden of homeowners vis-à-vis business. Under AB 80's reforms, property tax assessment became a nondiscretionary, administrative function; in the 1970s, as a result, "political discretion could not act as a buffer between homeowners and inflation" (Levin 1979:14).

The property tax increases engendered by reform in 1976 led quickly to a ballot measure calling for relief. Philip Watson, the Los Angeles County tax assessor, sponsored an initiative in 1968 that required that property tax revenues be used for property-related services only and that the state government assume the responsibility for such "people-related" services as education, health, and welfare. More important, property taxes could not exceed 1 percent of a property's current market value. The Watson initiative was opposed by the leaders of both major parties, including Governor Reagan, and lost by a two-to-one margin in November 1968. The defeat of this and a renewed effort by Watson in 1972 to use the initiative method to sharply reduce property taxes was due to the confluence of many factors: the ability of the state's leaders to agree on a rival, if more limited, approach to tax relief, the homeowner's exemption; bipartisan arguments that Watson's proposals meant a tax shift rather than a tax cut, since it would require increases in state income and sales taxes to pay for valued services; a modest rate of inflation in home values and assessments; public optimism about the general state of the economy; and a lack of widespread hostility to government spending. Under these circumstances, voters opted for the slice of tax relief prepared by their elected representatives rather than the loaf cooked up by Watson and his followers. In 1978, however, these conditions no longer prevailed.

Inflation prepared the ground for the new campaign against property taxes. Beginning in 1974–75 there was an unparalleled boom in the market for single-family homes in California. Prices in the San Francisco area, for example, grew by an annual rate of approximately 18 percent between 1973 and 1978; the more populous Los Angeles area experienced even faster growth (Oakland 1979:390). The procedures governing tax assessment ensured that the rise in real estate values was registered in one's tax bill. The average rate of growth in assessments was similarly high, reaching 28.9 percent per year in San Bernardino County and 30.1 percent per year in Orange

County for 1973-76 (Levy 1979:20). To illustrate the dramatic effect of such rapid inflation, the property tax bill on a $45,000 home in Los Angeles would have risen from $1,160 in 1973-74 to $2,070 in 1976-77, an increase of 80 percent over three years. Thus, property taxes in California, already high relative to the rest of the nation, escalated rapidly in the years immediately preceding the vote on the Jarvis-Gann initiative.

It is important to note that the sharp rise in real estate values was concentrated in the market for single-family housing. According to estimates made by the State Board of Equalization, the value of all owner-occupied single-family homes rose by an average annual rate of 12.8 percent between 1973 and 1976, while the average annual growth rate in the value of all other (mainly commercial) property on the rolls increased by approximately 7.6 percent. Because different kinds of property are taxed at the same rate, this differential rise in assessed valuation meant that the homeowner's share of the property tax burden grew—from 31.6 percent of total property tax receipts in 1973-74 to 31 percent in 1977-78 (Oakland 1979:379).

The operation of the uniform tax rate, combined with the difference in the growth rates for single-family and commercial property values, also helps explain the failure of local governments to lower their tax rates to offset the sharp increases in assessed valuation (Levy 1979). Between fiscal years 1974 and 1978, the average combined property tax rate in California fell from $11.24 to $10.68, a drop of only 1.3 percent per year. During the same period, local government expenditures grew by an average of 9.4 percent in per capita terms. Since the Consumer Price Index grew by an average annual rate of 8.1 percent, local government was gaining against inflation, but by less than 2 percent a year. But even if local governments had attempted merely to keep pace with inflation, the nature of the market for real estate would have necessitated a disproportionate rise in the tax bills of homeowners in order to avoid a substantial loss in revenues. Institutional factors and economic conditions thus created a context in which numerous homeowners faced escalating property tax bills without a corresponding rise in their income. Under such circumstances, Proposition 13 had a ready constituency.

Inflation contributed in other ways to the fiscal climate in California preceding the vote on Proposition 13. The total state and local tax burden in California is high compared to that in the rest of the nation; in 1976-77, for example, only Alaska, surely a special case, and New York had higher per capita taxes. Moreover, all state taxes grew rapidly between 1973 and 1978. Total state taxes rose by 88.6 percent. The largest increase was in personal income taxes. As money incomes rose, California's steeply progressive income tax subjected some residents to the tax for the first time and boosted others into higher brackets. As a result of inflation, therefore, income tax payments increased more rapidly than incomes; indeed, from 1973–74 to 1977–78 the average state income tax taken per $1,000 of personal income increased from $16 to $27, or 65 percent. During this period inflation provided the state treasury with a bonus of an estimated $4.5 billion in income taxes, thereby contributing to the surplus that figured so prominently in the implementation of Proposition 13 (California Roundtable 1979:5). What must be stressed, however, is that the vote on the Jarvis–Gann initiative occurred in the context of a high and rising level of state taxation. Proposition 13 went beyond its predecessors by requiring that a two-thirds majority of the legislature approve any new taxes, thereby enhancing its appeal to voters who would not themselves benefit from property tax relief but who were angry about the amount of other taxes they paid. And survey data indicate that antagonism toward the size of the tax burden was growing. In 1963, a Harris Poll found that 49 percent of the public thought their own taxes were too high; by 1976, fully 72 percent felt this way (Citrin 1979:114).

Other relevant polls depict widespread cynicism about the operation of government at all levels. One important manifestation of this disenchanted mood was the emergence of a majority belief that government rather than business or labor is mainly to blame for inflation. Another is that between 1968 and 1978 the proportion of Americans who believed government wastes "a lot" of the money paid in taxes rose from 47 percent to 78 percent; belief in the reliability, credibility, and competence of public officials registered a decline of the same magnitude (Citrin 1979).

Between 1973 and 1978 growing anger over high taxes and mistrust of government had created a climate favorable to cuts in the public sector. And although, as will be pointed out in detail later, public opposition to government spending *in general* coexisted with support for maintaining or increasing the state's budgetary commitment in numerous areas of social policy, the pervasive conviction that government is wasteful and inefficient meant that people often believed that taxes could be cut without reducing services. On the eve of the vote on Proposition 13, fully 38 percent of the California electorate felt that state and local governments could provide the same level of services with a 40 percent reduction in their budget. With such cynicism, warnings that the impact of Proposition 13 on public services and employment would be disastrous were easily rejected as false and self-serving. Moreover, as the campaign came increasingly to be portrayed as a struggle of the people against the politician and bureaucrat, voting in favor of Proposition 13 provided a handy vehicle for expressing frustration with government for reasons unrelated to the property tax.

The failure of state government to provide tax relief before 1978 was an important cause of the public's disillusionment with its leaders. In fact, Jarvis and Gann began circulating petitions for their initiative only after the legislature's efforts to pass a property tax relief bill during its 1977 session collapsed in an atmosphere of acrimony and disarray. These efforts foundered on disagreements among liberal legislators, their conservative counterparts, and Governor Jerry Brown over the amount of tax relief and the extent to which it should be directed to low- and moderate-income families. Uncertainty about the size of the state surplus made it difficult to agree on how much tax relief to provide. And with statewide elections approaching, how to apportion political credit for a tax cut became a bitterly contested issue. Specifically, Republican state legislators suspected Governor Brown of having allowed the state surplus to accumulate in order to be able to provide a tax rebate at the time of his campaign for reelection. Their interest in thwarting the governor's political ambition made them reluctant to accept compromise proposals for tax relief that Brown would be willing to sign. On the Democratic side, meanwhile, the governor's long-standing aloofness from the legislature reduced his ability to force a consensus between the liberal and the conservative members.

Finally, in early 1978, the specter of Proposition 13's passage elicited legislative action. After much squabbling, the Behr bill emerged. It proposed a property tax cut about half the size that Jarvis and Gann would require and created the opportunity for the state to tax residential and commercial properties at different rates. This measure appeared on the June 1978 ballot as Proposition 8. It was bitterly attacked by Howard Jarvis as a cruel hoax that represented yet another attempt of the politicians to deny citizens a tax cut. And when Los Angeles County released its 1978–79 assessment figures in

May and revealed that the total value of the property tax rolls had increased by 17.5 percent even though only one-third of the properties had been assessed, Proposition 13's victory was assured and the campaign against it crumbled. The determination to place a lid on property taxes that seemed on an inexorable growth curve overrode any concern about the risks of severely constraining the government's fiscal powers.

SOURCES OF VOTER SUPPORT
FOR PROPOSITION 13

In June 1978, 66 percent of the voting age population in California were registered to vote, 69 percent of those who were registered voted on Proposition 13, and 65 percent of the voters supported it. But although those who favored the Jarvis–Gann initiative constituted only 28.3 percent of the eligible electorate, the outcome of the vote cannot be termed unrepresentative. A California Poll conducted shortly after the election indicated that 62 percent of those who had not registered to vote favored Proposition 13, as did 57 percent of those who were registered but had abstained.

Group differences in support for Proposition 13 did exist: Owners were more favorable than renters, whites than blacks, Republicans than Democrats. What is more striking, however, is the widespread appeal of the Jarvis–Gann initiative to most social and political strata in California. Table 1–1 compares the results of surveys conducted just before the elections on the Watson initiative in 1968, Proposition 13 in 1978, and Proposition 4 in 1979. These data show that Proposition 13 won majority support among virtually every subgroup of the electorate. Among renters 47 percent voted for the measure and only blacks were, as a group, strongly opposed. Table 1–1 also indicates a continuing across-the-board shift toward increased support for cutting taxes and limiting public expenditures between 1978 and the present. Blacks were the only group to be more favorable to the Watson initiative than to Proposition 13, but one year later they too expressed majority support for Proposition 4.

The idea of self-interest is a natural starting point for analyzing variations in support for tax and spending limitation measures. A self-interest theory assumes that people decide where to stand on such issues by calculating the trade-offs between taxes paid and gov-

Table 1-1. Social and Political Basis of Support for Tax and Spending Limitation.

	Watson Initiative 1968[a]	Proposition 13 1978[a]	Proposition 4 1979[b]
Residential status			
Owners	42%	69%	73%
Renters	42	47	61
Income[c]			

1968	1978-79			
$0-5,000	$0-10,000	41	53	52
5-10,000	10-20,000	43	58	69
10-15,000	20-30,000	39	67	74
15,000+	30,000+	44	65	69

	Watson Initiative 1968[a]	Proposition 13 1978[a]	Proposition 4 1979[b]
Education			
Less than high school	37	67	67
High school/trade school	47	67	74
1-2 years college	49	64	70
3-4 years college	41	64	69
Advanced Degree	22	51	57
Race			
White	41	66	70
Black	51	18	58
Party registration			
Democrat	39	55	61
Republican	45	74	79
Ideological self-designation			
Liberal	31	42	57
Moderate	34	61	76
Conservative	52	74	76

a. Cell entries are the percentage who voted yes.

b. Cell entries are the percentage favoring the Gann initiative.

c. The income classifications differ for 1968 and the two later years.

Source: California Polls of October 1968, June 1978, and August 1979.

ernment services received and then acting to maximize their personal utilities. Group differences in preferences are hypothesized to reflect the social allocation between these costs and benefits.

We have already described the economic conditions and institutional factors that focused popular resentment upon the property tax. Clearly, homeowners, other things being equal, would gain directly from the massive relief promised by Jarvis–Gann. By the same token, public employees and heavy consumers of government services would be victimized if the passage of Proposition 13 were to lead, as many officials predicted, to painful cutbacks in the public sector. The election results clearly indicate the operation of these perceptions of self-interest. A survey conducted by the *Los Angeles Times* on election day indicated that 81 percent of homeowners without a state or local government employee in their household favored Proposition 13 compared to only 28 percent of the much smaller bloc of voters who rented their homes and did include a public employee in their households. Similarly, the intense opposition of black voters to Proposition 13 can be partly attributed to their interest in the continued growth of the public sector as a source of both employment and services.

Additional data underscore the importance of anticipated tax savings as a motivation for supporting Proposition 13. In August 1978, before property owners had received their first post-13 tax bills, the California Poll asked a representative sample of California residents to indicate the amount they believed they would save as a result of the passage of Jarvis–Gann. Table 1-2 shows that only 8 percent

Table 1-2.   Anticipated Tax Savings and Support for Proposition 13.

	$0	$1-199	$200-399	$400-999	$1,000+
Amount of Tax savings due to 13[a]	8% (n = 47)	23% (n = 119)	31% (n = 161)	21% (n = 110)	16% (n = 84)
Yes on 13 vote among owners[b]	49% (n = 16)	50% (n = 56)	77% (n = 87)	81% (n = 61)	83% (n = 54)

a. Proportions of all homeowners in the state.

b. Proportions of owners in a particular perceived savings category who voted in the June 1978 election.

Source: California Poll, August 1978.

of homeowners did not expect to realize any property tax savings, whereas 37 percent estimated they would save at least $400. And support for Proposition 13 increased with the size of one's anticipated tax reduction. For example, 82 percent of the homeowners who expected a tax savings of more than $1,000 voted for the Jarvis–Gann initiative compared to 49 percent of those who anticipated no property tax relief. Moreover, the relatively slight positive relation between income and approval of Proposition 13 reported in Table 1-1 was due largely to the higher level of homeownership among upper income groups. Among homeowners, being better off had no significant influence on support for Proposition 13. For example, among both the owners earning from $10,000 to $15,000 a year and those with an annual family income of more than $30,000, 69 percent voted for Jarvis–Gann.

In a previous study (Citrin 1979), probit analysis was employed to estimate citizen demand for public goods, using both social background factors and political identifications as predictors of three dependent variables: the vote on Proposition 13, the vote on Proposition 8 (the rival and more limited tax reform package produced by the legislature and Governor Brown), and expressed preferences for the level of public spending.

Table 1-3 reproduces the equations that predict the vote on the two tax relief measures.[1] The demographic variables included as predictors were race (on the assumption that blacks and Mexican-Americans rely more heavily than whites on services provided by local government and would be more likely to oppose a tax cut that would threaten the curtailment of such services), age, (control for life-cycle effects), level of education, income, and residential status. The indicators of political ethos included were the self-designation of respondents (in the June 1978 California Poll survey) as liberals, conservatives, or middle-of-the-roaders and party registration, on the grounds that Democrats are socialized to approve of an expansive role for the public sector in social policy and that the party's leaders were united in opposition to Proposition 13.

The results confirm that homeowners at all levels of income were more likely than renters to see themselves as benefiting from the property tax cut promised by Proposition 13. Interestingly though, homeowners were more likely than renters to *oppose* Proposition 8, apparently preferring to risk no tax cut at all to getting only half of what Jarvis–Gann promised. Indeed, the tendency for Proposi-

Table 1-3. Multivariate Analysis of Vote on Propositions 13 and 8.

Independent Variables[a]	Probit Coefficients and Standard Errors			
	Vote on			
	Proposition 13		Proposition 8	
	MLE	SE	MLE	SE
Home ownership	.30[b]	.12	−.23[c]	.11
Age	.01	.04	−.05[c]	.03
Education				
9–11 years	.04	.41	−.05	.36
High school graduate	−.24	.38	−.06	.34
1–2 college	−.34	.38	−.09	.34
3–4 college	−.41	.38	.28	.34
5+ college	−.84[c]	.39	.69[c]	.35
Income				
$ 7–10,000	−.35	.25	.54[b]	.19
10–15,000	−.13	.23	.31[d]	.17
15–20,000	.10	.23	−.06	.17
20–30,000	.22	.23	−.11	.16
30,000+	.25	.23	−.09	.17
Race				
Black	−1.27[b]	.28	.50[c]	.24
Hispanic or Asian	−.15	.19	.25	.18
Democratic registration	−.25[c]	.11	.18[c]	.09
Ideology	−.20[b]	.05	.15[b]	.04
Constant	1.10[b]	.44	−.43	.39
Estimated R^2	.25		.19	
N	911		911	

a. The votes on Propositions 8 and 13 are scored yes = 1 and no = 0. The independent variables are scored as follows: Age is scored 1 = 18–25; 2 = 26–35; 3 = 36–45; 4 = 46–55; 5 = 56–65; and 6 = 66 and older. Ideology is scored 1 = "strong liberal"; 2 = "moderately liberal"; 3 = "middle-of-the-road"; 4 = "moderately conservative"; and 5 = "strongly conservative." The remaining variables are dummy variables, all of which are scored "1" if the respondent is in the category named and "0" if not.

b. $p < 0.01$.

c. $0.01 > p < 0.05$.

d. $0.05 > p < 0.10$.

Source: California Poll, June 1978.

tions 13 and 8 to be viewed as antithetical was pervasive. Being a liberal, black, a Democrat, or college-educated boosted the probability one would vote no on 13 and yes on 8.

That the victory of Proposition 13 embodied the collective resentment of California's homeowners against sharply escalating property taxes is indisputable. Clearly, one message voters intended to send government was "Cut Taxes!" But as Table 1-3 shows, long-standing political predispositions such as party identification and ideological outlook as well as economic self-interest influenced support for the Jarvis–Gann initiative. This suggests we should probe further for additional meanings of the vote on Proposition 13. For example, was the election's outcome a manifestation of mass alienation from government per se? More important, was the revolt against high taxes also a protest against the current level and pattern of public spending?

We have already cited evidence of the widespread belief among Californians that government is wasteful. The June 1978 California Poll found that 89 percent believed the federal government was inefficient in its use of public funds; the comparable figures for state, county, and city governments were 69, 70, and 62 percent, respectively. Ironically, the federal government, which benefited from Proposition 13's impact on the total volume of property tax deductions from federal income taxes, had the least favorable public image. And despite the fact that Proposition 13 was directed primarily at the fiscal powers of local governments and school boards, as Table 1-4 shows, negative judgments about the efficiency of the federal government had the strongest association with support for the initiative. More striking, however, is the high level of support for Proposition 13 even among those who believed state and local governments to be efficient.

A similar pattern emerges when we examine the effect on voting behavior of opinions about the right level of public spending. People are understandably more willing to consume public services than to pay for them. Thus, despite widespread complaints about the amount of overall government spending, the public frequently favors maintaining or increasing expenditures for numerous classes of particular programs. Surveys conducted just before and just after the vote on Proposition 13 showed that California residents tended to favor *more* rather than *less* spending on police and fire departments, mental health programs, and education, while demanding cuts in spending

Table 1-4. Attitudes toward Government Efficiency and
Proposition 13 Vote.

	Percentage for Proposition 13	
Level of Government	Government Inefficient	Government Efficient
Federal	70[a]	31
State	68	44
County	69	49
City	68	54
School boards	70	48

a. Figures are the proportion of votes yes on 13 among respondents who viewed a particular level of government as inefficient or efficient, respectively.
Source: The California Poll, June 1978.

only in the areas of welfare and the government's own administrative
services (Citrin 1979). This pattern of preference conforms closely to
that provided by nationwide surveys in recent years: Programs whose
benefits are available to everyone, including the middle-class taxpayer, are more widely approved than those with specialized clien-
teles mainly comprising the poor and black. The irony, of course, is
that universal access to the programs that are favored makes them
expensive.

As Table 1-5 shows, there is an empirical correlation between the
belief that public spending should be reduced and support for Proposition 13. Leaving aside the important question of the direction of
causal influence, for it is quite plausible that some citizens decided to
vote for Proposition 13 simply to obtain lower taxes and then ration-
alized their choice by advocating reduced spending, the data indicate
that whatever the domain of expenditure one considers, supporters
of the Jarvis–Gann initiative were more likely than its opponents to
favor cutbacks.

It is noteworthy, however, that the difference in the preferences
for public spending of these two voting blocs are often quite small
and that, even among those who approved Proposition 13, advocates
of reduced spending were in the minority for most policy domains.
In other words, Proposition 13 enjoyed substantial support among
those who favored maintaining public expenditure at their current
rate or even increasing them. The status quo group comprised a
majority of the public in nine of the fifteen spending areas listed in

Table 1-5. Advocacy of Less Public Spending and Support for Proposition 13.

	Percentage Favoring Spending Cuts		
Domain of Spending	Total Sample	Voting Yes on 13	Voting No on 13
Higher education	27[a]	35	14
Public schools	27	32	11
Welfare	66	80	48
Medical care	30	36	19
Parks and recreation	24	30	14
Police	4	9	6
Highways	25	27	21
Prisons	17	21	12
Mental health	11	16	4
Environmental protection	40	49	22
Fire	6	8	3
Public transportation	27	35	15
Public housing	47	53	30
Courts	28	33	19
Government administration	73	80	62

a. These figures represented the proportion responding "less" when asked, "Do you think that state and local government should spend more, the same amount, or less of tax money in this area?"

Source: The California Poll, June 1978.

Table 1-5 and contributed heavily to the victory of Jarvis-Gann. Indeed, voters who favored spending cuts in only four or fewer policy areas (including the universally unpopular administrative spending area) made up 58 percent of the electorate—fully half supported the antitax proposal. And among those who favored more spending in at least three areas, 47 percent voted to curtail local government's fiscal powers drastically. The passage of Proposition 13 therefore did not depend on the presence of a large body of voters demanding across-the-board cuts in government spending and services. Its victory represented a cry for lower taxes and more arguably for less spending, but not for fewer government services.

Analysis of public opinion about the desirable level of government spending in selected areas of policy concluded that political ethos had a persistent influence on expressed preferences for increased expenditure (Citrin 1979). As might be expected, self-identified liberals and Democrats were consistently more favorable to a high level of government services; less obviously, however, indicators of economic self-interest such as income, homeownership, and occupation had weak and irregular effects. One plausible explanation for this contrast between the predictors of responses to spending issues and tax referenda (see Table 1-3) is that the informational contexts in which these choices are embedded systematically differ.

More specifically, what may be crucial in determining popular choice is the degree of certainty with which one can estimate the personal costs and benefits of a proposed change in the level of taxes or spending. In the case of Proposition 13, it was easier to accurately estimate one's gains from lower property than one's losses from a hypothetical reduction in government services. In general, public consciousness of taxes is likely to be more widespread than awareness of the content of government expenditures. When one is asked about the desirable level of public spending to deal with a widely recognized problem, ignorance of the nature of current expenditures and the programmatic character of any change makes it hard to know where one's self-interest lies. Under these circumstances, it is not surprising that voters are guided by their general attitudes toward a distant objective rather than by their immediate economic situation.

In an additional test for the influence of a person's tax liability on his choices on taxing and spending issues, we combined information about the background and attitudes of individual voters with data about the actual taxing and spending behavior of their local governments. Using the zip codes of respondents in the August 1978 California Poll to locate them in the appropriate county, city, and school district jurisdictions, we were able to identify the tax rate to which they were subjected and the pattern of expenditures within the relevant jurisdictions from official government documents (*Financial Transaction Yearbooks for California Counties, Cities, and School Districts*). Table 1-6 presents the results for an initial set of models. The dependent variables are self-reported vote on Proposition 13 and opinions about the right amount of spending on public schools and welfare; once again, the estimates were derived by probit analysis techniques.

Equation (I) of the table indicates that the higher the overall property tax rate in a locality, the more likely voters were to favor Propo-

Table 1-6. Impact of Local Taxes and Spending on Voter Choices.[a]

	Vote on Proposition 13 Equation (I)			Preferences for Public Schools Spending[c] Equation (II)			Preferences for Welfare Spending[c] Equation (III)		
Independent Variables	Probit Coefficient	MLE/SE[b]	Independent Variables	Probit Coefficient	MLE/SE	Independent Variables	Probit Coefficient	MLE/SE
Party registration	-.204	-2.20	Black	.218	.658	Black	.707	2.24
Ideology	-.284	-6.97	Hispanic	.142	.817	Party registration	.344	2.79
Black	-1.19	-4.81	Party registration	.126	1.09	Ideology	.123	2.18
Residential status	.432	4.23	Ideology	.112	2.15	Residential status	-.459	-3.65
Income	.009	2.00	Child under 18 in home	.468	4.68	Percent black in locality	.032	3.87
Combined local property tax rate	.044	2.66	Some high school	.257	.808	Welfare expenditure (in $1,000s)	-.00001	-.672
Constant	.409	1.94	High school graduate	.307	1.1	Combined local property tax rate	-.102	-3.25
			Some college	.272	.960	Constant	.0114	.035
			College graduate	.208	.720	μ_2	1.18	.07
			Postgraduate	.289	.983			
			Residential status	-.566	-4.68			
			Local school expen./child	-.092	-.559			
			Combined local property tax rate	-.007	-.301			
			Constant	.753	1.598			
$(n = 943)$			μ_2	1.63	.09	$(n = 548)$		
			$(n = 478)$					

a. These figures are the probit coefficient divided by its standard error and may be viewed as the equivalent of the t-coefficient in OLS. Proposition 13 vote is coded: yes = 1, no = 0. Spending preferences are coded: more spending = +1, the same = 0, less = −1. Other variables are coded as in Table 1–3.

b. *Source:* California Poll, June 1978, *Financial Transactions of California Counties, Cities, and School Districts.*

c. *Source:* California Poll, August 1978.

sition 13, even after one controls for the effects of other individual attributes that influenced the vote. When we consider opinions about spending on welfare [Eq. (II)], the tax rate once again is influential, with high tax rates boosting support for cutbacks. The level of actual county and city expenditures on welfare had no impact on expressed preferences for spending in this area. Finally, Eq. (III) indicates that neither the tax rate variable nor the level of educational expenditures independently influenced the likelihood one would favor cutbacks (or increases) in government spending for public schools. Whether or not a respondent's household included a child under 18, an obvious index of self-interest, did have the predicted impact: Households with children understandably favored *more* spending on schools.

On balance, we take these results to confirm the greater sensitivity of voters to the tax side of the trade-off between lower taxes and reduced spending on government services. Obviously this is not to say that bond issues will always fail to win public approval and tax cuts always succeed. However, as long as perceptions of the consequences of changes in public spending are cloudy, the experience with the Jarvis–Gann initiative suggests it is likely that people will opt for a certain tax savings.

LIFE AFTER 13: REVENUES
AND EXPENDITURES

An immediate consequence of Proposition 13's overwhelming victory was to elevate tax and spending limitation to a status previously accorded such symbols of virtue as motherhood and the flag. Led by Governor Brown, whose dizzyingly rapid reversal of position on the Jarvis–Gann initiative is generally acknowledged to have secured his reelection, officials at both the state and local level scurried to embrace the new religion of "lean" government and to seek the blessing of its prophet, Howard Jarvis. Jarvis's endorsement apparently played a crucial role in the defeat of at least five incumbent liberal Democratic state assemblymen in the November election, the results of which not only returned to office a governor who honored his pledge to be stingy but also strengthened conservative forces in the ensuing legislative debate over how to implement Proposition 13.

The first two years of fiscal life in California under Proposition 13 almost completely confounded the initiative's critics on the central issue. Despite a reduction of almost $7 billion in property tax collections per year, local government operations remained relatively intact and the loss of employment in the public sector was minimal. Meanwhile, statistics from the State Board of Equalization show that the typical homeowner received a cut of 52 percent in property taxes during the first year after the passage of Proposition 13, while taxes on commercial property dropped almost 60 percent. The tax cut promised by Howard Jarvis had been delivered.

To Jarvis's chagrin, however, Proposition 13 had only a modest effect on the amount of local government spending in the short run. Allowing for the fact that property tax revenues provided 40 percent of all local revenues, the projected $7 billion shortfall implied a 23 percent reduction of expenditures. In fact, Oakland (1979) estimated that in fiscal year 1978–79 local governments lacked only $857 million in the revenues required to maintain previous service levels, a deficiency of only 2.8 percent. One reason for this relatively small gap is that higher assessments produced additional property tax revenue. Since the passage of Jarvis–Gann, assessed values have grown by 13.8 percent (Fitzgerald 1979), partly because the three-year reassessment cycle had not fully registered the effect of the upsurge in housing prices and partly because new construction and property transfers were exempted from Proposition 13's rollback requirements. In the context of a continuing boom in the real estate market, these factors produced an additional $405 million in 1978–79 (Oakland 1979: 397).

The main reason that Californians have been able to enjoy the benefits of reduced taxes without suffering painful disruption in services, however, is the earlier accumulation of an enormous state surplus. In 1977–78 the state's tax collection was $14.85 billion, an increase of 40 percent since 1975–76. During this brief period, personal and corporation income taxes grew by 48 percent and the receipts from the sales tax by 34 percent without any change in the rates. These burgeoning revenues resulted from the state's strong recovery from the recession of 1974 and from the previously cited impact of inflation on personal income taxes. Since state expenditures grew by only 23 percent over the same two years, the accumulation of a large surplus was inevitable. Indeed, the size of the surplus was sufficient to enable the state government to provide $4.4 billion of direct assistance to local governments. In the following fiscal year, the "bailout" assistance for local governments rose to $4.85 billion and local budgets rose by amounts ranging from 4 percent to 12 percent (Fitz-gerald 1979). The state also was able to provide a one-time tax cut of $500 million in 1979–80.

In part because of Governor Brown's determination to freeze state hiring and limit wage increases, the *growth* of state government expenditures slowed significantly after the passage of Proposition 13. But those supporters of the Jarvis–Gann initiative whose objective was to reduce the size or alter the shape of public spending have been disappointed. The emergence of new programs has virtually ended, but few existing programs have been severely reduced. Despite the pervasive unpopularity of expenditures for welfare and public assist-ance, for example, no major changes in state policy have been en-acted and in 1979–80 welfare recipients were able to obtain a 15.1 percent increase in their monthly grants. The terms of the state's financial assistance to local governments in 1978–79 required that the quality of the universally approved police and fire services remain at current levels. Since these services, which used up as much as 60 percent of local budgets, could not be cut, the main reductions were borne by services with weaker constituencies: libraries, summer schools, and park and recreation programs.

Proposition 13 has had a number of unanticipated consequences. Discontent and militancy among public employees has grown. Be-cause renters have failed to reap a significant portion of the property tax savings enjoyed by their landlords, a strong organized move-ment calling for rent control has developed. Rent control measures have passed in San Francisco, Santa Monica, Los Angeles, and Berke-ley, and a statewide initiative qualified for the 1980 ballot and was defeated. Proposition 13 has accentuated the shift in the property tax burden from business to the single-family homeowner. Oakland (1979) estimates that the homeowner's share of the property tax will rise from 43 percent in 1978–79 to 48.6 percent in 1981–82. Own-ers of business property, as a class, have probably been the main ben-eficiaries of Proposition 13; in the event there emerges a deficiency in the revenues required to maintain the state's current program of tax relief for localities, the constituency for a split roll that allows business properties to be taxed at a higher rate than residences is likely to grow. Indeed, the February 1979 California Poll reported that 46 percent of the respondents in a representative sample of California adults favored such a measure, 43 percent preferred the existing single-roll system, and 11 percent were undecided. Finally, although surveys have repeatedly shown that voters in California viewed their local governments as more efficient and responsive than the state government, the new financial preeminence of the state raises the possibility of enhanced centralized power over programmatic decisions too. For example, the share of educational expenditures financed locally dropped from 52 percent to 28 percent as a result of Proposition 13. In this area, there have been no significant inroads on local control to date. Elsewhere, however, the state government has flexed its fiscal muscles. Thus, the first bail-out bill prohibited cost-of-living increases for local employees and reductions in public safety.

On the other hand, the state chose not to attempt to eliminate disparities in local spending that existed prior to Proposition 13. The long-term bail-out program passed in 1979 took as its base the funding levels and programs that existed in 1977-78. The state's approach therefore rewards localities with relatively high levels of expenditure regardless of efficiency considerations. So, for example, Berkeley was allowed to retain its city public health department, the only such body in the state. Similarly, substantial layoffs at the local level occurred only when, as in Alameda County, county officials seized on Proposition 13 as an opportunity to implement long-desired changes. It was this failure of Proposition 13 to transform either the size or the shape of the public sector that led Paul Gann to sponsor Proposition 4, which does impose a ceiling on government spending.

THE PUBLIC MOOD AFTER PROPOSITION 13

More than two years after the passage of the Jarvis-Gann initiative, the public remains convinced of its merits. Polls have repeatedly shown that the public continues to approve of Proposition 13 by a margin better than two to one (*Los Angeles Times*, October 31, 1979: 1). More specifically, Table 1-7 indicates that 56 percent of the public believe that Proposition 13 has had a favorable overall effect on the taxes they paid, whereas only 6 percent reported negative tax consequences. The balance of opinion was negative when people were asked about the proposition's impact on government services or their jobs, but on these questions about two-thirds of the public reported no effect on their immediate family.

Table 1-7.   The Perceived Impact of Proposition 13.

	On Taxes, %	On Services, %	On Wages, Jobs, %
Favorable	56	7	12
No effect	33	63	66
Unfavorable	6	27	19
Don't know	5	3	3
	(n = 983)	(n = 983)	(n = 983)

Source: The California Poll, March 1979.

As this suggests, the reality of relief has eroded public concern about and resentment of property taxes, at least for the moment. Before the passage of Proposition 13, 60 percent of the affected California residents complained that their property taxes were unfairly high (Advisory Commission on Intergovernmental Relations 1978). Eighteen months later a statewide poll showed that only 27 percent felt they were paying more property taxes than they should, while 72 percent believed they were paying the right amount.[2] It should be stressed, however, that dissatisfaction with other taxes remained widespread: 68 percent felt their overall tax burden was too high and 51 percent believed they were paying too much in state income taxes.

Although largely convinced of the merits of Proposition 13, the public expressed considerable dissatisfaction with its implementation. In the March 1979 California Poll, for example, of respondents with a definite opinion, 42 percent believed that cuts in local government spending after Proposition 13 had been insufficient, 35 percent believed the right amount had been cut, while only 23 percent believed that spending reductions had been too substantial. However, fully 82 percent believed that the budget cuts had been made in the wrong places. Supporters of Proposition 13 complained about the cuts in fire and police services; opponents bemoaned the elimination of teachers and the budgetary squeeze faced by the public schools. Interestingly, both sides agreed that too few cuts had been made at the top of the bureaucratic hierarchy; the public seems to have been dimly aware of the trend toward the presence of more local government employees in high positions (Pascal et al. 1979).

As this suggests, there has been no erosion of the pre-Proposition 13 sentiment that state and local governments are inefficient and unresponsive. Indeed, the failure of the doomsday predictions made by the state's political leaders seems certain to have reinforced public cynicism about the credibility of government leaders. In this vein, the August 1979 California Poll found that 18 percent of the California electorate thought that government "never" pays attention to the public's desires in deciding policy, an additional 37 percent thought that government was responsive "just a little of the time," and only 7 percent replied "most of the time." The state government was perceived as inefficient by 72 percent of those polled in March 1979 as compared to 68 percent before the vote on Proposition 13; 63 percent regarded local governments as inefficient. Since public attitudes in the aftermath of Proposition 13 continue to favor a substantial governmental role in dealing with problems in "health, education, jobs, the environment, and energy" (43 percent of the sample in the California Poll of August 1979 thought government should be "doing more" in these areas, and another 25 percent thought government should maintain its present level of activity), these perceptions of government as wasteful are likely to be crucial in determining responses to upcoming tax reform initiatives.

In the context of a growing state surplus and the prevailing image of government as bloated, it is not surprising that Proposition 4 passed without any serious opposition. With the lesson of Proposition 13 in mind, no politician dared to condemn this constitutional amendment to limit the amount of state and local government spending. Indeed, the ballot argument for this complex measure was signed by both the Democratic speaker of the California State Assembly and the Republican minority leader. Proponents of the "spirit of 13" measure outspent its opponents by an estimated 126 to 1 (personal communication from the secretary of state's office). In a desultory campaign that drew only 34 percent of the registered voters to the polls, Proposition 4 won a majority in every county in the state.

At the time of the election the state's legislative analyst tentatively concluded that if passed, Proposition 4 would cause "state appropriations subject to limitation" to be modestly lower in the future (California Sample Ballot, November 1979, p. 21). More recently the staff of the Assembly Revenue and Taxation Committee have testified that in view of the rapid liquidation of the state surplus, the estimated revenues in upcoming years, and the requirement that the state balance its budget, it is unlikely that the state or most local governments will be able to spend the amounts permitted by Proposition 4.

FUTURE PROSPECTS

To recapitulate, the property tax revolt erupted in California because the combination of soaring real estate prices and inflexible, if efficient, assessment procedures produced large and seemingly inexorable increases in people's tax bills. Inflation fed the public resentment that culminated in the passage of Proposition 13, but it also produced the state surplus that has enabled citizens to enjoy lower property taxes without inflicting serious expenditure or employment cuts on local governments.

The persistence of this outcome clearly depends largely on the continuance and growth of the state government's relief program. This in turn requires large surpluses in future state budgets. Are these likely to materialize? Here we enter into the uncertain worlds of economic and political forecasting. A major recession would certainly wipe out much of the remaining surplus that funds the state's bailout program. And if the economic slowdown extends to the housing market, the rate of growth in the property tax base will also diminish. On the other hand, substantial inflation is likely for the foreseeable future, and other things being equal this should continue to feed the state treasury.

It is no longer clear, however, that other things will remain equal. For one thing, the terms of Proposition 4 may prohibit the accumulation of a surplus by requiring annual rebates of revenues in excess of allowable expenditures. For another, state legislators, severely burned by their failure to enact tax relief before the passage of Proposition 13, have moved vigorously to liquidate part of the state surplus through an array of changes in the state's tax system. These changes include one-time tax cuts of $1 billion in 1978–79 and $500 million in 1979–80; renter's relief; and abolition of the business inventory tax, most significantly, legislation (AB 276) that provides for indexing of state personal income taxes to take account of inflation. For taxable years beginning in or after December 1, 1979, but excluding those beginning in 1980 and ending on November 30,

1982, the "inflation adjustment factor" takes account of the annual change in the California Consumer Price Index in excess of 3 percent. For 1980–82, there is full indexing.

Taking these reforms and the program of fiscal relief for local governments into account and assuming there will be *no* recession in California, the state's legislative analyst has projected that the state's surplus will be almost completely liquidated by 1981–82. These preliminary projections anticipate a year-end surplus of $1.36 billion for 1979–80, $304 million for 1980–81, and only $104 million for 1981–82.[3] The 1979–80 operating budget estimates a deficit of $1.5 billion. It must be emphasized, however, that these estimates ignore the potential impact of the passage of other initiatives that would raise or reduce personal income taxes.

Because Proposition 13 requires that state taxes can be increased only by a two-thirds majority in the legislature and that new local taxes might win the support of two-thirds of the qualified electors in a district, it is unlikely that other taxes will be raised. A statewide initiative enabling localities to tax residential and business properties at different rates may provide an escape route for those seeking to avoid cutting expenditures, but the passage of such a measure might also result in countervailing effects on tax collections by slowing down business activity. Cutting bureaucratic "fat" by eliminating jobs and freezing public sector wages would doubtlessly be a popular response, but the experience on Proposition 13 suggests that the political obstacles in the way of this goal are formidable.

What other developments that substantially reduce the state's revenues would be sure to bring is the intensification of political conflict between public employees and their constituencies on the one hand, and the tax-paying middle class on the other. In that context, people will finally face the trade-off between taxes and services that has so far been avoided, and we may learn whether the trend in modern society toward an expanding public sector can not only be slowed, but reversed. Whatever the outcome, government officials in California already know that budgeting by the people and budgeting for the people are not the same.

NOTES TO CHAPTER 1

1. Probit analysis was employed because when the dependent variables are dichotomous or trichotomous a heteroscedasticity problem arises and the assumptions of ordinary least squares (OLS) regression that the error term has zero mean and constant variance are generally not met. The probit coefficients reported in Table 1-3 are maximum likelihood estimates that translate into the increment in probability of being in a higher response category for the observed dependent variable brought about by a unit change in the independent variable. (See McKelvey and Zavoina 1975 for a full explanation of the probit analysis technique employed here.)

2. These results are derived from a statewide telephone poll conducted by the Survey Research Center of the University of California, Berkeley, as part of a research grant awarded to Jack Citrin, Merrill Shanks, and David Sears by the Hewlett Foundation. We are indebted to the Foundation and Professors Shanks and Sears for permission to report these findings.

3. We are grateful to Ted Clement of the legislative analyst's office for providing these figures.

REFERENCES

Advisory Commission on Intergovernmental Relations. 1978. *Changing Public Attitudes on Government and Taxes.* Washington, D.C.

California Roundtable. 1979. *California Tax Study.* Burlingame, California. California Roundtable Task Force.

Citrin, J. 1979. "Do People Want Something for Nothing?" *National Tax Journal* 32, no. 2 (June).

Fitzgerald, M. 1979. "Living with Proposition 13." *Tax Revolt Digest* (November).

Levin, M. 1979. "How Property Tax Reform in the Sixties Fueled the Tax Revolt of the Seventies." *Taxing and Spending* II, no. 2.

Levy, F. 1979. "On Understanding Proposition 13." *Public Interest* 56 (Summer).

McKelvey, R.D., and W. Zavoina. 1975. "A Statistical Model for the Analysis of Ordinal Level Dependent Variables." *Journal of Mathematical Sociology* 4.

Oakland, W. 1979. "Proposition 13: Genesis and Consequences." *National Tax Journal* 32, no. 2.

Pascal, A. et al. 1979. *Fiscal Containment: Who Gains? Who Loses?* Santa Monica, California, RAND Corporation.

Paul, D. 1979. *The Politics of the Property Tax.* Lexington, Mass.: D.C. Heath.

COMMENTS — *Jack H. Beebe*

The adversary role of the critic normally focuses on finding fault with assumptions, methods, or even subjects addressed. I was pleased in reading the foregoing chapter that I did not have such reactions, for it takes a sensible, almost eclectic, approach to an important issue. The conclusions — although not terribly strong — are well supported by the analysis.

There are several reasons for the chapter's success in explaining Proposition 13 and the California tax-limitation movement. Foremost, it has evolved from earlier studies done separately by the two authors, one by Jack Citrin in the *National Tax Journal* (June 1979) and one by Frank Levy in *The Public Interest* (Summer 1979). It also has benefited significantly from a study on the same subject by Bill Oakland in the *National Tax Journal* (June 1979). The new Citrin–Levy study shares the strengths of each of these earlier analyses and demonstrates the perspective that comes with blending different approaches.

The present analysis also benefits simply from the passage of time. All of the earlier essays were written in 1978, so that the analyses were being conducted about the time the proposition was brought before the voters. Bill Oakland was visiting scholar in the research department of the Federal Reserve Bank of San Francisco at the time, where I was working on the effects of Proposition 13 on California bonds. I am well aware that these early studies all required some true *ex ante* hypothesizing. The mere passage of time has rendered an analysis of Proposition 13's meaning and consequences far more tractable.

The new Citrin–Levy study presents an interesting amalgamation of the earlier methods of Citrin, Levy, and Oakland. Citrin's work is foremost a political analysis derived principally from results of opinion polls. The Levy contribution, particularly his earlier paper, is based on what he calls a "micro" approach — that is, a detailed case study of the economic and political factors in the evolution of the California tax-limitation movement. This method contrasts starkly with Oakland's "macro" approach, which focuses primarily on hypotheses that can be tested using time series and cross-sectional data showing the growing tax burden in California relative to other states.

At the time that Bill Oakland was doing his analysis I was concerned with the simplicity of the macro approach. There appeared to be some notable counterexamples such as Texas and, I believe, Arizona, where strong pressures were bearing on the state legislatures despite relatively low taxes and expenditures. Levy's micro approach is not likely to lead to such sweeping conclusions. But then Levy's approach does not generalize well either. By integrating the Levy and Oakland approaches with the Citrin opinion-poll analyses, Citrin and Levy create a rich explanation of the California government-limitation movement in a fairly general framework.

The study has a few weaknesses worth mentioning. First, it is difficult to bring the three approaches together in a cohesive set of hypotheses. Being of limited mind, economists prefer a limited menu of hypotheses. By observing the problem from different angles, the authors give a very complex picture, at times befuddling the reader. Although I believe that this complexity has more strengths than weaknesses, it creates the difficult expositional task of making a single picture from the various directions.

A second problem arises from the fact that the study gives far more emphasis to Proposition 13 than to Proposition 4 and the future. This weakness is understandable in that we have had little experience with Proposition 4 and the future is subject only to speculation. However, the discussion could go further in these directions.

With these general comments, I shall turn to some specific issues that sparked my thinking. In a number of places, the chapter raises interesting points regarding the public's perception of "fat" in government; in fact, this is one of its central themes. The Citrin–Levy attitudinal surveys are based on extensive poll results over the 1957–78 period. (These polls are elaborated on in the earlier Citrin paper.) It is clear that there was a shift in attitudes during the 1960s such that respondents increasingly thought that government wasted money, taxes were too high, and that government was not trustworthy or responsive. Citrin and Levy link these changing attitudes partly to the surge in inflation over the same period and to the public's realization that government policies are the ultimate source of inflation. Although I agree with this hypothesis, it is worth speculating on whether there might be an alternate hypothesis that is perhaps more fundamental. Might these increasingly negative attitudes toward government be part of a larger distrust of institutions? Suppose one had asked respondents the following questions about corporations: (1) Are corporations charging prices that are too high? (2) Are corporate managers trustworthy and responsive to your needs? (3) Is there excess "fat" in corporations? I believe that the 1960s would have revealed a similarly negative shift in the public's attitude. I am not suggesting that corporations are responsible for the acceleration in inflation. But I am suggesting that the shift in attitudes in the 1960s might have been against institutions in general and not against only governmental institutions.

If the Proposition 13 movement is part of a wider tide against institutions, then the consequences are far-reaching, for we should see legislation expropriating profits and promoting restrictions on large private as well as public institutions. There seems to have been a trend in this direction, at least through the mid-1970s, although the more recent period may show mixed results. In particular, during later California elections, antibusiness initiatives met with only mediocre success, whereas Proposition 4 breezed through. So it appears that the strongest grass roots pressures presently are aimed at government.

In analyzing Proposition 4 and other developments subsequent to Proposition 13, the authors correctly point out that Proposition 13 did not turn out to be what voters had anticipated. Rather than a lid on government, it became a fiscal reform package. Many voters apparently felt that they had been fooled by Proposition 13. I suspect, however, that even fewer persons understood Proposition 4 when they voted for it. (There was almost no public debate of Proposition 4 largely because politicians feared the consequences of opposing it.) The new amendment is potentially very powerful in that it places a *permanent* ceiling on real per capita appropriations (spending) at the 1978-79 level. There is thus no leeway for real economic growth in government (except for voter-approved three-year temporary spending overrides) to match real economic growth in the private sector. Moreover, the restriction applies *separately* to each individual governmental unit, from the state through special districts (excluding many small special districts with little taxing power). For school districts, the amendment places a permanent ceiling on real per pupil expenditures at the 1978-79 level.

I do not believe that the few analyses done so far have delved very deeply into the probable effects of Proposition 4. For example, budget projections by California's legislative analyst office were taken through 1984 and were for the state budget only. On this basis, the effects of Proposition 4 were found not to be drastic. However, the nature of Proposition 4's limits suggests that its constraints will be felt over the long term—beyond the period analyzed by the legislative analyst—and that the most severe problems may occur at the local level. It is also not obvious that voters intended to reform government by increasing its centralization, as occurred under Proposition 13, or by imposing rigid constraints on every local governmental body, as occurred under Proposition 4. Thus there appears to be little rational connection between the spirit of grass roots government limitations and the actual form of the limits.

Citrin and Levy make the very important point that in enacting further tax and spending limits California voters will have to face the trade-off between taxes (or spending) and real government services. Budget surpluses and any existing fat no longer exist. Indeed, the trade-off may have been decided by Proposition 4, although the bite may not be felt for several years. In this context, failure of the more recent Jarvis II (which would have reduced state income taxes by half and indexed the tax rates to inflation) indicates that voters are not interested in another dramatic cutback at this time. Perhaps voters now appreciate the large reduction in government services that Proposition 4 and the reduced capital expenditures resulting from Proposition 13 may ultimately impose.

2 PROPOSITION 13
Genesis and Consequences

William H. Oakland

The voters of the State of California enacted in 1978 what has been hailed as a revolutionary measure for reducing the level and growth of state and local government expenditure as well as sharply restricting the use of the property tax as a source of government revenue. The Jarvis–Gann amendment, or Proposition 13 as it has come to be known, 1) restricts the property tax rate to no more than 1 percent of assessed value;[1] 2) sets assessed value for a property that has not been transferred since 1975–76 equal to its fair market value in that year plus 2 percent per year (compounded); in the event that the property has been transferred since 1975–76, the market value at the time of sale is used (plus the 2 percent growth factor); and 3) requires that new taxes or increases in existing taxes (except property taxes) receive a two-thirds approval of the legislature in the case of state taxes, or of the electorate, in the case of local taxes.[2]

The potential fiscal impact of these provisions is enormous. Since the statewide average effective rate of property tax had stood at approximately 2.5 percent, the rate limitation alone would reduce property tax collections by one-half.[3] Moreover, the rollback of assessments to 1975–76 applied to a period of rapidly escalating

This study was previously published in the *National Tax Journal*. It is based upon a study published in the Winter 1979 issue of the Federal Reserve Bank of San Francisco's *Economic Review*.

property values. Hence, the overall impact on property tax receipts amounted to a reduction of 57 percent, or $7 billion. This constitutes nearly 20 percent of the total revenues raised by all levels of California government, and 37 percent of the own-source revenues of local governments alone.

Critics of Proposition 13 predicted that the fiscal consequences of such a massive reduction in local government revenue would prove disastrous. Assuming slightly more than half of the $7 billion would be spent on payroll (the national average is 57 percent), more than 200,000 public sector jobs would be lost. Allowing for indirect effects (from the money employees would no longer spend) the total employment (private plus public) loss was estimated at 400,000. Equally important, a massive disruption of public services was predicted to accompany the revenue shortfall. The city of San Francisco, for example, estimated that outlays on police and fire services would be cut by one-third, the budget for libraries cut by 80 percent, the city zoo entirely eliminated, and funds for other recreation and cultural activities reduced by two-thirds (San Francisco Bureau of the Budget 1978).[4] Because of substantial state relief and a host of factors discussed in this chapter, these dire forecasts have not yet materialized. Nevertheless, there are many who argue that these consequences may still be in the offing, since the state program was enacted only for one year and the surplus from which it was financed may not recur.

Although the employment and public expenditure effects of Proposition 13 have received the most attention, there are numerous other ramifications of the amendment. There are, among others, implications for financial markets; taxpayer equity; efficiency of the housing market; the structure of state and local government; and perhaps, most dramatically, for other governments, including the federal government. Because of this complexity it would be foolish to attempt a comprehensive evaluation in the limited space available here. Instead, this chapter will focus upon three broad questions or issues:

1. What was the general fiscal climate during the period in which the amendment was formulated and debated?

2. To what extent has (or will) Proposition 13 succeed in reducing the size and growth of public expenditure in California?

3. What are the broad implications of the amendment for the revenue structure of California government?

The answer to the first question helps to resolve the controversy of whether Proposition 13 was a result of fiscal conditions that characterize state and local government in general or whether it was a response to fiscal tensions unique to California. The evidence supports the latter position; more specifically it is argued that the California fiscal climate in the pre-Proposition 13 period had three outstanding elements.

1. A heavy and growing state and local tax burden during a period when such burdens had leveled off in most other states.

2. A massive shift of property taxes toward homeowners.

3. A rapidly expanding state budget surplus.

Although difficult to quantify, each factor undoubtedly contributed to the emergence of Proposition 13. More important, however, is the fact that the second and third factors are not commonly present in most other states. The fact that similar measures are under consideration in other states, therefore, is more a reflection of an attempt to replicate California's "success" with voter-induced tax reduction than a response to similar fiscal pressures. Largely for this reason, California's experience provides little guidance as to the consequences of such measures in other states. For example, without a substantial budget surplus somewhere in the state–local fiscal system, painful disruptions in public services, as yet avoided by California, will inevitably follow.

This leads us to the second question—the impact on the size and growth of public expenditure. Some of the advocates of Proposition 13 have argued that one of its major impacts will be to restrain the growth of the public sector. Evidence is that such effects are and will continue to be relatively minor. Specifically, in its first year, Proposition 13 is estimated to have reduced the level of public services by a scant 2.8 percent. In subsequent years, the estimated reduction in the growth rate of public services is less than 1 percentage point. Such results primarily reflect the significant budget surplus the state government had accumulated in recent years, the highly responsive character of the state revenue system, and the substantial growth of future property tax revenues.

Despite the small size of its expenditure impacts, Proposition 13 has had major effects upon the revenue structure of California governments. Because it largely substitutes state revenues for local revenues, the share of local government expenditures financed by local sources drops precipitously. This has obvious consequences for home rule. In addition, the progressivity of the state-local revenue system is increased because state revenue sources tend to be more progressive than the local property tax. Finally, an important, although unintended, consequence of the change in revenue structure is the de facto sharing of property tax proceeds by local government units within a county area. In effect, Proposition 13 has introduced tax-base sharing at the county level. This will have the effect of strengthening fiscally weak jurisdictions (central city governments) at the expense of the more affluent (the suburbs).

CALIFORNIA TAX CLIMATE

In this section I will focus upon three major facets of the California fiscal climate: 1) the behavior of the total state-local tax burden over the past two decades, 2) the behavior of the relative property tax burden of owner-occupied residential property, and 3) the growth of the state surplus since 1975–76 and its prospects for the near-term future.

Total State-Local Tax Burden

California governments collected $20.8 billion in taxes in the fiscal year 1975–76, more than any other state (U.S. Bureau of the Census 1977). Its per capita tax collection of $965 placed it behind only Alaska ($1,896) and New York ($1,139). Accordingly, per capita taxes in California stood 32 percent above the national average and 44 percent above the median state. Measured against personal income, a similar picture emerges. Californians paid 14.9 percent of their personal income in 1975–76, ranking behind only New York and Vermont. In terms of this index, California stood 19 percent above the national average in 1975–76. Thus, regardless of the measure, California emerges as a high tax state.

Not only is the tax burden in California relatively high, but it has increased sharply in recent years. Table 2–1 shows that without Proposition 13, California governments would have absorbed nearly 16 percent of the state's personal income in the fiscal year 1978–79 as compared to 9.3 percent in 1957—an increase of more than 6.5 percentage points. Although this measure for the United States as a

Table 2-1. State and Local Taxes as a Percentage of Personal Income, 1957–78.

Year	U.S.[a]	California	California = U.S.
1957	8.14	9.31	1.17
1962	9.32	10.46	1.14
1963–64	10.13	12.07	1.94
1964–65	10.24	11.98	1.74
1965–66	10.43	12.47	2.04
1966–67	10.32	11.98	1.66
1967–68	10.49	13.37	2.88
1968–69	10.91	13.71	2.80
1969–70	11.44	13.38	1.96
1970–71	11.66	13.73	2.07
1971–72	12.42	14.94	2.52
1972–73	12.71	14.91	2.20
1973–74	12.16	14.01	1.85
1974–75	12.00	14.59	2.59
1975–76	12.17	14.89	2.72
1976–77	12.38[b]	15.78[d]	3.40
1977–78	12.11[b]	15.96[d]	3.85
1978–79	11.93[c]	15.97[d] (12.64)[e]	4.04 (0.71)[e]

a. Excluding California.

b. Based on estimates of U.S. Commerce Department as reported in the *Survey of Current Business.*

c. Same as b, but first quarter 1978 used to project entire year.

d. 1976–78 tax receipts based on author's estimates using California State Comptroller Reports. Personal income for 1978 taken from *Economic Report of the Governor,* 1978.

e. After Proposition 13.

Sources: U.S. Bureau of the Census, *Government Finances,* 1957–78.

whole also increased during the period, it did so much less rapidly. The net result was that the differential between California and the rest of the nation widened from 1 percentage point to more than 4 percentage points over the two decades. Even more striking, however, is that much of the gap between California and the rest of the United States occurred during the second half of the 1970s. Whereas the effective tax rate in the rest of the country had stabilized and even decreased slightly during the seventies, California's effective rate continued to grow at rates similar to the sixties. This suggests that California was out of step with the rest of the country. Proposition 13 may thus reflect the taxpayers' attempt to bring their government back into line with historic relationships.[5] The reader will note from Table 2-1 that even after the adoption of the amendment, California's tax rate remains above the average for the rest of the nation.

Property Tax Burdens

The preceding discussion suggests that pressures for tax relief were building in California during the 1970s. The figures, however, are much too aggregative to offer any insight into the direction that a tax reduction would take. Evidence to be presented will show that property tax burdens, particularly upon homeowners, had risen sharply in the five years prior to passage of the proposition. Thus, it is not surprising that the taxpayers chose this particular avenue for tax reduction.

The property tax plays a major role in the California tax structure, constituting approximately 41 percent of total state-local tax revenue in 1975-76 (U.S. Bureau of the Census). The corresponding figure for the United States as a whole is 36 percent (U.S. Bureau of the Census). Given that it is a high tax state, therefore, it is not surprising that California's property tax burden is relatively high. In per capita terms, California's 1975-76 property tax receipt of $415 stood 57 percent above the national norm and was surpassed only by New Jersey ($446) and Alaska ($1,048) (U.S. Bureau of the Census). As a share of personal income, the relevant figures are 6.4 percent for California and 4.5 percent for the nation as a whole. The introduction of general revenue sharing narrowed this gap in the early seventies, but it began to widen again after 1973.

The most interesting property tax development, however, is not with respect to total collections, but for receipts from homeowners. Column 5 of Table 2-2 shows that, in the absence of Proposition 13, the share of property taxes accounted for by single-family dwellings would have risen from 32 percent in 1973-74 to 44 percent in 1978-79. This sharp increase meant that relative to *total* state personal income, homeowners' property taxes increased by 38 percent over the same period.[6]

The precipitous increase in homeowners' tax burden directly reflects the growth in single-family assessments relative to other property types as columns 1-4 of Table 2-2 indicate. The single-family share had been relatively constant during the sixties and early seventies despite substantial adjustments in the shares of other groups. An increase in the homeowner's exemption caused the share to dip momentarily in 1973-74. However, beginning in 1974-75, the homeowners' share grew rapidly due to an unparalleled boom in the market for single-family homes. Prices for existing homes in the San Francisco area, for example, jumped by 120 percent over the five-year period ending April 1978, an annual rate of increase of approximately 18 percent per year (Real Estate Research Council of Northern California 1978). Such increases were not confined to San Francisco; the Los Angeles area experienced even faster growth. Nor were they the result of inflation alone since the GNP deflator increased by only 55 percent over the same five-year period. The behavior of the nonresidential share also suggests that the real estate boom was confined primarily to single-family housing.

Because reassessment in California is conducted on a three-year cycle, the full effects of the housing price upsurge had yet to be felt by the fiscal year 1978-79. Assuming that, in the future, all property appreciates at 9 percent per year and that new construction continues its present pace, it is estimated that the single-family share of assessments would have grown (without Proposition 13) to 48.6 percent for the year 1981-82. In the space of only seven years, then, the homeowners' share of the property tax would have risen by 54 percent. The 48.6 percent figure is given sharp relief when one considers that, as of 1975, the share of homeowners and renters *combined* amounted to only 47 percent for the nation as a whole.[7]

Given the preceding evidence, it is not surprising that the taxpayer revolt focussed upon property tax reduction. Not only were property

Table 2-2. Distribution of Net Assessed Value and Property Tax Burden on Single-Family Dwellings, California, 1964-65 to 1978-79.[a]

| Period | Share of Total Net Assessed Value | | | | (5) Share of Property Taxes: Single-Family Dwellings | (6) Taxes on Single-Family Dwellings as a Percentage of Personal Income |
	(1) Single-Family Residences	(2) Other Residences	(3) Non-residential	(4) State Assessed[g]		
1964-65	34.8%	12.3%	40.8%	12.1%	36.2%	1.97%
65-66	34.5	12.6	41.4	11.5	34.8	2.01
66-67	34.0	13.3	41.8	10.9	35.3	2.04
67-68	33.6	13.7	42.6	10.1	35.0	2.05
68-69[b]	34.0	13.8	42.6	9.7	35.4	2.11
69-70[c]	32.2	14.4	44.0	9.5	33.5	1.98
70-71[d]	33.5	14.8	42.9	8.8	34.8	2.24
71-72	33.7	14.5	43.8	8.1	35.0	2.37
72-73	34.0	13.9	44.4	7.6	35.2	2.35
73-74[e]	31.6	13.8	46.9	7.7	32.1	1.88
74-75[f]	32.9	13.4	46.4	7.3	33.9	1.98
75-76	35.2	13.2	44.7	6.9	36.2	2.16
76-77	39.5	12.9	41.0	6.6	40.4	2.48
77-78	41.0	12.6	39.6	6.7	42.2	2.53
78-79	43.0	12.6	38.3	6.4	44.3	2.60

Notes to Table 2-2.

a. Net of exemptions.

b. First significant "open space" assessments.

c. Introduction of $750 homestead exemption; 15 percent inventory exemption.

d. 30 percent inventory exemption.

e. $1,750 homestead exemption; 45 percent inventory exemption.

f. 50 percent inventory exemption.

g. State-assessed property is mainly personal property of utilities. Beginning in 1964 and ending in 1974, the assessment ratio on this class was lowered until it reached the ratio applying to other classes.

Source: California Board of Equalization and the author's estimates for years 1975–76 to 1978–79.

taxes relatively high in California but there was a massive shift of the property tax burden toward homeowners, spawned by rapidly escalating real estate prices. Although homeowners as a class were made better off by the capital gains on their homes, most were not in a position to realize them. Consequently, a large number of homeowners found themselves with property tax bills that were doubling and even tripling without a corresponding increase in their income flow. Thus considerable pressures arose for some form of property tax relief.

State Budget Surplus

No story about the California fiscal climate would be complete without a discussion of the budget surplus the state government had begun to accumulate by 1975-76. Table 2-3 shows that without the passage of Proposition 13 (which applied to 1978-79), the budget surplus would have accumulated to at least $10.1 billion by 1979-80.[8] The magnitude of this can be better appreciated if one considers that the combined yield of the state's two major revenue sources, the personal income tax and the general sales tax, was expected to be $11 billion in the calendar year 1979 (*Economic Report of the Governor* 1978: A-55). Thus, the surplus by the fiscal

Table 2-3. Budget Surplus of the State of California prior to the Adoption of Proposition 13, 1975-76 to 1979-80 (*$ millions*).

Fiscal Year	Surplus at Beginning of Fiscal Year	Change in Surplus from Preceding Year
1975-76	570	
1976-77	1,211	641
1977-78	3,800	2,589
1978-79[a]	7,100	3,300
1979-80[a]	10,100	3,000

a. Does not allow for $4,100 million state Proposition 13 relief and temporary income tax cut of $1,000 million, both for fiscal year 1978-79.

Source: For 1975-76 and 1976-77, California Legislature, *Analysis of the Budget Bill, July 1, 1978 to June 30, 1978*; for 1977-78 to 1979-80, the *San Francisco Chronicle* (August 25, 1978).

year 1979-80 would almost be sufficient to permit suspension of the income and sales tax for that year.

The growth in the state's surplus reflects a virtual explosion of tax revenues in the recent past. Table 2-4 shows the behavior of the major state revenue sources over the two-year period 1975-76 and 1977-78. Three of the taxes showed growth rates of 43 percent or more and a fourth grew by about one-third. Overall, growth of revenues amounted to a staggering 40 percent. What makes this impressive is that it was accomplished without any rate increases and was accompanied by a growth in state personal income of only 23 percent. In the aggregate, the latter implies a revenue elasticity of 1.75. Although state expenditures also grew rapidly over the same period (27 percent), this growth was not sufficient to prevent the accumulation of a considerable surplus.

Much of the explanation for the rapid growth of California taxes rests with the fact that the national economy was recovering rapidly from a substantial recession whose trough occurred in the first quarter of 1975. It is well known that corporate profits and taxable personal income are highly sensitive to aggregate economic conditions. As the economy approaches full employment, revenue increases from these sources will slow down. However, there is one factor that tends to keep state revenue growth above that of personal income: infla-

Table 2-4. Growth of Major State Taxes in California, 1975-76 to 1977-78.

Tax Source	Receipts 1977-76, $ Millions	Change Since 1975-76, $ Millions	Percent Growth 1975-76 to 1977-78
Personal income tax	$ 4,391	$1,432	48%
General sales tax	5,020	1,278	34
Selective sales taxes	2,234	672	43
Corporation income tax	1,900	616	48
Death and gift taxes	369	48	17
Property (auto excise) tax	445	70	19
Total	14,359	4,116	40
Item: California personal income growth.			23

Source: U.S. Bureau of the Census, Governmental Finances, and Economic Report of the Governor, 1978.

tion. Since the state's personal income tax is steeply progressive over a wide range, increases in income due to inflation generate dispropor- tionately larger increases in tax receipts. Specifically, the elasticity of the state income tax with respect to personal income has averaged about 1.7 over the last decade. This means that for every 1 percent inflation-induced growth in personal income, income taxes increase by 1.7 percent—a bonus for the state of 0.7 percent. At inflation rates of 7 to 8 percent this translates into an additional 5 percent real revenue growth for the state government.

Since recent inflation rates can be expected to continue into the near future, the short-term outlook for state revenue growth is par- ticularly bright. Continued inflation should enable the state to sus- tain a growth of personal income of 11 percent, its average for the past five years. Assuming that taxes other than the personal income tax also grow at 11 percent, total tax revenue can be expected to expand by 13.5 percent per year—or nearly doubling within five years.[9] More important, if state government expenditure grows in proportion to state personal income, the state budget surplus will continue to expand. Table 2-5 shows that by the year 1983-84 the annual surplus will rise to $6.3 billion and the total surplus to more than $30 billion. It appears, therefore, that the budget surplus would grow to untenable levels without some action to reduce taxes. Of course the state government could respond to increasing expendi- tures more rapidly than the 11 percent assumed in these projections. But this would run counter to national trends; the share of income absorbed by state and local taxes has been falling (see Table 2-1).

Table 2-5. Projected Budget Surplus of the State of California, 1978-79 to 1983-84 (*$ millions*).

Fiscal Year	End-of-Year Surplus[a]	Yearly Surplus[a]
1978-79	$ 7,100	$ 3,300
1979-80	11,202	4,102
1980-81	15,767	4,565
1981-82	20,846	5,079
1982-83	26,489	5,653
1983-84	32,780	6,291

a. For derivation see text. No allowance is made for state relief or tax cut programs enacted for the fiscal year 1978-79.

Although one might argue that the state could provide greater financial relief to local governments, this would only shift the locus of the surplus. Tax reduction, of some form, appears inevitable. Indeed this goes a long way toward explaining the recent one-time-only state income tax cut of $1 billion at a time when government finances were supposed to have been in a state of crisis. A glance at Table 2–5 suggests that this action was no more than a drop in the bucket.

Recapitulation

We can now weave together the three major strands of our fiscal climate story. Not only have taxes in California been considerably higher than elsewhere but they have been diverging from the national norm in recent years. Pressures have therefore been developing to bring the state back into line. In effect this amounts to resistance to abnormally high levels of government expenditure.[10] At the same time, the combination of economic recovery and inflation had produced a substantial budgetary surplus, which, if left unchecked, would have grown to unreasonable proportions in the near future. Hence, pressures were building to bring taxes back into line with expenditure. Finally, a boom in the market for single-family homes produced a sharp jump in the homeowners' share of the property tax burden. Thus, there was considerable pressure to provide tax relief to this subset of taxpayers.[11]

Proposition 13, then, was California's method of dealing with these diverse pressures. It accomplished the necessary tax reduction and at the same time provided a change in tax structure that was felt to promote equity. This is not to say, however, that the amendment was the optimal way of achieving these goals. The fact that no provision was made for a redistribution of taxes from the state to local governments created the possibility of considerable disruption of the delivery of public services. However, given the diverse objectives to be served and differences of interests among voters, a comprehensive approach may not have proven politically feasible. Moreover, the state *did* redirect substantial revenues to local government. Viewed in this light, Proposition 13 did successfully liquidate the state surplus.

EXPENDITURE IMPACTS

More than anything else, Proposition 13 has been interpreted as a measure to reduce the level and control the growth of government spending. In this section, I offer quantitative estimates of the expenditure impacts of the amendment in both the short and medium term. It will be seen that the preelection estimates were grossly exaggerated and that Proposition 13 has had a modest, if not insignificant, impact on the size of the public sector in California.

Early Estimates of the Impact

As pointed out earlier in this chapter, initial estimates were that the Jarvis–Gann amendment would reduce local government property tax revenues for the fiscal year 1978–79 by $7 billion or 57 percent. Allowing for the fact that the property tax produces 40 percent of all local revenues, the implied reduction in local expenditure is 23 percent. A reduction of such a magnitude was not required, however, because the state government liquidated some of its surplus and allocated $4.1 billion of direct assistance and $0.9 billion in emergency loans to local governments. Since the loans would have to be repaid and because no local unit availed itself of them, it is more accurate to measure the state relief package at $4.1 billion. Accordingly, local governments were expected to face a shortfall of $2.9 billion in the first year after the passage of Proposition 13. In terms of total expenditure this amounts to a 9.5 percent reduction.

Although an across-the-board cut of 9.5 percent would be painful, it would not appear to be unmanageable. However, the problem is more serious than the 9.5 percent would indicate. A large fraction of local expenditure is out of the control of local authorities because of federal or state mandates and/or grant funds that are not fungible. Consider, for example, public welfare. Half of the support for the welfare program comes from the state. Moreover, support levels and eligibility requirements are in the hands of the U.S. Congress and the state legislature. Hence, the major discretion left to the localities lies with administration, which amounts to less than 5 percent of total welfare outlay.[12] And efforts to trim administration may backfire because payments to ineligible households may increase.

Adding to this problem is a requirement that local communities maintain the quality of police and fire services as a condition for receiving the emergency state assistance. It is likely, therefore, that uncontrollable expenditure amounts to as much as 60 percent of local budgets. Hence, the remaining 40 percent would have to bear the full brunt of the $2.9 billion revenue shortfall. Since this involves cuts of nearly 25 percent, serious disruptions may be expected to follow. Thus, the 9.5 percent revenue gap greatly understates the magnitude of the difficulty that would confront local governments.

Despite these somber circumstances, local government employment dropped by only 7,000 workers during July (Federal Reserve Bank of San Francisco 1978). Even though this reflects only the first month of operation under Jarvis–Gann, the permanent character of the amendment would require much of the adjustment to take place early. If there was a $2.9 billion shortfall, local employment would have been expected eventually to drop by 80,000, more than ten times what actually occurred. Although local governments undoubtedly have some flexibility in substituting workers for other inputs, reducing overtime, and so on, a discrepancy of 73,000 could not be due to such factors. As I shall show, the problem rests with the $2.9 billion figure itself—it is a gross exaggeration of the revenue gap remaining after the state relief measure.

Impact on Existing Service Levels

There are two ways to estimate the public expenditure impacts of Proposition 13. The first is to compare public service levels with those that had prevailed in the fiscal year prior to implementation of the amendment—fiscal year 1977–78. Such a comparison is relevant for the issue of whether a substantial disruption in the flow of public services resulted from the action. A second approach is to compare public services with what they would have been in the absence of Proposition 13. This enables us to discern the expenditure impact of the amendment. Clearly the two measures will be the same if the level of public services remains constant over time. However, some growth in public services has been occurring and can be reasonably expected to continue into the future. Hence, to obtain the expenditure impacts the first measure must be adjusted for such growth.

We begin with the first measure—the impact on the existing level of public services. The calculations used to derive the service level impact are summarized in Table 2–6. The first block of the table

Table 2-6. Reduction in the Average Level of Local Public Services Caused by Proposition 13 (*$ millions*).

Changes in local revenues caused by Proposition 13		
1977-78 property tax collection	$11,452	
1978-79 officially estimated property tax collections	5,404	
Net change		-$6,048
Adjustments		
State relief	4,100	
Additional property tax revenue due to higher assessments	405	
Total		4,505
Projected increase in other revenues, 1977-78 to 1978-79		1,716
Net change in revenues		173
Changes in revenue necessary to maintain 1977-78 service levels		
1.08 × 1977-78 expenditure	2,288	
Less wage share (55%)	1,258	1,030
Revenue deficiency	857	
Percent revenue deficiency	2.8%	

shows that Proposition 13 was expected to reduce local government revenues between the 1977-78 and 1978-79 fiscal years by $6,048 million. From this must be subtracted the state relief package of $4,100 million. A second adjustment must be made for the fact that officials underestimated actual property tax collections for 1978-79. Recall that the amendment required that assessed values be rolled back to their 1975-76 levels if the property had not been sold since that time or at the value at time of sale if it had been sold. This prompted officials to project the growth of assessments at 1.3 percent, as compared to the 12.5 percent that was expected before Proposition 13 was passed (Legislative Analyst 1978). In fact, assessments for the fiscal year 1978-79 have increased by 9 percent, more than 70 percent of what was originally projected. This apparently reflected the fact that, despite a three-year reassessment cycle, many properties had been underassessed relative to their 1975-76 value as late as Spring 1978, when the rolls for the 1978-79 fiscal year were taken. Furthermore, because of the assessment lag, many of those properties transferred during the 1975-78 period were not reassessed at their value at time of sale. Since market values were rapidly escalating, the degree of underassessment would be considerable. In both of these cases, Proposition 13 allows assessors to adjust prevailing assessments for past errors. The result was that a large number of properties showed higher assessments after Jarvis-Gann passed than they would have without it.[13] The upshot is that property tax revenues will be $405 million higher than initially projected.[14]

The next step is to allow for the growth of non-property tax revenues. Since the latter are not directly affected by the amendment, I assume that they will grow by 10 percent between 1977-78 and 1978-79—their average rate of growth since 1974-75. This will produce an additional $1,716 million for use in 1978-79. Thus, the net change in *total* local government revenue between 1977-78 and 1978-79 is $173 million.[15]

The last step is to compute the growth of revenues that would have been necessary to sustain 1977-78 public service levels. Since inflation is expected to amount to 8 percent over the period, a revenue increase of $2,288 million is necessary to maintain services. However, as part of its relief measure, the state legislature prohibited cost-of-living adjustments for local government employees. Thus, revenue needs to be increased only to cover higher costs of materials and supplies. Since wages constitute 55 percent of total expenditure, the requisite increase is $1,030 million.[16] Thus, the revenue deficiency is $857 million, or 2.8 percent.

One might object to the preceding adjustment on the grounds that the wage freeze will have to be made up sooner or later and should therefore not be taken into consideration. If local governments purchased labor services on competitive markets, there would be considerable merit to this objection. However, a review of relative wage levels for local public employees shows that California ranks only behind Alaska in public sector compensation levels, with wages 23 percent above the national average (U.S. Bureau of the Census 1977b). Private sector wage differentials, as measured by the manufacturing wage, were much lower, standing at 9 percent. It would seem, therefore, that the wages of California public sector workers have been considerably above those dictated by a free market and that a one-year wage freeze would not necessarily need to be made up.

In summary, although Proposition 13 was initially estimated to produce a 23 percent shortfall for local governments, its actual effect may be only 2.5 percent. Even allowing for the fact that mandates push the brunt of the adjustment upon 40 percent of local governments' budgets, the implied reduction amounts to 7 percent for those activities that are subject to cuts. Such an adjustment would seem to be possible without major disruptions. Since many local governments have responded to the revenue shortfall by adopting a spate of fees, much of the remaining reduction may be avoided.[17]

The employment data cited here are consistent with the finding that the public service level impact of the Jarvis–Gann amendment was small. Further support is provided by the budget of the City and County of San Francisco. Although accounting procedures make year-to-year comparisons difficult, the total budget adopted for 1978–79 was $823 million, down only $8 million from the preceding year. Moreover, the budget for salaries of permanent employees remained unchanged from a year earlier—implying no layoffs. Furthermore, several emergency tax measures adopted at the time the amendment was passed were rescinded—which would hardly imply fiscal distress. Finally, there is some evidence that the City actually budgeted a considerable surplus.[18]

Impact on 1978–79 Service Levels

To determine the impact on 1978–79 planned local expenditure I assume that expenditures are reduced by the loss of local revenue caused by Proposition 13 plus any state-mandated reductions in expenditure. My calculations are shown in Table 2–7. The official estimate of the loss in 1978–79 property tax revenue is given on the first line (Legislative Analyst 1978). From this must be subtracted state relief and the property tax receipts not anticipated in the official estimate. The resulting sum—$2,539 million—is thus the reduction in local government revenues below what would have been realized in 1978–79 without the amendment. This figure overstates the impact on public services because it fails to allow for the wage freeze imposed by the state legislature. This action frees funds that can be used for other purposes—including new personnel and mate-

Table 2-7. Local Public Expenditure before and after Proposition 13, 1978-79 (*$ millions*).

Changes in local revenues caused by Proposition 13		
Officially estimated 1978-79 property tax collections		$12,448
Officially estimated 1978-79 property tax collections under Proposition 13		5,404
		7,044
Less		
State relief	$4,100	
Additional property tax because of higher assessments	405	
Savings because of prohibition on cost-of-living increases	1,258	
Total		5,763
Net revenue shortfall		1,281
Projected 1978-79 local revenue		31,473
Percent net revenue shortfall		4.0%

rials. In effect, then, it is similar to a state grant to local governments of an amount equal to the wage savings. Hence, it must be subtracted from the revenue shortfall. This yields a net reduction in public services of $1,281 million below the level that would have prevailed without Jarvis-Gann. Since total 1978-79 revenues were expected to be $31,473 million, this amounts to a 4.0 percent shortfall. This would seem quite modest compared to the figures one frequently sees in the popular press and well below what many of Proposition 13's supporters had hoped to achieve.

Future Service Level Impacts

Even though the first year expenditure impact is minimal some would argue that the major impact will be felt in subsequent years. This view is based upon several considerations: 1) the state relief package was for a single year only; 2) the state surplus from which existing relief was drawn will be depleted; 3) the assessment growth restrictions of the amendment will inhibit future growth of property tax receipts.

First, although it is true that future state action cannot be predicted with certainty, the availability and the extent of future state assistance will undoubtedly be dictated by the existence of surplus state funds. Second, although the surplus available to the state legislature in July 1978 was the result of several years accumulation, there is ample reason to believe that the state could continue or even *increase* existing levels of assistance without increasing tax rates. To show this, I project the state surplus under two alternative sets of assumptions about the growth of personal income and state relief. The first assumes these to be 12 percent and 10 percent, respectively. The second uses 10 percent and 8 percent. The two sets of assumptions enable the reader to judge the sensitivity of the results. Although 12 percent personal income growth is slightly higher than the 11 percent experienced over the past 5 years, the recent upsurge in inflation makes such an assumption quite plausible. The 10 percent growth in aid, on the other hand, would maintain state relief as a constant fraction of the property tax revenue that would have prevailed in the absence of Jarvis–Gann; that is, in the absence of Proposition 13, aggregate property tax receipts would likely have grown at 10 percent per year—their average growth during the seventies. If state aid grows at a 10 percent rate, therefore, any reduction in the growth of local expenditures would be the result of the failure of *locally* raised revenues to keep pace with the growth they would have experienced without the amendment.

The second set of assumptions is made to bracket the range of possible outcomes. The 10 percent personal income growth figure has been surpassed each year since 1973, when it was 9.6 percent. The 8 percent growth of state relief, on the other hand, was chosen so as to maintain the *real* value of relief under present inflationary conditions.

In order to project the state surplus, a procedure similar to that used for Table 2–5 is employed. In other words, state expenditure is assumed to grow at the rate of personal income, while revenues grow at the same rate multiplied by the revenue elasticity. However, allowance must now be made for two post–Proposition 13 developments in the state income tax. The first is a one-time-only tax cut of $1 billion for fiscal 1978–79. The second is the indexation of income tax brackets for the first three percentage points of inflation. Hence, the elasticity of the income tax will be lowered below the 1.7 used to construct Table 2-5. To allow for this, we assume the elasticity to be reduced to 1.5. This produces a total state revenue elasticity of 1.166.

The projections under the two sets of assumptions are shown in Table 2-8. It is seen that under the first set of assumptions, the state can adequately fund the program without an increase in tax rates.[19] Although annual expenditures exceed revenues in the 1978-79 to 1984-85 period, the carryover surplus is sufficient to fund the deficits. Moreover, by 1985-86, the situation is turned around, as annual revenues begin to exceed expenditures.

The situation is very similar under the second set of assumptions. Although cumulative deficits begin to emerge by 1983-84, they are sufficiently small to ignore. For example, the $170 million annual deficit in 1984-85 amounts to only 0.006 percent of state revenue and 2.6 percent of the state relief program. Since the annual deficit

Table 2-8. Projected Surplus of the State of California, 1978-79 to 1986-87 (*$ millions*).

Fiscal Year	Assumption A [a]		Assumption B [b]	
	Yearly Surplus	Cumulative Surplus	Yearly Surplus	Cumulative Surplus
1978-79	-$1,800[c]	$2,000	-$1,800[c]	$2,000
1979-80	-468	1,532	-516	1,434
1980-81	-427	1,105	-474	1,010
1981-82	-372	733	-420	590
1982-83	-298	435	-354	236
1983-84	-203	232	-271	-35
1984-85	-33	149	-170	-205
1985-86	65	214	-49	-254
1986-87	n.c.[d]	n.c.[d]	96	-158

a. Assumption A: 12 percent growth of state personal income; 10 percent growth of state aid.

b. Assumption B: 10 percent growth of state personal income; 8 percent growth of state aid.

c. Reflects a $1 billion tax cut for 1978-79 only.

d. Not calculated.

Source: See derivation in text.

disappears by the next year, it seems reasonable, as an approximation, to argue that the program is fundable.

Whether or not the state can maintain its relief as a constant fraction of local government property tax losses, then, hinges critically upon the growth of personal income. If this growth is as high as 12 percent, such an objective is attainable without an increase in statutory tax rates. If, on the other hand, income growth is only 10 percent, aid can grow at only 8 percent per year without an increase in tax rates. In this event, relief will fall 2 percentage points below the level necessary to sustain local public expenditure growth at the level that would have prevailed in the absence of Proposition 13.[20] The quantitative significance of this will be discussed shortly, after local revenue growth has been discussed.

Let us turn now to the potential problems caused by the amendment's limit on property reassessments to 2 percent per year (unless the property is transferred). On its face, this might also seem to limit property tax revenue to 2 percent growth. However, such is not the case. The growth of property tax receipts will reflect the degree of underassessment as of 1978-79, the rate of increase of property values, the turnover rate of existing property, and the rate of new construction. Consider first the growth of residential property assessments.

It can be shown that under a plausible set of conditions, the growth of aggregate assessments for existing houses will grow at a rate equal to 90 percent of the underlying appreciation rate of housing prices in the *first* year following the reassessment limitation. Moreover, in subsequent years, the growth of assessments will continue to increase until it reaches the appreciation rate. Thus, if housing values are increasing at a 10 percent annual rate, the assessed value of the housing stock in place during 1978-79 will grow by 9 percent in 1979-80. The set of conditions that give rise to this outcome are as follows: 1) The existing housing stock is initially underassessed relative to its 1978-79 value by 25 percent; 2) The turnover rate of existing houses is 15 percent. Given the rapid growth of housing prices in recent years, the first condition should be easily satisfied. The 15 percent turnover rate, on the other hand, corresponds to the statewide average in recent years (San Mateo County Manager 1978).[21]

The rapid increase in the assessed value of the existing housing stock reflects the fact that although homes are reassessed less frequently under the amendment, the magnitude of the reassessments that occur will be much larger. For example, if a house is sold every seven years and housing prices grow at 10 percent per year, the assessed value of such a house will double at the time of sale. If, on the other hand, the house were annually assessed, the increase in assessments would be only 10 percent each year. Thus, Proposition 13 will have a much smaller effect on the growth of the assessed value of existing homes than perhaps some of its framers intended. To measure the effect on the total residential property tax base, the growth caused by new construction must be taken into account. Such activity amounts to between 2 and 4 percent of the existing housing stock in California. If housing prices are growing by 10 percent per year, which is modest by recent standards, the total residential property tax base will then increase by 11 to 13 percent per year, not much below its recent performance.

The situation for nonresidential properties is much different. Such properties are much less frequently transferred than housing. Hence, the growth of the taxable base of this class of property will likely be closer to the allowed 2 percent per year plus any growth due to investment. Since the latter has averaged 2 percent of the existing stock, a growth of 4 percent per year of the nonresidential property tax base can be expected to emerge.

To determine the expected growth of the *total* property tax base, one needs to take a weighted average of the growth of the residential and nonresidential components. Since the latter are of roughly equal magnitude, a simple average will do. Therefore, if housing prices rise by 10 percent per year in the future, the property tax base should grow by 7-1/2 percent to 8-1/2 percent—say 8 percent. This is only 2 percentage points below what would have been expected without Proposition 13. Such a gap will pose a much less serious problem, however, than before the adoption of Proposition 13. In the preamendment period, the property tax accounted for 40 percent of total revenues of local governments. Now, however, the share amounts to only 20 percent. This means that the annual revenue shortfall caused by the reassessment provision should amount to only 0.4 percent—scarcely a startling effect.

To determine the total effect of Proposition 13 on the growth of public services, we must combine our results for state relief with those for the reassessment limitations. If the state is able to sustain a growth in its relief of 10 percent per year (as in Assumption A in

Table 2-8), the reduction in the growth of public expenditure will reflect the reassessment provision alone; hence, it will be only 0.4 percent. If on the other hand, the state is only able to expand relief at 8 percent (Assumption B), the total reduction will be 0.7 percent.[22] Since the growth of local public expenditure would have been expected to be 10 percent per year, such a reduction would appear to be insignificant.

Recapitulation

This section has shown that Proposition 13 has and will likely continue to have only minor effects upon the size of the public sector in California. My estimates are that 1978-79 public service levels were only 2.8 percent below those prevailing in the year before the amendment took effect. Even if allowance is made for increases in public services that would have occurred in the absence of Jarvis-Gann, the reduction for 1978-79 is a modest 4.0 percent. The future expenditure effect, on the other hand, will hinge largely upon the continuance and growth of the state relief program launched in the first year of the amendment's operation. Since future state budget surpluses can be expected to materialize, it is not unreasonable to expect the necessary aid to be made available to local governments. The major source of constraint on expenditure in the future will result from a somewhat slower than necessary growth of property tax revenues. The shortfall, however, should amount to only 0.4-0.6 percent of the total revenue requirement of local governments. Since other revenue instruments such as charges, fees, and wage taxes are available, it is possible that even this minor shortage can be resolved. Hence, contrary to widespread opinion and the objectives of its framers, Proposition 13 has and should continue to have a small impact on public expenditure levels in California. Before moving to the next section two caveats are in order. First, the calculations of this section were done entirely at the aggregate level. It is quite possible, therefore, that some individual government units may experience considerable reductions in expenditure. The second is that no allowance was made for the possibility of recession in making projections in future state surpluses. A major recession may wipe out much of the carryover surplus from which the early deficits of the state relief program are funded. However, it is important to point out that even during the 1975 recession, California personal income grew by 10-1/2 percent—which is above my minimum growth assumption. This was largely due to inflation, which kept nominal incomes rising, despite the downturn. Since substantial inflation is likely for the next four or five years, even the occurrence of a recession during this period may not invalidate these conclusions.

IMPACTS UPON TAX STRUCTURE

Although Proposition 13 may have a relatively minor effect upon the level of government expenditure, it will have a substantial impact upon the state and local tax structure as well as upon the distribution of revenue raising responsibility between the state and local governments. In Table 2-9, alternative breakdowns of total state and local own-source revenue by level of originating government are presented. The first column shows the division that would have prevailed for 1978-79 in the absence of the amendment *and* assuming no action to cut state taxes. The local share of 49 percent compares with 52 percent for 1975-76 and a national average of 46 percent (1975-76). In column (2) an estimate of the actual 1978-79 breakdown is shown. The local share is seen to drop by 12 percentage points to 37 percent. This understates the extent of the reduction, however, because without the amendment the state would probably have taken steps to liquidate its surplus. Assuming it did so by $4.1 billion, the amount of local relief, column (3), shows the resultant local share. Proposition 13 is seen to have lowered the local share of state-local revenue by nearly 20 percentage points.

The situation is even more dramatic for specific local functions. Columns (4) and (5) show the share of education financed locally, with and without Proposition 13. The local share drops from 52 percent to 28 percent, falling by nearly half.[23] The significance of this reduction is highlighted by the fact that in only six other states was the local share below 30 percent (Advisory Commission on Intergovernmental Relations 1978).

It is widely believed that the control of public expenditure ultimately rests with the body responsible for raising the revenue. If this is correct, Proposition 13 will lead to a major shift towards state control. The prohibition against employee cost-of-living increases and against reductions in public safety may be just the tip of the

Table 2-9. State–Local Division of Revenue-Raising Responsibility, California, 1978–79.

| | Source of Total Own-Source Revenue ($ millions) | | | Share of Elementary and Secondary Education Costs | |
| | Without Amendment | With Amendment | Without Amendment[a] | Without Amendment | With Amendment |
	(1)	(2)	(3)	(4)	(5)
Local	$16,933 (49%)	$10,483 (37%)	$16,983 (55%)	52%	28%
State	17,675 (51%)	17,675 (63%)	13,575 (44%)	n.c.[b]	n.c.[b]
Total	34,653	28,158	30,558		

a. Assumes $4.1 billion in State tax reduction.
b. Not calculated.
Sources: U.S. Bureau of the Census, Government Finances; also estimates by the author.

iceberg for future state interventions. Local control or "home rule" may become a thing of the past in California.[24] Any judgment here, however, must remain in the realm of speculation. Experience with federal revenue sharing has shown that separation between revenue raising and expenditure authority is sometimes possible.

Less uncertainty surrounds the tax structure consequences of the amendment. If my reasoning has been correct, the net effect of Proposition 13 is a substitution of state tax sources for the local property tax. More specifically, it is likely that in the absence of the measure, the state would have cut income taxes.[25] Since the income tax is generally agreed to be more progressive than the property tax, such a substitution can be presumed to have favorable equity consequences.[26]

There are yet other implications of the shift toward state finance that arise from the character of the relief measure. Under the latter, relief is shared roughly in proportion to previous property tax collections.[27] Given that the major alternative to Jarvis–Gann was income tax reduction, areas that are relatively property intensive will gain relative to those areas that are income intensive. Since cities and rural areas have a larger share of the statewide property tax base than of the income tax base, taxes will be shifted toward the suburbs. Given the poor fiscal condition of many central cities such a shift will provide welcome relief.

Further relief for fiscally disadvantaged jurisdictions will come from a little noticed feature of the state relief measure. Because of the massive reduction in property tax receipts, it was necessary to specify how the remaining property tax revenues were to be allocated. Basically, the state legislature decided to allocate these proceeds among counties in proportion to their total assessed valuation. This precludes intercounty tax transfers. Within a county, however, tax proceeds are to be divided up roughly in proportion to previous property tax collections: Each local unit suffers the same percentage revenue loss. The implication of this arrangement (if continued) is that *future* increases in assessable base will be shared by all units within a jurisdiction. In effect, therefore, we have a system of tax base sharing similar to that in operation in the Minneapolis–St. Paul area in which increments to the metropolitan tax base are shared by all local units within the urban area. The major difference is that the latter is on a metropolitan basis as opposed to a county basis.

Base sharing has been widely touted as a technique to cope with the adverse fiscal consequences of suburbanization. Under this arrangement a central city would not suffer revenue losses if its tax base moves to the suburbs.[28] Moreover, the city will reap part of the benefit of whatever net growth occurs in the metropolitan area. Perhaps unwittingly, therefore, California, through the implementation of Proposition 13, has radically changed fiscal relationships in its metropolitan areas.[29]

To summarize this section, the adoption of Proposition 13 may profoundly affect the system of governance of California. On the one hand, it could lead to a substantial loss in local control, while on the other it may significantly affect fiscal relationships within metropolitan areas. Finally, it should increase the equity of California taxes both among persons and among political jurisdictions.

CONCLUSION

As its title indicated, this chapter examined the origins of Proposition 13 and its major implications for the growth of public expenditure and for the revenue structure of California governments. One of its principal findings is that the amendment cannot be attributable to a single cause, but reflects several forces. First was a high and growing state-local tax burden during a period when similar burdens in other parts of the country were leveling off. Second was a substantial shift in the distribution of property tax burdens toward homeowners at a time during which inflation was already causing budgetary problems for many households. Last was the emergence of a significant state surplus, which, if left unchecked, would have grown to unreasonable proportions.

Each of these factors contributed to the particular form of the measure that was presented to the voters. By placing a ceiling on the property tax rate, restricting the growth of assessments, and increasing the political majorities required for new taxes, it promised to restrict the size and growth of the public sector. By focusing tax reduction upon property taxes, it provided the relief sought by homeowners. And finally, by placing local governments in an intolerable fiscal situation, it forced the state to liquidate much of its surplus.

Although Proposition 13 appears to have achieved its property tax reduction and surplus liquidation objectives, it will probably have a minimal effect upon the growth of public expenditure. In its first year, it only required a 2.8 percent reduction in the average level of public services; in the near future, barring a major recession, it will have little or no effect unless the state withholds the relief it can afford and which it seems already committed to provide.

Since expenditures are insignificantly affected, Proposition 13 emerges as a tax reform measure, shifting emphasis from the property tax to the income tax. Moreover, by shifting a major portion of local revenue raising responsibility to the state, the amendment may seriously erode local control. The measure has also had some unintended consequences for fiscal relations at the local level since the property taxes that remain are to be shared on a countywide basis. This will tend to augment the resources of fiscally weak governments at the expense of the more affluent.

These unintended consequences aside, Proposition 13 emerges as a unique California phenomenon. The combination of factors that gave it birth are unlikely to be matched in any other state. The same can be said of its consequences. The existence of a significant state surplus mitigated its potentially disruptive impacts upon the delivery of public services. This carries an important lesson for other states that are considering measures similar to Proposition 13. Unless a considerable surplus already exists somewhere in the state-local system, the relatively smooth transition experienced by California cannot be expected to be shared. If not, citizens and public officials must be prepared to face considerable disruptions in the flow of public services.

NOTES TO CHAPTER 2

1. This rate limitation does not apply to the debt service on outstanding debt.
2. This description of the amendment is only meant to be suggestive.
3. It is estimated that a levy of 0.25 percent would be necessary initially to service outstanding debt.
4. The unevenness of these cuts reflects the fact that not all services are equally funded by the property tax as well as the existence of a myriad of state and federal mandates.
5. This conjecture is rejected by the U.S. Congressional Budget Office (1978), which using unpublished data concludes that tax burdens in California have been growing about the same rate as elsewhere. Curiously, a

67 percent difference in growth rates of tax burden is interpreted as a 2.2 percent differential (that is, 5.5 percent versus 3.3 percent).

6.   Since the homeowners' share of state personal income is unknown it was not possible to construct an index of homeowners' tax burden per se. Nevertheless, if income shares were constant over the period, the 30 percent figure is a measure of the *increase* in homeowners' burden.

7.   1975 is the latest year for which national data are available. Although the California number for that year is close to the national average, the recent upsurge in residential share in California is unlikely to be matched nationally because the boom in real estate prices was much more pronounced in California than elsewhere (Advisory Commission on Intergovernmental Relations 1978:106).

8.   The term "at least" is used because the state's projections, from which figures here were drawn, have proved markedly conservative in the past.

9.   To arrive at this figure, multiply the 11 percent by 1.7 to obtain the growth of personal income tax receipts—18.7 percent. Since the latter accounts for 1/3 of total general revenue, the growth of total revenue is simply $(1/3 \times 18.7) + (2/3 \times 11.0) = 13.5$.

10.   Although this argument has been couched in terms of taxes, it applies equally well to government expenditures because taxes and expenditure move together. An exception to the latter occurs after the 1977–78 fiscal year when substantial surpluses emerge. However, the gap between tax burdens in California and the rest of the United States had already opened substantially by 1977–78.

11.   Another element that may have played a role is the Serrano decision on the finance of elementary and secondary education. To implement Serrano, the state had planned to redistribute property taxes from rich to poor districts. Such action was to begin in the fiscal year 1978–79, but because of Proposition 13's restriction on property tax receipts, it had to be tabled. One might argue that support for Proposition 13 came from those who saw the impending state action as eliminating the connection between their property tax payments and the level of educational services they received. It should be noted, however, that under the state plan, local overrides to increase educational expenditures were permitted. (See California State Legislature 1978: 720.)

12.   The localities also have control over a modest general relief program. However, the amounts here are too small to warrant explicit discussion.

13.   Since the California Board of Equalization makes annual surveys of assessment ratios, one would have expected such widespread underassessment to show up in their data. However, figures for fiscal year 1977–78 only indicated underassessment of 8 percent in terms of *current* prices. (See California State Board of Equalization 1977.)

14. Total assessments for 1978-79 were $116.2 billion compared with the estimate of $108.1 billion. At a tax rate of $5 per $100 valuation, the extra $8.1 billion would yield $405 million.

15. Excluding special districts, for which data were unavailable, non-property tax receipts grew as follows: 1974-75 to 1975-76 — 12.6 percent; 1975-76 to 1976-77 — 10.2 percent; 1976-77 to 1978-79 — 20.7 percent.

16. The 55 percent wage share was taken from U.S. Bureau of Census 1977a: 30. Subsequent to the completion of this study the Supreme Court of California ruled that the wage freeze was unconstitutional. Data are yet unavailable as to the quantitative effect of this decision. However, local governments cannot be expected to grant substantial wage increases during such a period of stress.

17. A survey by the *Los Angeles Times* (October 1, 1978) showed that California cities increased expenditure by 4.6 percent and counties by 5.3 percent over 1977-78 levels. By my estimates such increases were sufficient to maintain *real* 1977-78 spending levels.

18. The city auditor is quoted as saying that the city "would probably have a surplus of $51 million" (*San Francisco Chronicle*, September 6, 1978). The situation with the San Francisco Unified School District is similar. The budget for 1978-79 actually appears to be higher than for the preceding year.

19. Of course, because of the progressivity of the income tax, effective rates increase.

20. This assumes locally raised revenue also grows at without-amendment rates. Otherwise, the 2 percentage points is added to the gap left by the latter revenues.

21. Although one would expect turnover rates to be reduced somewhat because reassessment is triggered by transfer, the effect is likely to be small. Most property transfers involve employment transfers, retirement, or death. Moreover, the maximum savings from maintaining ownership is 1 percent of the value of the home — a figure that may be small compared to the benefits of upgrading one's housing.

22. To arrive at this figure the shortfall in relief growth of 2 percentage points must be translated into a fraction of total local revenue. This is done by observing that state relief is 70 percent of the size of local property tax receipts. Hence, the shortfall in state relief is equivalent to a 1.4 percentage point shortfall in property tax receipts. Since property taxes constitute 20 percent of local revenues, we have a *revenue* shortfall of 0.28 percent because of state relief. The latter is then added to the reassessment result and rounded.

23. There is some reason to believe, however, that the figures in Table 2-9 may overstate the effects of the amendment on education finance. In

response to the Serrano decision the state had decided to redistribute property tax receipts among local school districts beginning with fiscal year 1978–79. Because of the limitation on the level of property taxes imposed by Jarvis–Gann, this action had to be shelved. Strictly speaking, funds that were to be redistributed should be counted as state as opposed to local funds. Unfortunately, estimates of the extent of such redistribution were not available at the time this chapter was written.

24. These home-rule effects of Proposition 13 are reinforced by the Serrano school finance decision, which requires greater uniformity of expenditures among school districts.

25. While any of the major state taxes could, in principle, be cut, the California legislature has cut income taxes three times in the past decade. It seems reasonable, therefore, to view income taxes as the marginal instrument.

26. Recently, it has been argued that the incidence of the property tax rests upon the owners of capital. However, this outcome is based upon the premise of a nationally applicable property tax. Since the case at hand is restricted to a single state, its major consequences will be upon output and input prices, as the orthodox theory would predict.

27. An exception is aid to education. Here relief was allocated according to a complex formula that reflected an attempt to equalize resources between school districts. See SB 154, California State Legislature 1978.

28. Unless the suburb is located in another county. Note that city–counties such as San Francisco obtain no benefit from this provision.

29. Since the relief measure is for the first year only, it is conceivable that the state legislature might change the distribution formula in future relief measures. For example, county property tax revenues could be divided among local units in proportion to a unit's share of aggregate assessments. Because the jurisdictional boundaries of many local units overlap, however, such an approach might produce nonsensical results. Moreover, if the objective of the relief was to minimize disruption of public service flows, the present allocation formula may be optimal.

REFERENCES

Advisory Commission on Intergovernmental Relations. 1978. *Significant Features of Fiscal Federalism, 1976–77*, vol. II.

California State Board of Equalization. 1977. *Annual Report 1976–77*. Sacramento.

California State Legislature. 1978. *Analysis of the Budget Bill*. Sacramento.

Economic Report of the Governor. 1978. Sacramento.

Federal Reserve Bank of San Francisco. 1978. "Recent National, Regional, and International Developments." September 5.

Legislative Analyst. 1978. "An Analysis of Proposition 13: The Jarvis–Gann Property Tax Initiative." Sacramento. May.

Real Estate Research Council of Northern California. 1978. *Northern California Real Estate Report*, vol. 30, no. 1.

San Francisco Bureau of the Budget. 1978. "Analysis of the Fiscal Impact of the Proposed Jarvis–Gann Amendment." Report to the San Francisco Board of Supervisors. March.

San Mateo County Manager. 1978. Study. May.

U.S. Bureau of the Census. 1977a. *Government Finances in 1975–76*.

_____. 1977b. *Public Employment in 1976*.

U.S. Congressional Budget Office. 1978. "Proposition 13: Its Impact on the Nation's Economy, Federal Revenues, and Federal Expenditures." July.

3 PROPOSITION 13, PROPERTY TRANSFERS, AND THE REAL ESTATE MARKETS

Frederick Balderston, with
I. Michael Heyman and
Wallace F. Smith

BACKGROUND

Proposition 13 has lowered the annual costs of owning real property in California. The larger this cost reduction to the owner, the more important the immediate consequences for particular ownership decisions: to buy, sell, or lease; to build a new building; to renovate or add to an existing building. At the same time, changes in financing and, in some cases, of the amount and quality of public services follow from Proposition 13 and will also affect real estate markets in various ways.

Real estate decisions, many thousands of them, may have large macroconsequences for the California economy and will affect governmental revenues and responsibilities. Yet there is wide uncertainty as to the specific meanings of the new implementing legislation and as to the responses to the new conditions that may be made by millions of California households, thousands of business enterprises, and many hundreds or thousands of governmental and public organizations. (Relatively modest shifts of assumptions fed into a UCLA forecasting model produced large predicted changes in rates of em-

This report is part of a project on impacts of Proposition 13 initiated by Professor Eugene C. Lee and supported by the U.S. Department of Housing and Urban Development.

ployment, unemployment, and total income in California.) (Kimbell 1978.)

For the purposes of this research report, property transfers are transactions that shift control of real property from one economic unit to another and are regarded as *substantive property transfers within the meaning of Proposition 13 and the 1978 implementing legislation*. An ownership change registered with the recorder of deeds is a typical example; but the state legislature, in Senate Bill 154 and Senate Bill 1212, excluded some transfers from consideration on the ground that they were essentially technical. Interspousal transfers and deed recordings to convey title of previous joint-tenancy property to the surviving spouse are two cases in point. If these nominal transactions had not been excluded, the property would have lost "base year" treatment and a new assessment would be made as of the date of the technical property transfer.

Our definition emphasizes change of control, not change of ownership, because, for example, leases of more than ten years are included as property transfers within the meaning of Proposition 13. (See Senate Bill 154, sec. 29.)

Two not very surprising conclusions can be reported concerning what happened in response to Proposition 13 immediately after its passage in June 1978. First, this change in tax exposure, having come about without the long seasoning that a significant change in the rules of the game often has through protracted hearings and incremental action, was difficult for decision makers to absorb and it increased business uncertainties for a time. Second, specific effects of the property tax change were confounded with many other forces and events in real estate markets. Even when data become available from several years of market activity after passage of Proposition 13, its effects will be very difficult to distinguish from those of numerous other variables that affect the volumes of property transfers, the amount of new construction, and the prices of real property.

It is revealing, however, to analyze the reasons why uncertainty has increased and to examine some temporary consequences of this uncertainty. Some elements of the market response to Proposition 13 can be analyzed, and the constitutional validity and the potential use of legal devices for property transfer can be discussed.

It is of interest to observe of the housing as well as other real estate markets that this decrease in the cost of holding real estate assets is expected by businessmen, other things being equal, to stimulate the real estate markets, both for existing property and for new construction. Holding these types of assets becomes more attractive relative to other asset types and relative to the situation before passage of Proposition 13. Yet the problem is, of course, that other things do not remain the same. The high uncertainty of which there was nearly universal testimony immediately after passage of Proposition 13 arose from the perception of a number of offsetting variables. These in turn may affect both the transaction volumes and prices for existing real estate and the rates of new construction.

An ideal way to approach the evaluation of Proposition 13's impact would be to begin from a fully defined econometric model of the market (say, the housing market) and inject the change in property assessment and tax cost into that model. From this, the change in values and the transaction turnover rate could be calculated from the relation in the model. The model might also permit calculation of the rate of convergence to full "1 percent of market value" treatment of the whole stock of housing.

It is not possible to follow this econometric approach, either for housing or for nonhousing real estate. Therefore, our investigation consists of a series of efforts to clarify elements of the impact of Proposition 13 by means of microeconomic analysis.

PROPERTY TURNOVER RATES

Property turnover is important in the interpretation of Proposition 13 because a property transfer triggers reassessment as of the date of transfer and therefore changes the property tax liability from base year treatment, or the previous assessed valuation adjusted by 2 percent per year. This, in turn, changes the costs of holding that property as compared with the costs prior to the transfer. (In today's generally inflationary climate, the assessment rises, and the tax liability and costs of property holding also rise. But it is quite conceivable that the transaction could take place at a lower price than the fair market value upon which the assessed value was based, thus resulting in a reduction of the property tax.)

Property turnover rates, therefore, must be used for future estimates of the revenue from property taxes. In particular, turnover rates offer a signal of the extent to which base-year treatment is replaced by current fair market value as the basis of assessment.

Therefore, the extent of convergence of total property tax revenue in a county toward a level based on current fair market value depends upon the turnover rate in that county. (Of course, the *average* rate of property turnover does not tell the whole story. Some parcels of property may change hands repeatedly whereas others remain in the same continuous ownership indefinitely. Thus, the base-year treatment extending back to 1975 will never be eliminated completely from a county assessor's rolls.)

Total property tax revenue in a county will, under foreseeable economic conditions, inevitably lag behind the tax yield based upon current fair market valuation even if every parcel of real property changes hands at the average turnover rate. Proposition 13 provides for a 2 percent per year increase of assessed value from the last previous assessment based upon a transaction. Thus, if the average rate of price inflation for real property is greater than 2 percent per year, each parcel is valued for assessment purposes at less than the current year's fair market value most of the time. It catches up briefly when there is an ownership change, and then it begins to lag behind again in subsequent years. The more frequently the property changes hands, the smaller the reduction of property tax payments below each year's current valuation. Property turnover rates in California counties have ranged from 8 percent to 20 percent. In this range the maximum valuation lag on a property is between five and twelve years. How big the reduction in tax yield to the county and local governments will be, however, depends also upon the size of the difference between the average annual rate of price inflation in real property and the allowable adjustment of 2 percent per year. Figure 3-1 illustrates this.

County-by-County Turnover Rates in California

Table 3-1 shows gross property turnover in each county of California for three assessment years. (The assessment year runs from March 1 to February 28 of the year following; the data come from county assessors to the State Board of Equalization as part of the standard workload reporting system.) Table 3-1 shows substantial variation in gross property turnover between one year and another for a given county. It also shows big differences between one county and another. Finally, even though 1974-75 was a recession year and 1976-77 was a good year in real estate markets, Table 3-1 does not

Figure 3-1. Lag in Assessed Value behind Current Fair Market Value.

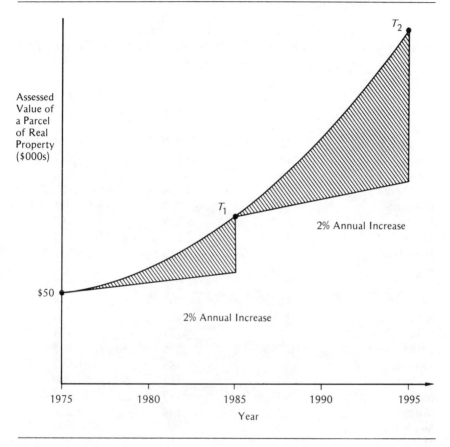

T_1, T_2 are transactions.

Shaded area denotes assessment lag.

show indications of the presence of a well-defined cyclical tendency—for example, to have low turnover in 1974–75 with steady increases thereafter. The statistical portrayal of overall property turnover, as shown in Table 3–1, does imply that a great deal of data gathering and analysis will be required to arrive at an accurate interpretation of the influences on turnover and the consequences of turnover.

The statistical presentation in Table 3–1 is based on available data that were reported for workload calculations by county assessors to the California State Board of Equalization. For each county, this is

Table 3-1. Gross Property Turnover Rates, California Counties, Selected Years.

County	March 1, 1974– February 28, 1975	March 1, 1975– February 29, 1976	March 1, 1976– February 28, 1977
Alameda	.135	.141	.171
Alpine	.183	.077	.139
Amador	.120	.143	.166
Butte	.163	.238	.203
Calaveras	.100	.092	.106
Colusa	.151	.188	.241
Contra Costa	.140	.130	.235
Del Norte	.290	.338	.185
El Dorado	.199	.200	.231
Fresno	.153	.192	.167
Glenn	.157	.140	.113
Humboldt	.188	.113	.357
Imperial	.094	.102	.091
Inyo	.258	.236	.257
Kern	.122	.103	.138
Kings	.117	.097	.144
Lake	.158	.151	.134
Lassen	.234	.238	.143
Los Angeles	.137	.144	.163
Madera	.140	.113	.200
Marin	.187	.173	.215
Mariposa	.138	.134	.264
Mendocino	.099	.107	.124
Merced	.175	.154	.165
Modoc	.091	.234	.163
Mono	.142	.160	.189
Monterey	.146	.156	.178
Napa	.145	.190	.193
Nevada	.223	.219	.254
Orange	.248	.247	.213
Placer	.145	.142	.186
Plumas	.268	.282	.271
Riverside	.147	.143	.236
Sacramento	.151	.146	.209
San Benito	.123	.127	.164
San Bernadino	.130	.156	.149
San Diego	.148	.137	.203

Table 3-1. continued

County	March 1, 1974–February 28, 1975	March 1, 1975–February 29, 1976	March 1, 1976–February 28, 1977
San Francisco	.174	.126	.139
San Joaquin	.135	.143	.179
San Luis Obispo	.158	.183	.223
San Mateo	.117	.123	.155
Santa Barbara	.138	.171	.161
Santa Clara	.240	.233	.233
Santa Cruz	.165	.150	.208
Shasta	.244	.241	.267
Sierra	.114	.137	.164
Siskiyou	.123	.114	.121
Solano	.153	.156	.141
Sonoma	.141	.150	.186
Stanislaus	.164	.178	.210
Sutter	.113	.123	.141
Tehama	.254	.292	.295
Trinity	.153	.124	.162
Tulare	.167	.179	.194
Tuolumne	.121	.112	.121
Ventura	.153	.182	.220
Yolo	.183	.193	.192
Yuba	.177	.179	.205
Average	.161	.165	.183

Source: California State Board of Equalization, Assessors' Budgets and Workloads Summaries, 1975–76, 1976–77, 1977–78 calendar years. Property turnover rates for each of the 58 California counties were calculated by dividing the total number of property transfers (for the corresponding assessment years) by the number of secured roll units.

calculated by dividing the total number of parcels on the "secured roll" into the total number of property transfers. These are data reported to the State Board of Equalization by county assessors. The 1976–77 turnover rates vary from a low of 0.091 in Imperial County to a high of 0.357 in Humboldt County—a remarkable range for such a gross statistic.

The statewide average of 0.183 for all property in all counties is, however, an interesting statistic. If this rate of property transfer is maintained in the future, the implication is that within five to six years, 100 percent turnover of property will have occurred. There may be some considerable number of real estate parcels that remain in the same ownership, of course, and other parcels having two or more ownership changes. Thus, the implication of 100 percent turnover cannot be taken to mean that base year treatment is eliminated entirely.

Property transfers as reported in these data, however, include many more items than are covered by Proposition 13 and in the implementing legislation enacted during June 1978. In future, the interpretation of property turnover can be improved by obtaining measures that reflect an analytically defined turnover concept. First, it will be important to separate the measures of the number of parcels between housing, on the one hand, and nonhousing real estate on the other, and to disaggregate further as follows: 1) single-family, from one to four family parcels, and five or more family parcels; and 2) in nonhousing real estate, to distinguish types of property as industrial, agricultural, office, or commercial. A uniform classification for use by all counties would be needed, and prior to its adoption there should be consultations with urban planning officials, real estate economists, financial institution professionals, and other interested users of real estate data.

Four alternative concepts could also be considered, for use on the data of each property category. For that category, let S be the number of existing parcels, E be the number of sales made, and C the number of new parcels created through subdivision and construction activity. Then

(1) E/S is the turnover rate with no construction.

(2) $(E + C)/S$ is the adjusted turnover on the preexisting number of parcels.

(3) $(E + C)/(S + C)$ is the adjusted turnover on the end-of-year stock.

and

(4) $(E + C + N)/(S + C - W)$ is the fully adjusted turnover on the fully corrected end-of-year stock, where N is the number of parcels created by subdivision but not built on and W is the number of parcels withdrawn from the deed register through property consolidations, government condemnations, and so on.

Table 3-1 is based on measures in accordance with concept (3). Concept (4) is the ideally satisfactory one, if the most comprehensive view of overall turnover is needed. For housing-market analysis, however, housing economists sometimes wish to analyze the turnover on existing property separately from the impact of newly built housing. For this purpose, then, they might wish to have, for each housing category, a separate measure according to concept (1) for comparison with new construction in that category. The reason is that economic variables affect transactions on existing houses differently from their effect on new buildings.

We will continue with exploratory investigation of variables correlated with property turnover and of possible causal relationships. Among the variables under investigation as possible correlates of county turnover rates are total population and population growth; employment; construction activity, including both housing starts and dollar volume of nonresidential construction awards; and retail sales.

One example of the differences in turnover rates for different categories of property is shown in Table 3-2. For calendar years 1976 and 1977 single-family housing turnover was 13.9 percent and 14.1

Table 3-2. Comparison of Single-Family House Turnover Rate and Other Property Turnover, Santa Clara County.

	1976	1977
	Jan. 1-Dec. 31	*Jan. 1-Dec. 31*
Number of sales transfers[a]	43,026	44,399
Number of single-family sales	37,229	39,113
Single-family sales as a percentage of all sales	86.5%	88%
Number of single-family parcels	268,824	277,407
Single-family sales as a percentage of all parcels	13.9%	14.1%
Number of all other real property sales	5,797	5,286
All other sales as a percentage of all sales	13.5%	12%
Number of all other parcels	61,169	60,813
All other real property transfers as a percentage of parcels	9.5%	8.7%

a. Includes sales of existing properties and of new parcels by subdivision; excludes quit-claim deeds and other technical transfers not qualifying as property transfers under Proposition 13. State Board of Equalization tables for the assessment year from March 1, 1976, to February 28, 1977 show 78,221 total property transfers of all types.

Source: Loren Leavitt, M.A.I., Chief Appraiser, Santa Clara County, California.

percent, respectively, in Santa Clara County, a very active county in real estate volume and new housing construction. The same table shows turnover in property other than single-family housing; for 1976 this rate was 9.5 percent, and for 1977, 8.7 percent. Many particular categories of business property—factory and office buildings, for example—are said to have still lower turnover rates. There is good evidence to substantiate the view that disaggregated data on the number of parcels and on number of sales should be gathered for each county from now on, in order to facilitate analysis.

As a final note on the problems of statistics, it should be pointed out that the statistics of real property diverge from the statistics of housing in important respects. For example, the number of housing *parcels* is the number of separately recorded ownerships; each multi-family rental structure is counted in housing statistics by the number of dwelling units it contains. When a change in the rules of the real estate game occurs, as has happened in Proposition 13, there is creation of new real property parcels and ownerships through conversion of rental housing to condominiums. We are not yet sure how the statistics will reflect the conversion to cooperative (stock) ownership, which also occurs. We now turn to detailed consideration of turnover in residential real property.

TURNOVER OF OWNER-OCCUPIED DWELLINGS*

Since there is great interest in the effect of Proposition 13 on the turnover rate of single-family homes, it would be useful to have data on what that rate had been prior to the election and its change in assessment practices. Unfortunately, little data exist except for partial counts of sales, through multiple listing services, for example. What is lacking is the inventory base from which those sales came. Another frequently cited piece of information is the average life of a single-family home loan, usually assumed to be about eight years; not all home purchases are institutionally financed, however, and loans may be refinanced for reasons other than sale.

A recent regression study in Alameda County provides information that may be more significant than a turnover rate per se, namely that cross sectionally over census tracts the census-based turnover

---

*Written by Wallace F. Smith.

rate was not significantly influenced by common socioeconomic variables (such as family income, race, family size), so that the best predictor of the turnover rate is in fact the average turnover rate: approximately 10 percent per year. Again, this is a cross-sectional constant; there are undoubtedly seasonal and cyclical fluctuations in the rate that remain to be described.

Owner-occupancy turnover rates can be calculated from the decennial census. Counts of owner-occupied dwellings on the enumeration date can be compared with the number of homeowner households that moved in during the fifteen-month period preceding enumeration; the number of owner-occupied dwellings constructed during that same fifteen months can be subtracted from both entries in order to restrict the turnover rate to the existing inventory. With this adjustment and a correction for the fifteen-month period, estimated annual homeownership turnover rates for California metropolitan areas in 1969–70 are as shown in Table 3–3.

The 1975 Annual Housing Survey suggests possible explanations for the variation in turnover among metropolitan areas—namely that

Table 3-3. Estimated Annual Homeownership Turnover Rates for Metropolitan Areas, 1969-70.

Anaheim–Santa Ana–Garden Grove	.13
Bakersfield	.08
Fresno	.07
Los Angeles–Long Beach	.07
Modesto	.08
Oxnard–Ventura	.11
Sacramento	.09
Salinas–Monterey	.08
San Bernadino–Riverside–Ontario	.10
San Diego	.09
San Francisco–Oakland	.07
San Jose	.08
Santa Barbara	.09
Santa Rosa	.09
Stockton	.06
Vallejo–Napa	.08
All California metropolitan areas	.08
All California urbanized areas	.08
All California	.08

lower rates occur for central cities as opposed to suburban areas, for older housing units, and for elderly homeowners as opposed to child-rearing families. The rates shown in Table 3-4 were calculated from the 1975 survey, which does not permit the extraction of newly constructed units and so is not entirely comparable to the 1970 information. Sample sizes in the Annual Housing Survey are very small, and these rates—particularly for elderly households—have large standard errors.

Available home turnover data are inadequate for development of reasonably robust model from which the impact on turnover of property tax changes could be inferred. Some insight into likely response can, however, be gained from consideration of hypothetical but realistic options for homeowners under assessment practices and property tax rates before and after passage of Proposition 13.

Table 3-4. Turnover Rates for Metropolitan Area, 1975.

	Central City	Not in Central City	Total
San Francisco–Oakland Standard Metropolitan Statistical Area (SMSA)			
All owner-occupied units	.07	.10	.09
Built 1939 or earlier	.05	.06	.06
Husband–wife households			
no nonrelatives	.07	.10	.10
head age 65 or over	.01	.01	.01
One-person household, age 65 plus	.01	.04	.02
San Diego SMSA			
All owner-occupied units			.12
Built 1939 or earlier			.06
Husband–wife households			
No nonrelatives			.12
Head age 65 or over			.05
One-person household, age 65 plus			.05

Source: 1975 Annual Housing Survey.

EFFECTS OF REASSESSMENT ON SALE
OF OWNER-OCCUPIED HOUSING

Proposition 13 provides that property is to be assessed at its 1975–76 market value plus 2 percent per year so long as ownership remains unchanged. A change of ownership means that assessed value is changed immediately to accord with market value at that time (presumably as indicated by the price paid). This means that a family desiring to change its dwelling—because of a change in its job situation or family size, perhaps, or simply to upgrade its housing—incurs a financial penalty in the form of stepped up property tax liability. Quite apart from legal questions arising from this provision of Proposition 13 (which are treated elsewhere in this chapter), reassessment on sale might seem likely to discourage homeowner mobility. If this effect were substantial, the replacement demand for housing might be weakened and the level of new construction would fall. Families would be more likely to stay put, perhaps undertaking improvements in their present homes rather than shopping for new ones. How strong is this effect?

This question was put to a number of well-informed persons in the California housing industry—real estate brokers, mortgage lenders, builders, and others. The procedure was very informal, but the view was unanimous: There is pervasive uncertainty among buyers and sellers about how this provision will affect the housing market and strong belief on the part of industry professionals that it will not prove to be significant.

Informed professionals are not able to cite housing turnover rates per se; industry data in common use do not include such rates. But home sales indicators—numbers of listings and sales, trends in average prices and in loan volumes—do not yet reflect any clear impact of Proposition 13 as of September 1978. Most of these indicators were off somewhat during the spring of 1978 in comparison with the hyperactive preceding spring; this could have reflected uncertainty about the upcoming Proposition 13 vote, but the belief is that it reflected other factors such as some increase in the cost of mortgage money and substantial fall-off of speculative/investor purchases of single-family homes. The rate of increase in average home prices sold through multiple listing was thought to be sharply lower in the summer of 1978—probably generally under 10 percent per year—than it had been in early 1977, approximating 30 percent in some areas, but that decline had begun in mid-1977.

As for the direct impact of the reassessment rule on potential home sellers and buyers, informed practitioners believe that the generally lower level of tax *rates* robs changing *assessments* of their importance. As soon as one starts to attach numbers to the relationship, however, it becomes obvious that "it all depends" on expected rates of appreciation and other partly subjective factors.

Table 3-5 carries out a hypothetical case in point. It assumes a family owned a home worth $50,000 in 1975 that by 1978 had risen in value (at 10 percent per year) to $66,550; the family now contemplates selling the home to purchase one valued at $90,000. Under Proposition 13 what is the property tax effect of the move, and how will this effect change if the move is deferred to 1983 or 1988?

The table assumes market values rise uniformly at 10 percent per year, and that pre-Proposition 13 tax rates are 10 percent of assessed value. Beyond these assumptions it merely employs assessment and tax formulas written into law, including the homeowner's exemption. (Income tax consequences of changes in property tax payments are not included, however.) Acknowledging that "it depends" to a considerable extent on the appreciation rate and pre-Proposition 13 tax rate assumed as well as on the price gap between the new and the existing home, Table 3-5 points to three distinct kinds of effects:

1. Proposition 13 *lowers* the tax penalty for the family that wants to upgrade its housing. Before Proposition 13, the move in 1978 would have raised annual property taxes from $1,489 to $2,075, an increase of $586. Under Proposition 13 the same move would raise taxes by only $369 ($830 minus $461).

2. Proposition 13 provides a tax incentive for moving to a better house now rather than later. For the family that upgraded to the better house in 1978, the total property tax in 1983 would be $924, which is $408 higher than the old house's property tax for 1983. If the upgrade is postponed until 1983, the total tax on the new house in that year would be $1,379, or $863 more than if the old house had been retained.

3. Eventually Proposition 13's reassessment begins to "lock in" the homeowner in the sense that the tax penalty for buying a better house is greater under the new law than it would have been with-

Table 3-5. Effect of Proposition 13 on Hypothetical Homeowner's Decision to move.

	1975	1978	1983	1988	
Present home market value (mv)	$50,000	66,550	107,179	172,613	Inc. 10%/year
Assessed value (av)					
Pre-13	10,750	14,888	25,045	41,403	mv × 25% – 1,750
Post-13		46,060	51,583	57,680	1975 mv + 2%/year – 7,000
Property tax					
Pre-13	1,075	1,489	2,504	4,140	av × 10%
Post-13		461	516	577	av × 1%
New home market value		90,000	144,946	233,437	Inc. 10%/year
Pre-13 assessed value		20,750	34,487	56,609	mv × 25% – 1,750
Post-13 property tax		2,075	3,449	5,661	av × 10%
Post-13, buy 1978					
Assessed value		83,000	92,367	102,709	90,000 + 2%/year – 7,000
Property tax		830	924	1,027	av × 1%
Post-13, buy 1983					
Assessed value			137,946	153,032	144,000 + 2%/year – 7,000
Property tax			1,379	1,530	av × 1%
Post-13, buy 1988					
Assessed value				226,437	233,437 – 7,000
Property tax				2,264	av × 1%
Tax increase on move					
Pre-13		586	945	1,521	
Post-13, buy 1978		369	408	450	
Post-13, buy 1983			863	953	
Post-13, buy 1988				1,687	

out it, when a sufficient number of years has elapsed. The jump in property tax is greater under Proposition 13 than without it. The hypothetical family that put off its move to 1988 would then incur a tax penalty of $1,521 per year under pre-Proposition 13 rules, but $1,687 with Proposition 13 in effect.

The dollar difference may not seem great, particularly as it is a hypothetical comparison and one that ignores other factors that may enter into a decision to move. The financial penalty would also be at least partly offset by the years of post-13 tax saving in the older house.

The "locked-in" effect is clearest in the case of a family who must move for reasons other than a desire to upgrade its housing—because of a job change, for example. For such a family selling its home in 1978 for $66,550 and buying another for the same price, the assessed value of its home under Proposition 13 would have risen from $46,060 to $59,550 and annual taxes gone up from $461 to $596. The new figure is well below the pre-Proposition 13 tax of $1,489, however, and that is likely to color the thinking of people in the market for some period of time.

The interplay of factors involved in this comparison seems to justify the apparent widespread uncertainty among homeowners about what Proposition 13 really means to them. It is in fact a fairly complicated equation. That the absolute dollar amounts seem too small to worry about corresponds to the largely subjective responses we obtained from industry professionals.

PROPOSITION 13 AND THE CALIFORNIA HOUSING MARKET*

Homeowners—Basic Issues

Pending more definitive analysis of the Proposition 13 phenomenon it is reasonable to assume that California's 3.9 million homeowning households were a principal force encouraging introduction of the measure and that most homeowners voted for it. Owners of rental property stood to gain from reduction of property taxes, but they do not constitute a numerous nor cohesive group. Renter households

*Written by Wallace F. Smith.

could expect only indirect and partial benefits from Proposition 13 at best. But homeowners knew with certainty what Proposition 13 would do for them immediately; based on 1976-77 estimates from the legislative analyst's office, the average homeowner stood to gain $35.24 a month through the reduction in property taxes. This is 57 percent of the average monthly property tax cost to homeowners, $61.83. Both monthly figures would have escalated by 1978-79, of course.

Is this amount of saving sufficient to change the market behavior of homeowners, homebuyers, or homebuilders? Will other aspects of Proposition 13 — the rule regarding reassessment upon sale, in particular — counteract these effects? Will the immediate benefits to homeowners be weakened, offset or perhaps intensified by changes in the provision of local government services, or by further fiscal reforms?

We can gain perspective on these questions by looking briefly at what was happening to the California homeowner's situation in the few years prior to Proposition 13. Household incomes had been rising sharply, reflecting not only general inflation but also a composite demographic factor of declining birthrates and increased labor force participation by married women. For example, in Santa Clara County between 1970 and 1975 household income per capita had risen 50.4 percent, of which 22.5 percentage points was attributable to this demographic factor and the remaining 27.9 percentage points reflected wage gains including inflation (Urban Land Institute 1977). Taken together, these two effective demand factors explain most of the price escalation of homes in California from 1970 to the present and help us understand why the resale and construction markets during most of the period have been strong despite the appearance that families were being priced out of the homeowner market. Certain families were indeed being priced out, but they were being replaced by other households for whom homeownership might not have been considered a "normal" housing choice.

By informal estimates upward of 80 percent of new houses in California have been sold over the past four or five years to childless, two-income households. According to a study of demographic characteristics of house purchases for comparable four-bedroom houses in San Jose, 43 percent of the buyers in 1968 were two-persons-employed households. In 1976, two-persons-employed households constituted 88 percent of house purchasers, and the household size averaged 2.8 persons (Urban Land Institute 1977: Table 9).

For childless couples who both work, the traditional reason for wanting a single-family home—to rear children—is absent. Tax and investment incentives, however, more than compensate for this; the single-family house is well suited to the tax needs of an employed couple unwittingly moving into onerous personal income brackets and also provides an excellent inflation hedge for savings. (If the working couple do later decide to have children, they will at least have been able to benefit by rising equity values and tax savings during the interval when both had wage incomes.) The demand for new houses spilled over into the market for existing houses. As market values rose, the assessed values of houses also rose, given the principles that assessors are required to follow and the improved techniques at their disposal for updating their rolls of single-family dwellings. Tax rates did not fall in proportion, so property tax burdens rose, not just for those who were buying new or existing houses,

Table 3-6. Inflation and Property Tax Burden on Hypothetical Fixed-Income Homeowner.

Market value of home (mv)	$40,000	$70,494	12% appreciation rate
Assessed value	8,250	15,874	mv × 0.25 - 1,750
Property tax	825	1,587	Assume 10% rate
Fixed income	10,000	10,000	
Property tax as percentage of income	8.25%	15.87%	
Income after property tax	9,175	8,413	
Purchasing power (1973 $)	9,175	5,726	Assume 8% inflation rate
Loss of purchasing power due to property tax and inflation		3,449	= 37.6% of $9,175
Effect of Proposition 13: Suppose 1975 market value of home =		60,000	
then 1978 assessed value =		56,672	60,000 × $(1.02)^3$ - 7,000
and property tax =		567	
leaving for other living costs		9, 433	
an increase in 1978 $'s =		1,020	

but for all homeowners, including those with single incomes and fixed incomes.

Table 3-6 describes the situation of a hypothetical but generally realistic fixed-income homeowner between 1973 and 1978. A retired person, for example, would be likely to be living in a debt-free home worth more than his or her current income would justify purchasing; property taxes would be the principal housing cost, taking 8.25 percent of income in 1973. Five years later, if home values increase at 12 percent per year (which approximates reality), assessments are updated, property tax rates do not fall, and the householder's money income remains fixed, property taxes take 15.87 percent of that income. Inflation, together with rising taxes, reduces nonhousing purchasing power by almost 38 percent. This person is faced with a choice between homeownership and food, let alone the other good things of life. *Any* tax relief would be desperately desired. Sufficient tax relief would allow the person to remain in his or her home. Since elderly people have less occasion to move than younger people, who are making job changes or enlarging their families, the threat of reassessment upon purchase of another dwelling has little meaning to them. Hence for the hypothetical retired homeowner Proposition 13 is a nearly unmitigated Godsend. In the example of Table 3-6, supposing market value had reached $60,000 by 1975, the new property tax expense in 1978 would be $1,020 per year less. Proposition 13 clearly helps these households stay where they are, which in itself should cause the inventory turnover rate to fall. In the five years prior to its passage, undoubtedly, many fixed-income households in California were forced to sell their homes because of rising property values, assessments, and taxes.

For other homeowning households the pre–Proposition 13 situation is far less clear. Property taxes are only a part of the fiscal burden on homeowners that statewide measures can deal with, about 40 percent of the total taxes (property, sales, and state income) paid by homeowners in 1976-77 (from a study by the State of California, legislative analyst 1976-77). The combined impact of these three taxes was moderately progressive, rising from about 8.5 percent of income at the $10,000 to $20,000 income level, to just under 11 percent of income when income was between $50,000 and $75,000. In terms of household income the property and sales tax burdens were regressive, but this was more than offset by the structure of state income tax rates.

For households whose current incomes were at least keeping up with inflation and whose homes were appreciating faster than the general inflation rate while property tax rates were relatively stable or even falling, it is not easy to see great concern about property taxes per se. Putting the three major taxes together, however, and taking into account the combined effect of inflation (even if incomes rise at the same rate), the progressive structure of unindexed state income tax rates, and the accelerated rise in property values, we can construct a picture of the overall tax burden that homeowners in 1976-77 might have forecast five years hence, by 1981-82. Figure 3-2 traces the composite tax burden as a percentage of income for three situations—the actual pattern in 1976-77; the pattern that would exist in 1981-82 assuming 8 percent per year increase in incomes and in the Consumer Price Index and escalation of house prices at 12 percent per year without reductions in property tax rates; and finally the 1981-82 situation adjusted for the Jarvis-Gann amendment's direct effect, lower property taxes.[1] The two forecast lines thus assume real household income remains unchanged; inflation and the tax system cause the proportion of income required for these taxes to rise.

The pre-Proposition 13 projected escalation of tax burden is massive. (If federal income tax burden were taken into account, the projection would be still more alarming. Since Proposition 13 affected only state fiscal burdens, the role of the federal income tax has been omitted from this analysis.) The homeowner in the $10,000 to $15,000 bracket (real, 1976-77 income) who paid 8.7 percent of income for property, sales, and state income taxes together in 1976-77 could expect to pay 15.2 percent in five years. For the $40,000 to $50,000 household (again, in 1976-77), the burden increases from 10.2 percent to a projected 23.2 percent of income. By earning enough to stay even with inflation, the household promotes itself into ever higher income tax brackets. Despite the more rapid (assumed) increase in house prices and therefore in the property tax, in the aggregate by 1981-82, that tax still would account for just about 40 percent of the three-tax total. The unindexed income tax structure just about compensates for the difference in the inflation rates assumed—8 percent for incomes and 12 percent for houses.

The direct effect of Proposition 13 is to lower the whole structure of tax burdens relative to what might have been expected by 1981-82. With respect to the structure existing in 1976-77, however, we have no real income gain to the taxpayer while the structure becomes

Figure 3-2. Effects of Proposition 13 on Projected Tax Burden—
California Homeowners, Assuming Real Income Unchanged 1976–
77 to 1981–82.

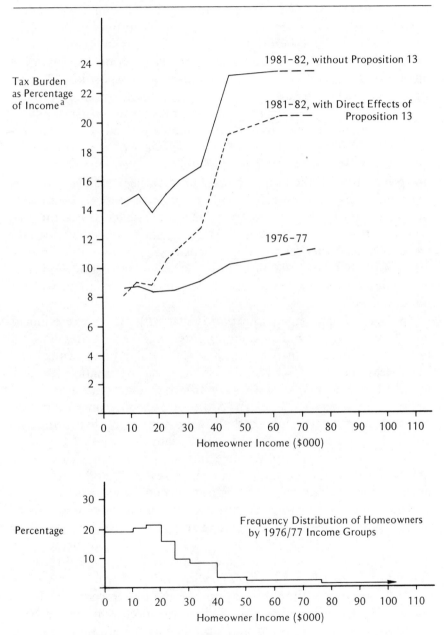

a. Sum of property, sales, and state income taxes.

sharply more progressive. The homeowner earning between $20,000 and $25,000 in 1976-77, paying 8.6 percent of income for these three taxes, will be paying 11.7 percent by 1981-82 *after* Proposition 13 (on the assumed inflation rates used here, and before indexing measures). That is better than the 16.1 percent burden that might have been anticipated before Jarvis-Gann, but it is still an increase in tax burden. Tax relief did not arrive with Proposition 13! (In developing these projections, secondary impacts of Proposition 13 upon state and federal income tax liability were not taken into account. The benefit of Proposition 13 to homeowners is thus overstated.)

This exercise, however hypothetical, does seem to have two important implications for the prospective behavior of the homeowner market. One is that the complaint of the non-fixed-income owner is not primarily with the property tax, but with the overall level of taxation. In a very real sense, it is not extravagance of local government that consumes the homeowner's real income so much as it is the progressive structure of state (and federal) income tax rates. This would say that homeowners supporting Proposition 13 were not necessarily asking for wholesale reductions in the level or the cost of local services. Local services will still play a role in the decision to select a home.

The second apparent implication is that without complete indexing of state and federal income tax rates, homeowning families are faced with continued increases in their real fiscal burdens, which may be at least partly offset by almost tax-free appreciation of their homes. This is a time to settle more firmly than ever into homeownership or to attain it if one can. Although it is difficult to translate appreciating property into cash flow to pay rising living and tax costs, that is the game toward which many households are being pushed—just about the only game in town. Proposition 13 encourages speculative holding and refinancing of real property, particularly in the context of inflation and lagging reform of other taxes.

Figure 3-3 shows projected 1981-82 tax burdens with and without Proposition 13's direct effect, in terms of current rather than real incomes. In 1976-77 a household with $35,000 income was paying 9.1 percent of that income for property, sales, and state income taxes; in 1981-82 a family with $35,000 would be paying about 9.5 percent without Proposition 13 and 6.4 percent with Proposition 13. They are different families, however. The family with $35,000 in 1976-77 would have an income of more than $51,000

Figure 3-3. Projected Current Income Burden of Major California Taxes on Homeowners, 1981–82, and Effects of Proposition 13.

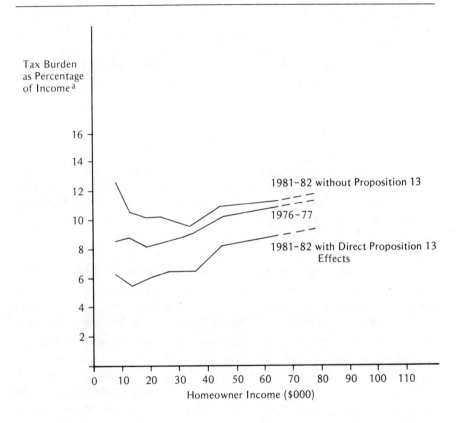

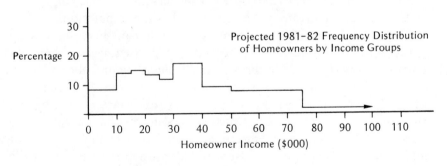

a. Sum of property, sales, and state income taxes.

five years later, assuming an 8 percent rate of increase. Figure 3-3 shows an apparent across-the-board easing in tax burden resulting from Proposition 13, but that is quite misleading.

It should be noted that both Figures 3-2 and 3-3 assume home-owners do not move their places of residence between 1976-77 and 1981-82. That is, the increase in property taxes post-Proposition 13 is limited to 2 percent per year after first being reduced by 57 per-cent of the initial level.

Property Transfer Mechanisms

Because most owner-occupied housing changes hands with the assist-ance of mortgage financing and of real estate brokers and title com-panies, the recording of a deed will surely continue as the dominant form of property transfer. Contracts of sale have on occasion been used in the past, however, for either of two purposes. First, there was a recent flurry of interest in them as a means of circumventing the due-on-sale clause that is standard in most mortgage terms. This clause enables the lender to force a new negotiation of mortgage terms rather than its acceptance, automatically, of assumption of the outstanding mortgage by the new buyer. One leading court case, Tucker versus Lassen Savings and Loan Association, upheld such an arrangement and invalidated a due-on-sale clause. Other cases may uphold the clause. A real estate brokers' association engaged a promi-nent attorney to draft a model contract of sale and promoted the idea of its use quite actively for a time, but it does not seem at all likely that this alternative to outright ownership transfer will become very important in ordinary residential real estate transactions.

The second way in which contracts of sale have been used is the conveyance of property in inner city, depressed areas, where the costs of property transfer through deed recording and the problems of financing are barriers to real estate transactions. There is deep objection among expert observers of the real estate market against the use of contracts of sale in such situations, for the normal protec-tions to both seller and buyer are not available; title may be clouded, and other aspects of the transaction may go wrong to the great dis-advantage of the parties.

The Diminished Lure of the Suburbs

Proposition 13 poses at least a potential threat to further development of suburban infrastructure, which could materially reduce the incentive or opportunity for urban households to leave central cities. This aspect of Proposition 13 seems far more likely to cause a slowdown in the turnover rate of owner-occupied housing than the change in assessment practices.

The urban property tax traditional in the United States makes suburban expansion essentially self-financing. A new tract of houses may require a new fire station, but it creates the locally controlled tax base to pay for the construction, equipment, and operation of that fire station. As the tract fills, the fiscal base beneath a central city fire station may weaken, but the suburban community does not have to solve that problem. Suburban infrastructure will perforce be newer and probably more attractive than that in the central city, which adds to the pull exerted by suburbs on households and contributes to the rate of turnover and of replacement of housing inventory.

Under Proposition 13, with its 1 percent limit on property taxes and restricted growth of assessment, new suburban infrastructure is not likely to be fiscally self-justifying. State funds may be allocated to support new infrastructure, but thus far no permanent assurances to that effect have even been suggested by state government. The automatic link between public infrastructure expense and public revenue has been broken. Suburban communities, where most construction of new single-family homes takes place, must henceforth be very cautious about approving or annexing developments. Such communities can levy greatly enlarged permit fees as a partial means of recouping the loss of property tax base for new developments, and this practice is apparently spreading very rapidly. It presents developers with an interesting dilemma; if they contest the increases in fees (on grounds that they are new taxes and thus prohibited by Proposition 13), they could force communities to suspend development permits altogether.

The removal of public school costs from the local property tax as a result of Proposition 13 is welcomed by some real estate brokers and developers—perhaps a majority. If there was one element in the pre-Proposition 13 fiscal equation that tended to make housing developments unattractive to the community it was the fact or belief that school expansion tended to raise average school costs and hence to increase taxes for present residents. Now the community need not concern itself about increased school costs. The remaining tax levy in addition to new development fees and user fees may cover the remaining public infrastructure and service costs, with a net improvement in the developer's fiscal impact argument for permits in some cases.

After the passage of Proposition 13 significant other factors entered the situation, and with the considerable lag between local approvals and construction, they obscured the impact of Proposition 13 on single-family home construction. Interest rates rose perceptibly in late Spring 1978, but there was a spurt of starts in June to avoid new energy requirements that took effect in July. By midsummer starts seemed somewhat low, but industry professionals did not attribute this to Proposition 13. Indeed it seems reasonable to suppose that there remains an inventory of serviced land that can keep construction going, perhaps at a modest level, while state government develops longer run systems for channeling suburban tax revenues back to the support of suburban functions. It seems unrealistic, however, to suppose that the set of fiscal relations that will eventually be created will perpetuate the lure of spanking new infrastructure and public services in the suburbs of California. That ought to diminish the replacement demand for housing to some extent and thus slow down the turnover of the inventory.

The Rental Market

Owners of rental housing stood to benefit significantly from lowering of the property tax rate through Proposition 13. From data developed by the California legislative analyst's office it appears that for 1976-77, 24 percent of gross rental income in such properties was going to pay property taxes. Given the normal leveraging of ownership, a reduction of nearly 60 percent in this expense would materially improve cash flow. Even allowing for the increase in income tax liability of owners, this change in the economics of ownership might have been expected to stimulate investment in and construction of rental housing.

It begins to appear that Proposition 13 has made the rental housing investment less attractive rather than more, according to comments of informed professionals. The reason is that rent control has become far more likely at some level and in some form because of tenants' complaints that they did not share in the benefits of Proposition 13 as many clearly expected they would. The issue is intensely political, but there is a perceptible effect upon the market; owners "want out." Conversion to condominiums or cooperatives has become even more attractive for these investors.

There may thus be a short-lived and aberrant spurt in the sale of residential rental properties as investors attempt to liquidate these holdings. The reassessment-on-sale provision of Proposition 13 does not seem likely to be a material consideration in these sales. Indeed, as the assessed values of California rental property appear to be based mostly on gross income multipliers, it is far from clear which way typical assessed values are headed.

Among California's renter households the percentage of income paid as rent decreases as income rises, but the proportion of rent that is accounted for by property taxes is virtually constant across income levels according to 1976-77 data from the legislative analyst's office (see Table 3-7). Thus, if landlords were forced to return their Proposition 13 windfall to tenants, the effect would be a greater proportional benefit for low-income tenants than for high-income tenants.

Table 3-7. Rent and Property Taxes in Relation to Tenant Income, 1976-77, California Renter Households.

Total Family Income	Renter Households, %	Rent Paid, as Percentage of Midpoint Income, %	Property Tax, as Percentage of Rent Paid, %
Under $5,000	26.9	n.a.	n.a.
$5,000-7,500	16.2	30	24
7,500-10,000	14.7	23	24
10,000-15,000	22.4	18	24
15,000-20,000	11.1	14	25
20,000-25,000	4.7	13	25
25,000-30,000	1.9	12	25
30,000-50,000	1.6	9	25
50,000+	0.5	n.a.	n.a.
	100.0		

Source: Legislative Analyst: 29.

PROPOSITION 13 AND NONRESIDENTIAL REAL ESTATE

Owners of business real property will benefit from both the base year treatment (1975–76 fair market value as the basis for assessment of property under continuous same ownership) and the 1 percent maximum of property tax on current fair market value. Base year benefits to business owners will be particularly large, of course, wherever a sharp escalation in actual economic value has occurred since 1975–76. Two examples follow:

1. Oil in the ground or coal reserves may already have ballooned in value since the base year and may be argued to qualify for base year valuation plus 2 percent per year.

2. "Improvements" may cost little when made but increase markedly in economic productivity with the passage of a few years. An example given by the State Board of Equalization is the treatment of orchards (and, presumably, vineyards). When young trees are planted, their cost per unit as property improvements is low. After five to seven years, they reach peak economic productivity, but assessed value is based upon fair market value (presumably, close to the installed cost) at the time of planting, plus 2 percent per year compounded. Thus, the orchard is taxed on a grossly understated basis for the years of peak productivity.

An irony ensues: Proposition 13 as passed in June 1978 contains no mechanism, according to the State Board of Equalization, for *reducing* assessed valuation when the economic value of real property falls, as indeed it can. In the orchard case, the declining value of older trees cannot be reflected in decreased property tax. On the contrary, the clock keeps ticking at a 2 percent per year *increase* in adjusted fair market value and thus in assessed value. Because the reduced productivity of old trees cannot be recognized in lower taxation, the orchard operator is rationally obliged to pull out the old trees sooner than he would otherwise do and replace them with new planting. The 1 percent limit on property tax does decrease the property tax costs of holding the asset by approximately 57 percent, as against the pre–Proposition 13 situation, and this factor gives the orchard owner incentives to hold the old trees longer. Figure 3–4 shows the effects

Figure 3-4. Economic Life of a Tree Having Varying Productivity over Time.

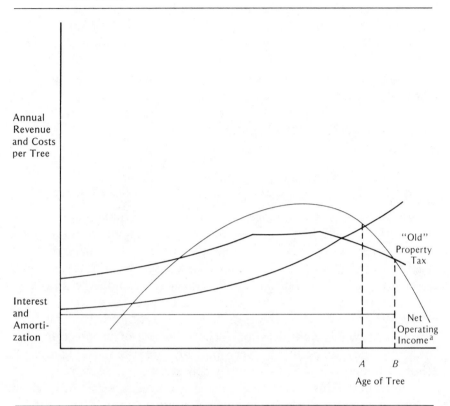

a. Annual net operating income = total revenue per tree minus labor and materials costs of maintenance and harvesting.

of the two factors. Here, the investment cost of the tree is assumed to be annualized as an interest and amortization charge. The economic life of the tree is shortened from B years to A years because property tax cannot be adjusted downward when the net operating income of the tree falls in the later years.

The size of the benefit of base year treatment will grow at a compounded rate over time if market values of business real property grow by more than 2 percent per year. Suppose, for example, that market valuation grows for ten years at the recent general inflation rate of 8 percent compounded. The 2 percent per year escalation provision is 6 percentage points less; thus the net differential grows by approximately 6 percent per year compounded. By the end of the tenth year, each dollar of base year value, compounded at 8 percent, will have grown to $2.1589. Assessed value will have grown to $1.2190. The differential is $0.9399, and the tax paid (at the 1 percent tax level) through base year treatment is only 56 percent of what would be paid at 1 percent of the tenth-year fair market value in this example.

Base year treatment is preserved by maintaining continuous same ownership. The example shows that advantageous tax treatment will grow to substantial proportions over time, and the incentive to preserve it will become greater and greater.

Types of Business Property Transactions

Business entities can arrange any of a wide variety of real estate transactions, including choice of the legal instrumentalities (corporation, corporate subsidiary, limited partnership, personal nominee) to act as seller and as buyer, and choice also of contractual device (straight ownership transfer, conventional leasehold, sale and lease back, contract of sale) (see Maisel and Roulac 1976). Timing and characteristics of business real estate transactions have long been influenced by tax considerations. The influence of Proposition 13 is only one case in point and very possibly not the most significant. (For example, the U.S. Congress is considering extensive reductions in the capital gains tax; if these become law, they may outweigh in significance for transaction making the reduced annual payment liability of property taxation.)

In order to preserve base year property tax assessment, business owners of real property will need to avoid property transfers as defined in Proposition 13 and in Senate Bill 154 and Senate Bill 2212, the implementing legislation passed in late June 1978. Change of ownership has been defined to include recorded and unrecorded transfers of legal or equitable title, with certain exclusions that are not pertinent to business transactions in general (see California State Board of Equalization 1978). Leases of more than ten-year term qualify as property transfers under these new rules.

As business executives and their legal and tax advisors become more familiar with the possibilities, there will no doubt be many ingenious solutions to the problem of defining contracts to greatest mutual advantage of owner and user. Financing agencies are often deeply involved also in the determination of the most advantageous treatment of business deals.

In one large-scale residential development, for example, complications from Proposition 13 are considerable concerning the property tax liabilities of the Irvine Company and of the many owners in the major development of the city of Irvine in Orange County, for example. Two factors produced special problems, the widespread use of long-term land lease agreements in that development and the sale of controlling interest in the Irvine Company in 1977. It will be some time before the issues are finally resolved.

Many commercial properties, in California and elsewhere, are occupied by tenants on rental contracts that are "net" contracts. The tenant agrees to pay all utilities, insurance, and property taxes (and may even agree to pay some other annual expenses). The owner receives a net payment for the use of the land (or land and structure) only. Owners often regarded such contracts as advantageous because they protected against inflation. With the passage of Proposition 13, there has been a dramatic reversal of form: The business *tenant* receives the benefit of the reduction in property tax to a 1 percent ceiling and the reduction to base year treatment to the date the lease came into force. Until the lease term is up, the property owner cannot obtain a share of the cost reduction; it goes as a windfall to the tenant. If the owner of the property should sell it, however, the new rules of the game call for reassessment at fair market value at the time of property transfer. The larger windfall is ordinarily the reduction of tax to 1 percent, but the owner can threaten to inflict on the tenant the loss of the base year treatment. With this leverage, the owner may be able to claim a share of the windfall immediately. The larger possibility for capture of a large portion of the property tax reduction comes, of course, when the lease expires and is due for renegotiation. At this point, the owner may take the position that lessor should be willing to pay occupancy costs as high as were implicit in the earlier lease agreement, including the effect of property taxes. In this way, the owner claims a gain that in due course should mean capitalization of the tax reduction into increased property value.

Business Property Transaction Volume

Whereas construction trends for nonresidential properties are measured and reported regularly from permit data for each region of California, there is no convenient source of regional or statewide data on transfer of business properties. The State Board of Equalization staff may soon collect data on business property transfer volume from county assessors. To be useful for analytical purposes, the total transfers would need to be broken into classes of business property: manufacturing or industrial, agricultural, extractive industries, office, and commercial.

The Real Estate Research Council of Northern California uses quarterly totals of deed recordings in each county obtained from county recorders as a measure of real estate market activity. (See Northern California Real Estate Council 1978:23-24 for an example.) County governments, in the offices of the recorder of deeds and of the tax assessor, have data on file from which measures of transaction volume in each property category could be constructed. But for maximum comparability of transfer data, the files of each county should be in a uniform property classification system, so that aggregation and comparisons could be undertaken.

Under Proposition 13 and the implementing legislation county assessors do have new problems of identifying some business deals that qualify as property transfers. In particular, business firms do not always need, from their point of view, to record leases and contracts, yet any lease of ten-year term or longer qualifies as a property transfer for the purposes of property tax treatment under Proposition 13. Assessors will probably use such clues as utilities hook-ups and mailing address changes to trace business transfers, as they already do for checking homeowners' tax exemption claims. In addition, the business property statement that each business entity is required to file will be expanded to include information on leases, so that assessors will ask for direct reports in future from the business entities themselves on the status of any lease on the property in question.

Business Property Exclusions from Proposition 13 Treatment

The State Board of Equalization has authority under California statute to undertake direct statewide assessment of certain types of business property. These include the real property owned by regulated gas and electric utility companies, telephone companies, and railroads. Also, radio telephone companies and some water companies fall under the board's direct jurisdiction, as does the assessment of timber values. The board has taken the position that Proposition 13 did not cover these special cases and that it may continue to assess these regulated industries on the basis of current fair market values. A superior court decision upheld that position, but appeals and other litigation may leave the issue unresolved for some years. With respect to gas, electric, and telephone utilities, if a reduction of property tax liability did occur because of the imposition of the base year and the 1 percent limit provided by Proposition 13, the public utilities commission would undoubtedly take account of the cost reduction and order a comparable reduction of utility rates. Thus, the chief effect of including the regulated public utilities under Proposition 13 would be, not to increase their profits, but to reduce utility rates and to reduce governmental tax revenues.

State law already provides a special basis for evaluation of timber, in that tax payment is made at the time of timber harvest. We cannot attempt here to explore further the possible consequences of Proposition 13 on the forest products industries.

Effects of Proposition 13 upon Other Business Investment Decisions

Some business investment decisions have a large component classified as real property, whereas others are mainly concerned with machinery and equipment or with the acquisition of other productive assets not considered to be real property. A general consequence of Proposition 13 is that the real property component of a business investment will now have a reduced annual holding cost. If no other changes of the cost and revenue elements of the investment decision occur, this reduced holding cost will cause some business investment possibilities to become attractive that were previously rejected.

Some campaign arguments for Proposition 13 before it was passed claimed that it would stimulate business investment in California. It is necessary to be cautious about the consequences. So far as new factory investment is concerned, most previous studies of industrial locational decisions put the annual cost of property taxation low on the list of considerations. Access to markets, availability of labor, and quality of local government services (including the quality of schools) have been found generally to be of greater importance in choosing location.

Another type of business investment decision also illustrates the current uncertainties. Developers choose sites for regional shopping centers on the basis of expected growth in the population of the region and the concurrent development of road systems and other infrastructure for residential communities. Although the post–Proposition 13 property tax costs of a new regional shopping center complex would be lower than before and this cost reduction would make the potential investment more attractive, the rate of population growth of an area might be slowed by the increased costs to the residential developer and by slower actions of local government agencies in approving residential developments. The sales revenue potential of a shopping center development is a far more crucial variable in the investment decision than is the annual cost of property taxes.

Thus, it will take further analysis and the unfolding of new evidence over a period of time to determine the consequences of Proposition 13 for business investments.

OTHER ISSUES

Proposition 13's impact upon real estate markets and property transfers needs to be analyzed with regard to several additional issues not already discussed.

County Assessors' Problems of Perfecting the Tax Rolls

At the time of passage of Proposition 13, county assessors faced two massive problems: to trace the appropriate base year assessed value of each parcel and to send to each taxpayer an up-to-date tax bill, including the effect of any transfer or improvement to the property as well as the permissible inflation increment of 2 percent per year. Many taxpayers apparently believed that the assessed value shown on their original 1975–76 tax bills would be correct. The State Board of Equalization was aware that assessments for that year were based upon varying practices, however. In some cases, comparable sales for previous years as well as for 1975–76 had been used. In others, a field appraisal from several years before had simply been updated by formula. Because Proposition 13 stated, and was interpreted to require, an assessment based upon 1975 only, the guidelines said that assessors should go back and recalculate the 1975 base year fair market value for each parcel. Then the 2 percent annual increment could be added to the corrected base year value. Any property improvement would be added to the assessed value as of the date of the improvement.

In addition, the assessor needed to trace any ownership transfers—including only those qualifying transfers as defined by the June 1978 implementing legislation and excluding purely technical transfers—and modify the assessed value to the fair market value at the time of the transfer. This is not a purely mechanical procedure, because identifying some transfers requires field work and other corroborating information.

County assessors did not have sufficient staff to undertake simultaneously both of these tasks before issuing new Proposition 13 assessed values to taxpayers, and each county assessor decided how best to deploy available staff. The law apparently permits supplemental tax bills to be rendered to taxpayers, based on corrected values at any time up to several years after the event. These problems created transitional uncertainties for property owners.

Appraisal Standards for Mortgage Financing

Mortgage underwriting for owner-occupied housing ordinarily involves primary attention to the fair market value of the property at the time of mortgage application, but there is also some consideration of the owner's income position and ability to cope with the costs of home ownership. Reduction in property tax payments eases these costs. Securities analysts, evaluating the profitability of savings and loan associations soon after passage of Proposition 13, offered the judgment that existing mortgages were improved in soundness for this reason.

Appraisers of rental housing for mortgage financing purposes are very specific in analyzing the ability of the property to "carry" the proposed loan. In the early months after passage of Proposition 13, however, appraisal standards and formulas were not adjusted to take account of the expected reduction in property tax liability. Instead, real estate appraisers continued to use the same multipliers as before in calculating the capital valuation of rental property. Until the county assessors made definitive determinations of assessed values, appraisers resisted reducing property tax payments. Also tenant groups, state political leaders, and city councils began almost immediately to talk of voluntary or compulsory rent rollbacks and possible rent control. A rent rollback approximately equal to the reduction in property tax payment would leave the owner of rental property in essentially the same net income position as before Proposition 13, and the conservative response of appraisers might well be, therefore, to leave appraised values unadjusted until the question of rent rollback became clarified.

CONCLUDING COMMENTS ABOUT PROPOSITION 13's IMPACTS ON REAL ESTATE MARKETS

The new conditions in the markets for both housing and nonhousing real estate include an unequivocal permanent reduction in the cost of holding existing property but a series of other effects that are uncertain in direction and magnitude. The early response of decision makers to this uncertainty has been, quite naturally, to "go slow" in adjusting to the new market conditions.

It appears that Proposition 13 imposes some penalty on an acknowledged property transfer. Thus we may see more use of contracts of sale and of unrecorded lease agreements unless participants in real estate markets become convinced that county assessors can quickly find and deal with such unrecorded transfers. Given the incentives for concealment, adequate enforcement will require more resources in county assessors' offices.

NOTE TO CHAPTER 3

1. The method of projecting tax burden for real income involves shifting the midpoint of each income class upward by $(1.08)^5$, calculating the enlarged width of that income class, and allocating the original frequency in that class uniformly among all classes within that new width starting from the original lower limit of the class. It is an arbitrary technique that approximates the shifting that would be possible with more complete data but that in this case slightly underestimates the upward shift in median income produced by an annual rate of 8 percent. Tax burden percentages for the lowest and highest classes are based on assumed midpoints and are consequently only generally representative. Income-related tax payment data were taken from an unpublished study prepared by the legislative analyst's office in Spring 1978.

REFERENCES

Aaron, Henry J. 1972. *Shelter and Subsidies: Who Benefits from Federal Housing Policies?* Washington, D.C.: The Brookings Institution.

Bartlett, Robert. 1978. "Proposition 13: Three Utilities Sue for Assessment Cuts." *San Francisco Chronicle* (July 26).

Bell, Douglas D., Executive Secretary. 1978. "Order Adopting Regulations of the State Board of Equalization." California: State Board of Equalization, Sacramento, July 3.

Bulkeley, William M. 1978. "Interest Rates on Prime Home Mortgages Are Cut by California's Two Biggest S & L's." *The Wall Street Journal* (August 15).

Calais, A. 1978. "Stable Taxes to Help Farmers Cut Losses." *Los Angeles Times* (July 24).

California State Board of Equalization. 1978. 78/120 (July 11).

_____ . 1976. *Taxable Sales in California: Sales and Use Tax.* Sacramento.

California, State of. 1978. *Proposition 13: Tax Limitation — Initiative Constitutional Amendment.* Sacramento.

_____ . 1978. *Senate Bill 2212, Chapter 332.* Sacramento, June 30.

_____ . 1978. *Senate Bill 154, Chapter 292.* Sacramento, June 24.

_____ . 1976-77. Legislative Analyst Study.

_____ . 1976. *California Statistical Abstract.* Sacramento.

Cohn, Lee M. 1978. "Analyzing the Ripple Effect of California Tax Cuts on Nation." *The Washington Star* (July 7).

Crocker Bank, Economics Department. 1978. "California and the Jarvis–Gann Amendment: An Economic Perspective of the Adjustment Process." *California Economic Report.* San Francisco, July 14.

Dunne, Finley Peter. 1978. "An Acid Test for Proposition 13." *Business Week* (September 4).

Ellickson, Robert C. 1978. "Why Housing Prices Went through the Roof. Pileup of Environmental Restrictions Found to Coincide with Climb in Costs." *Los Angeles Times* (July 24).

Hagman, Donald G. 1978. "How to Comply with Jarvis/Gann and Raise Taxes on Property at the Same Time." University of California School of Law, Los Angeles.

_____. 1978. "Proposition 13: A Prostitution of Conservative Principles." University of California School of Law, Los Angeles.

_____. 1978. "Reform of Local Government, California Style." University of California School of Law, Los Angeles.

Hall, Kenneth F., and Edward R. Gerber and Associates. 1978. "Legislature Faces Heavy Proposition 13 Agenda." *Proposition 13 Impact Reporter.* California Research, Sacramento, Calif., July 10.

Kimbell, Larry J. 1978. "The California Economy." *Research Conference on Proposition 13.* UCLA Business Forecasting Project, Graduate School of Management, University of California, Los Angeles, July 13 and 14.

League of California Cities, Committee on Community Development. 1978. "Action Plan for the Return of Home Rule and Fiscal Responsibility." *New League Action Plan—For Your Review and Comment. Action Plan for the Return of Home Rule and Fiscal Responsibility, Policy Committee Issues Papers.* Sacramento, July 17.

Lee, Eugene C. (with Terry Larson). 1978. "California Primary Politics: 1960–1978." Institute of Governmental Studies, University of California, Berkeley, *California Data Brief* 2, no. 3 (May).

_____. 1978. "750 Propositions: The Initiative in Perspective." Institute of Governmental Studies, University of California, Berkeley, *California Data Brief* 2, no. 2 (April).

Liebert, Larry. 1978. "A Proposition 13 Talk with Brown." *San Francisco Chronicle,* (July 26).

Los Angeles Times. 1978. "Nevada Group Claims Victory in Tax Drive." (August 8).

Maisel, Sherman J., and Stephen A. Roulac. 1976. *Real Estate Investment and Finance.* New York: McGraw–Hill.

Mark, Morris. 1978. "Housing and Construction Commentary, Proposition 13." Goldman Sachs Research, New York, *Investment Research*, June 30.

Mikesell, Stephen D. 1978. "Proposition 13: The Struggle to Save California's Way of Life." *Los Angeles Times* (July 23).

Real Estate Research Council of Northern California. 1978. "Market Trend—April 1978, Bay Area and Sacramento Residences." *Northern California Real Estate Report.* vol. 30, no. 1.

_____. 1978. *Northern California Real Estate Report.* vol. 29, no. 5.

Reilly, Ann M. 1978. "After Jarvis What?" *Dun's Review* 112, No. 1 (July).

Rivlin, Alice M. 1978. "Proposition 13: Its Impact on the Nation's Economy, Federal Revenues, and Federal Expenditures." Washington, D.C.: U.S. Government Printing Office, July.

San Francisco Chronicle. 1978. "EBMUD Won't Seek Bailout Funds." (July 26).

_____. 1978. "Mayor May Veto Repeal of Tax Raise." (July 26).

Security Pacific Bank Research Department. 1977. *California Construction Trends.* Security Pacific Bank, Los Angeles, December.

_____. 1977. "Economic Trends in the Seventies." *Central California.* Security Pacific Bank, Los Angeles, November.

_____. 1977. "Economic Trends of the Seventies." *Northern Coastal California.* Security Pacific Bank, Los Angeles, May.

_____. 1977. "Economic Trends in the Seventies." *Southern California.* Security Pacific Bank, Los Angeles, May.

Senini, Walter R., Chief of Operation, Property Tax Dept. 1978. "Proposition 13 Information: Answers to Some of the Frequently Asked Questions Regarding Proposition 13 Implementation." California State Board of Equalization, Sacramento, July 28.

_____. 1978. "The Valuation of Orchards and Vineyards." California State Board of Equalization, Sacramento, July 27.

_____. 1978. "Statutory Implementation of Proposition 13." California State Board of Equalization, Sacramento, July 11.

Shulman, David. 1978. "For Land's Sake, What's Prop. 13 Done? Ironically, It May Be One of the Most Sweeping Land-use Laws in the Country." *Los Angeles Times.* (July 23).

Sokolow, Alvin D. 1978. "The Redistribution of California's Population: New Growth in Nonmetropolitan Areas." Institute of Governmental Studies, University of California, Berkeley, *California Data Brief* 2, no. 1 (February).

Urban Land Institute. 1977. "Effects of Regulation on Housing Costs: Two Case Studies." Urban Land Institute Research Report 27, Washington, D.C.

4 FISCAL LIMITATIONS AND MUNICIPAL DEBT
The Extreme Case of Proposition 13

Ann R. Thomas

Imposing fiscal limitations on state and local governments has become a popular political idea in recent years. Because most governmental revenues are inflation-elastic and inflation is an increasingly permanent characteristic of our economic system, citizens are enacting constitutional or statutory constraints on the fiscal powers of governments in order to confine the increasing burden of taxation. In the rush to establish limits on operating revenues and expenditures, however, apparently the longer run effects on the ability of the governments to borrow long-term capital are being overlooked. The object of this study is to examine theoretically the effects of fiscal limitations on municipal credit, focusing especially on the impacts of Proposition 13.

Local and state governments traditionally finance capital projects by selling bonds to investors who are repaid in regular series of future payments. Since public facilities do not serve well as collateral, individuals who invest in the bonds are particularly concerned about the surety of payment, or conversely, the probability of default. To the extent that fiscal limitations reduce the ability of public officials to meet the debt service payments, investors will consider the debt to be more risky and will extract higher interest payments in order to compensate for the higher risk of default. In this way the cost or availability of municipal debt may be affected by fiscal limitations.

Proposition 13, a tax limitation on local governments in California, has severely affected the ability of local governments to borrow
long-term capital. Its effect may represent an extreme in degree of
effect on municipal markets, but all fiscal limitations have some
impact on credit availability, unless debt service is specifically exempt from the limitation.

This chapter consists of three parts. The first develops a theoreti-
cal framework derived from previous empirical studies of municipal
bond risk and financial theory. The second examines the effects of
Proposition 13 within this framework. The third summarizes the
findings and extends them to policy issues surrounding the problem
of the access of California local governments to the credit market.

MUNICIPAL BOND RISK

Yields on municipal bonds, as on other financial instruments, reflect
investors' evaluation of the riskiness of holding that debt. Unlike
other instruments, however, interest on municipal bonds is exempt
from federal taxes and usually from the taxes of the state in which
they are issued. The tax-exempt nature of the bonds causes the yields
to be lower than other types of bonds and also limits the market
of investors to those institutions or individuals for whom the tax
exemption is meaningful. Still, the riskiness of an individual bond is
evaluated relative to other municipal bonds and relative to other
financial assets.

Municipal bonds also differ in that the cost of information required for risk evaluation may be higher than for other credit instruments. The diversity of legal bond provisions, tax systems, and public
agency accounting methods, as well as the lack of reporting requirements, suggests that for an individual investor a thorough evaluation
of risk is difficult and costly. As a result investors often rely on commercial bond rating services to evaluate the riskiness of particular
issues. The economies of scale in the information gathering process
reduce the high costs for the individual in this market. The method
that the rating agencies use to evaluate the riskiness of bonds appears
to be a combination of subjective and objective processes, so that
financial accounting data are only one source of information. Nevertheless, the financial literature reports several studies that attempt

to test empirically for specific determinants of municipal bond risk using rating classes or bond yields as measures of risk.

Empirical Studies

Studies by Carleton and Lerner (1969), Michel (1977), and Hastie (1972), suggest that the relevant determinants of municipal risk are the size of the debt burden of the issuer, marketability of the issue, ability of the borrowing unit to service the debt and the unit's history of default. Carleton and Lerner used multiple discriminant analysis to attempt classification of bonds into rating groups. They were able to classify correctly 54 percent of a sample using a measure of debt burden and various financial measures of carrying ability as predictors. Hastie used a regression model to explain the level of municipal bond yield and found that default history, relative size of debt burden, and characteristics of issues that affected their marketability were significant factors, but the relative significance of the factors varied over time depending whether commercial banks or individuals were the major purchasers. Hastie also reported that variables that represent degrees of economic diversification and economic stability of the community were significant determinants.

Michel examined variables on which municipal officials and investment bankers traditionally depend to assess fiscal soundness. Attempting to predict bond rating groups, Michel was successful between 35 and 53 percent of the time. Factors used for the analysis included various fiscal measures of ability to carry debt. The results of these studies support the view that municipal bond risk evaluation is a complex process that is not totally dependent upon relative financial ratios. The results do indicate a conceptual framework for municipal bond risk analysis, however.

Municipal Risk Theory

From these studies emerges a three-component model of municipal bond risk to explain differences in riskiness for different municipal bonds. One determinant of risk is associated with the liquidity of the investment and is affected by such factors as size of issue. Another appears to be associated with investor dominance, which is caused by shifts over time between individuals and commercial banks as majority buyers. Hastie's work indicates that commercial banks tend to rely on a different set of financial information than do individual buyers, reflecting the fact that banks do some risk analysis themselves, whereas individual buyers tend to rely on bond rating agencies. Thus the importance of certain factors varies depending upon the dominant investor, and thus the riskiness of bonds varies over time.

The third component of municipal bond risk is financial risk, or the probability of default. It is the risk of default that is affected by fiscal limitations, although the degree of effect may be compounded by investor dominance. The financial risk associated with a security is primarily a function of the legal arrangement established to repay the bond. Secondarily, financial risk is a function of the ability and commitment of the issuer to repay the debt. Municipal bonds are legally classified by the sources of revenues from which interest and principal payments are made. For instance, general obligation bonds, usually considered the least risky class of municipals, are backed by the legal ability of the governmental unit to levy unlimited taxes, if necessary, to service the debt. This is the "full faith and credit" provision valued by investors. Other bond issues, which do not have the full faith and credit legal security, may rely on the revenues generated by the project (revenue bonds), incremental taxes arising from redevelopment (redevelopment bonds), special assessments (assessment bonds), or lease contracts (lease-purchase bonds). Such bond issues, often classified as nonguaranteed are generally considered riskier, because the legal provision for repayment is not as strong as is that for general obligation bonds. Among nonguaranteed bonds, legal provisions cause differences in riskiness. Within each class of bond as well, at another level of evaluation economic factors affect the abilities of governments to service the debt and thus affect the financial risk of the debt instruments. Such economic factors affect the expected level of future available revenues and the variations in those future streams over the lifetime of the bond. The concern is, of course, that at no time during the repayment period will available revenues of the issuing organization be less than the amount due to bondholders for that period.

Fiscal limitations may be written so that both the legal and the economic bases of municipal debt security are changed. In many cases bond repayments are totally exempt from the limitations, so that no changes occur in the legal or economic factors, and thus, there is no effect on the riskiness of municipal debt. However, when the limitations do not exempt debt service, the legal security as well as the economic factors on all categories of bonds may be affected, though in different ways and to different degrees. Also, the perception and evaluation of those effects may differ over time depending upon investor dominance.

EFFECTS OF PROPOSITION 13

Proposition 13 may prove to be as extreme as any adopted fiscal limitation on local governments in terms of the effects on municipal debt. Except for Proposition 2-1/2 recently enacted in Massachusetts, no other limitations either recently enacted or currently proposed so drastically change the cost and availability of local or state governments' municipal credit.

When Proposition 13 was approved by California voters as a state constitutional amendment in June 1978, it decreased local property tax revenues by about 50 percent across the state and effected considerable change in the ability of local governments to control future revenues. The amendment reduced assessed property values to 1975–76 levels, set the local property tax rate maximum at 1 percent, and established that assessed valuations can increase in the future at a rate no greater than 2 percent unless property changes ownership. The impact on municipal debt is broad. The ceiling on the rate of taxation effectively changes the legal security of general obligation bonds and redevelopment bonds and adversely affects the economic ability of local governments to service other classes of non-guaranteed bonds. The constraints on the growth of the tax base also diminishes the economic capacity for debt repayment. Since debt service is not exempt from the limitation, except for debt that was approved by voters prior to July 1, 1978, future accessibility of local governments to credit market is severely limited.

Legal Security

Because the tax rate ceiling is now inflexible, the legally provided security of full faith and credit cannot be attached to any new bonds. The amendment does allow, however, for new nonproperty-based tax systems at the local level with the approval of two-thirds of the qualified electors. Such tax revenues could be used to service debt, but the rate of taxation would be limited, not providing as much security as general obligation bonds.[1] Proposition 13 also changes the legal security behind tax allocation bonds in that the incremental property tax assessments from which the debt previously was repaid will not be as great and tax collection and control function have been shifted from the tax-allocation districts to the larger county level of government.[2] The effect is to limit severely, if not to eliminate, this form of financing future urban redevelopment projects.

Local governments in California also depend upon revenue bonds and lease-purchase bonds to finance public capital formation. Revenue bonds are the least affected of all classes of bonds if repayments are generated from the revenues of the financed project and are not dependent upon tax revenues legally. Occasionally revenue bonds are secured in part by funds from the operating budget of the issuing government in case the revenues from the project are not large enough. Such bonds become riskier under Proposition 13, because operating budgets that provide additional security are adversely affected.

Lease-purchase bonds that are totally dependent upon operating funds via lease contract payments are considerably affected by Proposition 13. Although the legal security of the bonds has not been altered, the ability of local governments to provide debt service has been bounded.

Economic Security

Other things equal, Proposition 13 increases the riskiness and therefore, the costs of lease-purchase bonds—both those currently outstanding and those to be issued in the future, as well as any other non-revenue-producing and nonguaranteed municipals. The impact of Proposition 13 is to reduce the level of available resources from which debt service is derived and to increase the variability of these future resources.

Consider a simple model of an operating budget of a local government that explicitly includes debt service.

$$\Sigma R_t - \Sigma E_t - D = \mu_t \quad , \tag{4-1}$$

where

ΣR_t = total revenues in period t;

ΣE_t = total expenditures in period t;

D = the debt service payment;

μ_t = the residual budget surplus or deficit for period t.

For a particular period, if revenues are greater than expenditures and debt service, the budget will be in balance or surplus ($\mu_t \geq 0$). If revenues are not as great, however, the budget will be in deficit ($\mu_t < 0$) and the debt service payment will be in jeopardy. Because most state and local budgets cannot be in overall deficit by law, the lease contract payment D, although a contractual obligation, may not be honored in times of fiscal stress. At those times debt service or the lease contract payment is just one of many claims on the limited resources of the governmental unit.

Most fiscal systems are designed to avoid budget deficits whenever possible. Nonetheless, because revenues are subject to economic variation and expenditures also may vary, the budget residual is a random variable. The probability of the residual being negative ($\mu_t < 0$) is a function of the design of the fiscal system that attempts to maintain a balance or surplus ($\mu_t \geq 0$), and it is a function of the variance of that expected stream over time. Between two fiscal systems that project the same expected budget residual μ_t, the system with the larger variance will be considered riskier from the viewpoint of a bondholder who is concerned about the surety of debt service D.

Thus the concern is with the effects of Proposition 13 on the level and the variance of the residual budget term μ_t. Assuming that government officials are quite aware that budgets cannot be in deficit, we will not be concerned here about the effects of the tax limitation on the level of budget residual.[3] Instead, the focus is on the effects of Proposition 13 on the variance of the budget residual μ.

Rearranging Eq. (4-1) and taking the variance yields

$$\text{Var } \mu = \text{Var } \Sigma R + \text{Var } \Sigma E - 2 \text{ Cov} (\Sigma R \Sigma E) \quad . \tag{4-2}$$

The variance of the residual is a function of the variances of both the revenues and expenditures modified by a covariance term that measures the degree to which the two streams vary over time with each other. If revenues and expenditures vary over time to the same degree and in the same direction, the covariance term (being negative) cancels the two individual variance terms and the net variance is zero. Realistically the covariance term will take on a wide range of values, depending upon the relative macroeconomic effects on revenues and expenditures and the degree of control the local officials have over revenues and expenditures.

Prior to the imposition of Proposition 13, local governments had some influence on the covariance of revenues and expenditures. Theoretically they could raise revenues when expenditure demands rose and cut expenditures when revenues declined. Thus the covariance term in Eq. (4-2) was probably large (and negative) and operated to reduce the overall variation in available resources. Under Proposition 13, however, local government revenues are under the control of the state legislature and the voters in the district in the future. Since control now resides with groups that have more diverse concerns, the expected effect is that the covariance term has decreased under Proposition 13, causing a greater variance in the budget residual. There is a greater probability that the residual will be negative. This suggests that funds that are to be available for debt service are less sure under Proposition 13 than before its enactment.

Going one step further, total variation in available revenues (Var ΣR_t) may increase because of the shift in the type of taxes that constitute local governments' total income. Revenues from the property tax are generally more stable over time than revenues from sales or income tax. This is because the base of the property tax—land values—does not vary greatly with the level of economic activity, but remains relatively stable even during recessions. On the other hand, both the sales and income tax bases vary considerably during periodic expansions and recessions, since employment, purchases, and incomes vary with the level of economic activity. Proposition 13 has caused local governments to give up a more stable source of revenue for a more variable system. Whether the eventual system involves state revenue sharing, voter-approved tax systems, or some combination of the two, the future tax base will be more variable. The portion of total local government taxes that consists of less variable property taxes will continue to decrease over time, being replaced by mroe variable sales and income taxes. This process suggests a gradual trend of increasing riskiness for local government debt.

Consider the total revenues R_t of a particular government unit for period t that result from three types of taxes: property R^p, sales R^s, and income R^i, so that

$$\Sigma R_t = a R_t^p + b R_t^s + c R_t^i . \tag{4-3}$$

where a, b, and c represent the relative proportions of each of the tax sources. Taking the variance of both sides,

$$\text{Var } \Sigma R = a^2 \text{ Var } R^p + b^2 \text{ Var } R^s + c^2 \text{ Var } R^i$$
$$+ 2ab \text{ Cov} (R^p R^s) + 2ac \text{ Cov} (R^p R^i)$$
$$+ 2bc \text{ Cov} (R^s R^i) . \tag{4-4}$$

Equation (4-4) shows that the variance of a total revenue stream is a function of the sum of the variances of each of the revenue sources and the sum of the covariances between the revenue streams.

Proposition 13 has reduced property tax revenues to local governments. Those revenues are partially replaced by state funds and by locally imposed sales or income taxes. The effect is to reduce the proportion of local government revenues based on property values and increase the proportion of revenues based on sales and income. Thus the relative weights of the variance and covariance terms shift. The proportion of property-based revenues, a, decreases and the proportions of sales and income-based revenues, b and c, increase. Since Var R^p, the variance in property tax is less than Var R^s and Var R^i, the variances in sales- and income-based revenues, the overall effect is an increase in the variance of total revenues. Of course, the shift in weight also affects the covariance terms. Since sales and income taxes both tend to depend on economic activity, the covariance of the two can be expected to be high. A shift from property tax to sales and income taxes increases the overall variance of available revenues and thus increases the riskiness of bonds secured by those revenues. This process continues as long as the property tax base increases at a rate less than the rise in overall prices. In other words, the effect of the tax base limitation on the riskiness of municipal lease-purchase bonds intensifies over time, as long as the inflation rate is greater than 2 percent.[4] The effect is proportional to the difference between the inflation rate and 2 percent.

In summary, under Proposition 13 lease-purchase bonds that are secured lease contracts with local governments have become riskier because the probability that the lease payments will not be met has

increased. Besides cutting the level of available resources, the variability of those funds has increased, because local government officials
have lost control over revenues and because the revenue sources have
shifted to more volatile tax bases.

CONCLUSIONS AND IMPLICATIONS

Traditionally state and local governments have borrowed in the municipal credit market to finance large, non–revenue-producing capital
using general obligation bonds and lease-purchase bonds. School
buildings, libraries, and fire stations are prominent examples of public facilities that provide collective benefits for the community and
are financed by tax-supported long-term debt. Proposition 13 has
severely limited the ability of local governments in California to
finance such capital in the future. This extreme and unplanned effect
on municipal credit availability may offer some incentives to citizens
of other states developing fiscal limitations to avoid damaging the
credit worthiness of governments. The policy challenge is to devise
methods that limit tax increases caused by inflation and yet allow for
the necessary fiscal flexibility that provides security for long-term
debt.

Limitation Measures

Recently enacted fiscal limitation measures reduce the degree of fiscal control traditionally held by elected officials and replace the
control with rules or electorate power. Rules may take the form of
quantitative ceilings on the growth of revenues or expenditures in
absolute terms (for example, the increase in the property tax base
cannot exceed 2 percent per year in California), or as indexed to relevant economic statistics (New Jersey state spending cannot increase
at a greater rate than the increase in state personal income) (Dansinger 1979). Electorate control, which may or may not accompany
the quantitative limits, is a shift in fiscal decision making power from
the elected officials to the electorate (for example, state and local
tax limits can be overridden by a majority of the electorate in Michigan) (Bowen 1979). In either case, the relevant factor with respect to
municipal bond risk is the effect on the ease with which additional

governmental resources can be obtained, if necessary, to assure that the indebtedness will be repaid on schedule.

Fiscal Flexibility

Neither of these approaches provides the required flexibility. Strict quantitative ceilings do not permit upward adjustment; voter control of taxes suggests that additional revenues will not be quickly available if necessary. In both cases, additional provision for debt security is needed.

One method of separating the desire for fiscal growth limits and the need for credit-securing flexibility is to exempt capital budgets and debt service from the limitation (as in New Jersey and Michigan). Another approach is to provide some mechanism such as legislative approval to override the limit in emergencies (as in Texas and Michigan). Assuming that potential bond default is considered an emergency, the override mechanism, if not too cumbersome, is useful in providing municipal bond security.

Perhaps the most reasonable approach to the problem of debt security in a fiscal limitation setting is to require that all debt issues be subject to voter approval, and once approved, that the tax levy associated with that debt be exempt from limitations. Then capital investment decisions can be made incrementally and separately from the operating budget decisions, and the security of the underlying bonds is not constrained by the limitations on the operating budget. Such a plan preserves the low cost of capital financing for local and state governments.

At the present time local governments in California have few options for long-term financing. Capital expenditures are being postponed, being financed through development fees on new private building, and to some extent being funded through lease-purchase bonds. In the long run the most reasonable option, however, is for local governments to regain the ability to issue general obligation bonds. This requires another voter-approved state constitutional amendment to counter the existing prohibition under Proposition 13.

In summary, fiscal limitations must be designed so that the credit worthiness of the governmental units is preserved. As an extreme example Proposition 13 has unintentionally limited the availability of credit because of its specificity and lack of debt service exemption. With some foresight, however, other states can achieve the objective of limiting fiscal activity without curtailing long-term capital market access. For California, meanwhile, the most efficient solution is to restore to local governments the legal ability to issue and service general obligation bonds.

NOTES TO CHAPTER 4

1. The state legislature must develop enabling legislation before such taxes can be proposed.
2. Property taxes are now collected at the county level and allocated to other local governmental units within the county by legislative direction.
3. Although Proposition 13 lowered local government revenues, state bail-out money replaced most of the funds during the first few years of adjustment.
4. The property tax base will increase at a 2 percent rate plus the effect of the increase in reassessments due to sales, improvements, and exchanges of property.

REFERENCES

Bowen, Frank M., and Eugene C. Lee. 1979. "Limiting State Spending: The Legislature or the Electorate." Institute of Governmental Studies Research Report 79-4, University of California, Berkeley.

Carleton, Willard T., and Eugene M. Lerner. 1969. "Statistical Credit Scoring of Municipal Bonds." *Journal of Money Credit and Banking* (November): 750-64.

Dansinger, James N. 1979. "Trends in Fiscal Limitations, Measures, a National and International Perspective." Unpublished manuscript.

Hastie, K. Larry. 1972. "Determinants of Municipal Bond Yields." *Journal of Financial and Quantitative Analysis* (June): 1729-48.

McWatters, Ann R. 1979. "Financing Capital Formation for Local Governments," Institute for Governmental Studies Research Report 79-3, University of California, Berkeley.

Michel, Allen J. 1977. "Municipal Bond Ratings: A Discriminant Analysis Approach." *Journal of Financial and Quantitative Analysis* (November): 587-98.

5 THE EFFECTS OF PROPOSITION 13 ON TAX-SUPPORTED MUNICIPAL BONDS IN CALIFORNIA
A Case Study of Bond Market Efficiency

Ronald Forbes, Alan Frankle,
and Philip Fischer

This chapter provides an empirical analysis of the interest rates on new issues of tax-supported bonds sold by California localities before and after the passage of Proposition 13. Our primary purpose is to use the event of Proposition 13 as a case study for examination of the efficiency of the municipal market.

A BRIEF SUMMARY OF EFFICIENT MARKETS: THEORY AND EVIDENCE FROM PRIOR STUDIES

As numerous past studies have noted, in an efficient market yields on securities fully reflect all relevant public information. In testing the efficient market hypothesis, previous studies have focused on the timing and magnitude of changes in prices or returns on securities in relation to the timing or announcement of significant new information. In a perfectly efficient market the timing of the new information and the market's response would be coincident. On the other hand, in a less than perfectly efficient market, security price or yield adjustments may lag behind new information; the length of the adjustment period can serve as one measure of departure from a fully efficient market.

Most of the numerous studies of the equities market conclude that stock market returns conform closely to the efficient market hypothesis. There are relatively few studies of the informational efficiency of bond markets, however, and the results have been somewhat mixed. (See for example Katz 1974, Grier and Katz 1976, Hettenhouse and Sartoris 1976, Weinstein 1978, and Pinches and Singleton 1978.) Most bond market studies have focused on corporate bonds, most commonly using the occasion of a change in bond rating as the timing of new information. One of the shortcomings of this approach is that a bond rerating is not considered new information. As noted by Weinstein: "We may conclude from this study that there is no evidence of a reaction of bond price to the announcement of a rating change. There is some evidence of price change during the period from 1/2 to 1-1/2 years before the rating change. This price change is the result of information which eventually leads to the rating change, rather than the rating change itself" (1978: 345). Although Weinstein's results contradict much of the prior work on bond market efficiency, they are not inconsistent with the results expected of a semistrong form efficient (public information efficient) bond market. The study of rating change has added little to our understanding of the details of bond pricing, however.

This study will use the event of Proposition 13, which was passed on June 6, 1978 and became effective later in 1978, as the effective date of publicly available new information relevant to the credit quality of tax-supported local debt in California. As the many current commentaries have noted, Proposition 13 is widely recognized as a major economic event in public finance. Thus, the behavior of municipal bond interest rates in response to this event should provide a less ambiguous test of the efficiency of the bond market.

A REVIEW OF PROPOSITION 13

The passage of Proposition 13 imposed new constitutional limits on the taxing power of the state of California and its political subdivisions, affecting primarily property taxes. The main limitations adopted by the voters are as follows:

1. The maximum property tax cannot exceed 1 percent of the market value of the property in 1975. This provision does not apply

to taxes levied to meet the debt service for voter-approved bonds sold prior to the effective date of the Proposition (July 1, 1978). The 1 percent limitation does not apply where a special tax is approved by two-thirds of the qualified voters.

2. Property assessments that were in effect on March 1, 1975 are the basis for determining market value for real estate tax purposes in 1978. Assessed valuation can increase only 2 percent per year unless there is new construction or a change in ownership of the property.

3. New state taxes must be approved by a two-thirds vote of the state legislature. New real estate taxes may not be imposed at either the state or local level.

The adoption of these taxing limits caused California local governmental units to lose a large proportion of the future revenues they could have reasonably expected to receive prior to the passage of the proposition. This future revenue decline resulted from the property tax ceilings that were added to the California state constitution. Current estimates indicate that without the assistance of state aid payments, local governments will lose approximately 60 percent of their 1977 property tax receipts or about 25 percent of their total 1977 revenue. As a result of Proposition 13, California local governmental units will lose approximately $7 billion per year in property tax revenue (Petersen 1978).

After the passage of Proposition 13, the state of California began to disburse state aid payments to local governments in order to provide time for the local governments to adjust in an orderly manner to the reduction in revenues. The state aid payments are being made primarily from a temporary state surplus of about $5 billion. These aid payments are designed to delay the full impact of the amendment for only one or two years, however; thereafter local governments will be required to live within the new taxing limitations.

There are two classes of tax-supported bonds that are immediately affected by the passage of Proposition 13: general obligation bonds and tax-allocation bonds. General obligation bonds issued by municipalities are backed by the full faith and credit of the issuer and by the power to levy property taxes without limit. If approved by voters prior to the effective date of Proposition 13 these bonds are specifically exempt from the voter-mandated cutbacks in property taxes.

That is, taxing entities are allowed by the terms of Proposition 13 to levy taxes as necessary to meet the debt service on "old" general obligation bonds. Moreover, the provisions of Proposition 13 effectively prohibit any new issues of general obligation bonds in the future.

A very specialized form of tax-supported bond that has been significant in California is the tax-allocation bond (also called the tax-increment bond). This type is generally issued by redevelopment agencies of city governments as part of a financing program designed to revitalize urban core areas.

Tax-increment bonds work as follows: The city declares a section of its jurisdiction as a redevelopment district. Under statutory powers available, the city can then acquire and condemn properties and proceed to redevelop and rehabilitate the area. As part of this process, the *assessed valuation* of *properties* will be fixed at some *base value* prior to redevelopment.

The agency then attempts to draw private investment capital into the district to build hotels, office buildings, industrial parks, and housing as a result of the infrastructure of services provided through the redevelopment program. In essence, the agency serves as a land developer providing public improvements.

To carry out the public improvements, the agency issues bonds payable solely from the incremental tax revenues generated from the incremental assessed value that results from private investment. The agency has no authority to levy taxes. Instead, the taxing process works as follows:

1. The units of government with taxing power (city, school district, county) levy taxes as established in the budgets of each unit on all assessed properties in the redevelopment district.

2. But the levying units collect *only* that portion of the levy produced by the *base year* valuations.

3. The taxes received over and above the levy on base year valuations are deposited in a *special fund* dedicated to the repayment of the tax-increment bonds.

Tax-allocation bonds were not exempted from the taxing restrictions of Proposition 13, and, as a result of voter-mandated cutbacks in property taxes, it has been estimated that such bonds may lose up to 60 percent of their former expected revenues. As noted by Standard and Poor's in discussing the case of the Park Center Projects of the San Jose Redevelopment Agency: "Proposition 13's effect on the tax increment securing these bonds was significant. In 1977–78, the Park Center Project generated $957,000 in tax increment revenues, but this was cut by 51% to $474,000 for fiscal year 1978–79. With annual debt service of approximately $814,000, the net effect is a $317,000 shortfall for debt service requirements in 1979" (1979: 823).

Measuring the impact of Proposition 13 on yields of both general obligation and tax-allocation bonds is the principal task of the empirical sections that follow.

DATA AND METHODOLOGY

Data for this study were compiled from the data base maintained by the Municipal Finance Study Group. The original sample consisted of all new California local bond issues reported in the *Daily Bond Buyer* "Results of Bond Sales" section for January 1976 through February 1979. Industrial revenue bonds and new issues with missing information were excluded.[1]

In an efficient bond market, yields fully reflect all new relevant public information. In testing the public information efficiency of the bond market, two questions present themselves; 1) Was the event under study "news" that the market had not already fully absorbed as reflected in prices? 2) If the event was news, what was the market's response to it? Both of these questions will be addressed by an analogue of the residual analysis procedure initiated by Fama et al. (1969).

In Fama et al. (1969), as here, residuals are computed as follows:

$$\hat{e}_{j,t} = R_{j,t} - E[R_{j,t}|I_{CP}] \quad , \tag{5-1}$$

where

$\hat{e}_{j,t}$ = the residual on security j in period t;

$R_{j,t}$ = the return observed on security j in period t;

I_{CP} = the information set available to the market in a control period CP, when information about the event is assumed to be unavailable;

$E[\cdot]$ = the expectations operator.

Equation (5-1) is a general formulation of the calculation of residuals. Stock market studies in general have used the least squares estimated market model to obtain the expected return, $E[R_{j,t}|I_{CP}]$.[2] The market model relates the return on a security with the return on the market.

The successful application of the market model relies upon the homogeneity of the securities in question and upon the availability of a complete time series of periodic returns for these securities in the secondary market. Bond returns are difficult to gather and examine because of the lack of continuous secondary market prices (or new issue yields) of municipal bonds. In this case, the traditional market model must be altered to accommodate newly issued bonds over time.

This study employs a municipal bond interest rate model to estimate $E[R_{j,t}|I_{CP}]$ in Eq. (5-1). The interest rate model that we use has been employed in many bond market studies and has consistently displayed its robustness.

The observed response of California bonds may be attributable to other changes affecting the entire market for municipal bonds and only indirectly California. Because the model does not control for all factors affecting the California bond market, it is necessary to establish a control group of bonds for comparison. The control group contains new issues from comparable Western states (Arizona, California, Nevada, Oregon, and Washington).

If the passage of Proposition 13 contains information that was not fully reflected by prices prior to the event, residuals before the event will be different from residuals after the event. This test focuses on the response of the California new-issue bond market in 1977-79 as compared with a control group of newly issued municipal bonds from other Western states. The residuals are computed as follows:

$$\hat{e}_{j,t} = NIC_{j,t} - E[NIC_{j,t}|I_{1976}] , \qquad (5-2)$$

where

$\hat{e}_{j,t}$ = the residual on issue j sold during month t;

$NIC_{j,t}$ = the net interest cost on issue j sold during month t;

$E[NIC_{j,t}|I_{1976}]$ = the expected NIC on issue j sold during the month t given the 1976 information set I.

Equation (5-2) states that the estimated residual $\hat{e}_{j,t}$ equals actual $NIC_{j,t}$ on a new issue of bonds minus the NIC that would have been expected for that issue in period t given only the information set available in 1976. We assume that the passage of Proposition 13 was not anticipated in 1976, which precedes the period of study by a year and one-half. Additionally, the assumption that the actual enactment of Proposition 13 was unforeseen in 1976 is reasonable because California voters had on two prior occasions rejected similar propositions. We also assume that structural differences, if any, in the primary market for municipal bonds between the years 1976 and 1978 will be small compared to the effects of Proposition 13.

Net interest cost is used as a proxy for the internal rate of return (IRR) because the IRR is generally not available and NIC and IRR are highly correlated.[3] An interest rate model for NICs is thus used in this study.

Regression analysis is used to compute the expected NIC for issue j in period t, $E[\text{NIC}_{j,t}|I_{1976}]$. A one-stage linear regression model is fitted to the 1976 data and the independent variables used in the regression model represent the issue, issuer, and market characteristics at the time of the bond sale. The variables used are similar to those employed in other studies of the municipal bond market.

The independent variables used in the regression model are as follows:

Variable

Amt (ln)	Amount of issue in thousands
Mat (ln)	Dollar-weighted average maturity of the issue in years
Index	*Daily Bond Buyer* 20 index in percent for the week of issuance
GO	(1) if the issue is general obligation, (0) otherwise
Cal	(1) if the issue is from California, (0) otherwise
Rating (Moody's)	
Aaa	(1) if Aaa, (0) otherwise
Aa	(1) if Aa, (0) otherwise
A-1	(1) if A-1, (0) otherwise
A	Omitted category
Baa-1	(1) if Baa-1, (0) otherwise
Baa	(1) if Baa, (0) otherwise
UR	(1) if not rated, (0) otherwise

EMPIRICAL RESULTS

As Table 5-1 points out, the results of the regression model explain over two-thirds of the variation in NIC for the sample bonds in the control period. Of particular importance, the results indicate that the NICs on California bonds in 1976 were not significantly different from the NICs for bonds from other Western states. With the exception of the variable representing the size of the issue, the coefficients of all other variables are significant and the signs correspond to theory.

As the second step in the analysis, the regression coefficients derived in Table 5-1 are then used to estimate the NIC that would have occurred in 1977 and 1978 if the same issues were sold during 1976. That is,

$$\hat{\text{NIC}}_{j,t} = E\left[\text{NIC}_{j,t} | I_{1976}\right] . \qquad (5-3)$$

Table 5-1. Western Net Interest Cost Model, 1976 Data, Regression Results.[a]

Variable	Estimated Coefficient
Amt (ln)	0.01
Mat (ln)	0.97[b]
Index	-.06[b]
GO (dummy)	-.31[b]
Cal (dummy)	0.05
Rating	
AAA	-.58[b]
AA	-.46[b]
A-1	-.17[c]
A	Omitted variable
BAAA-1	0.65[b]
BAA	0.40[b]
UR	0.55[b]

a. 281 observations: $R^2 = 0.68$; adjusted $\bar{R}^2 = 0.67$; constant = 3.32; standard error of the estimate = 0.45.

b. Significant at 0.01 level or below.

c. Significant between 0.10 and 0.01.

Residuals are then computed using the actual $\text{NIC}_{j,t}$ and the estimated $\hat{\text{NIC}}_{j,t}$ as follows:

$$\hat{e}_{j,t} = \text{NIC}_{j,t} - \hat{\text{NIC}}_{j,t} \ . \tag{5-4}$$

These residuals $\hat{e}_{j,t}$ are averaged cross sectionally to obtain mean monthly residuals.

$$\bar{e}_{c,t} = \frac{\sum_{j=1}^{k} \hat{e}_{j,t}}{k} \ , \tag{5-5}$$

where

$\bar{e}_{c,t}$ = the monthly mean residual;

$\hat{e}_{j,t}$ = the residual for issue j in month t from Eq. $(5-4)$;

k = the number of issues in month t.

Average monthly residuals are calculated separately for three subsamples of bonds in the 1977–79 period: 1) general obligation bonds from California, 2) tax-allocation bonds from California, and 3) bonds from all other Western states. The two subsamples of California bonds are selected because of the expectation of different effects on these groups owing to the limitations of Proposition 13 on California tax-exempt bonds. General obligation bonds are protected by a grandfather clause, and the passage of Proposition 13 should not alter the risk characteristics of these issues. Tax-allocation bonds, on the other hand, have been seriously affected, and we expect, therefore, to observe positive residuals reflecting the higher NIC on these issues.

The differences between the average residuals for California and those for the rest of the West should reflect any Proposition 13 effects and remove any bond market industry effects. Monthly average residuals for the Western states are computed in the same way that the monthly average California residuals were computed in Eqs. $(5-3)$–$(5-5)$. The difference between the California mean residuals $\bar{e}_{c,t}$ and the other Western states' mean residual $\bar{e}_{w,t}$ is computed as follows:

$$D_t = \bar{e}_{c,t} - \bar{e}_{w,t} \ . \tag{5-6}$$

This difference D_t will be examined over time and by class of bond.

Table 5-2 presents the monthly average residuals for California general obligation bonds, California tax-allocation bonds, and bonds from all other Western states from January 1977 to February 1979.

As the residuals for the control group suggest, all of the Western states appear to have increasing risk premiums beginning in February of 1977. This suggests that there were structural changes in the overall tax-exempt market in 1977–79 compared with 1976.

A comparison of the average residuals for California general obligation bonds and the control group of Western states indicates that the NICs for California general obligation bonds have generally decreased. This would be expected if voters anticipated that fewer California general obligation bond issues would be sold in the future. (See Figure 5-1 for cumulative residual analysis, the cumulative sums of Table 5-2's residuals over time.)

California general obligation bonds have also clearly outperformed the California tax-allocation bonds. This would be expected if the market accurately perceived the effects of Proposition 13.

To test whether the patterns of monthly mean residuals evidence a significant difference between subsamples in different periods before and after Proposition 13, the Mann–Whitney U test was performed. The results are summarized in Table 5-3. For the first six months of 1977, there was no significant difference in average residuals between California general obligation bonds and tax-allocation bonds versus the control group of other Western states. During the last six months of 1977, the average residuals for both types of tax-supported California bonds were significantly *lower* than the average for the control group (see Table 5-2). Over the January–June 1978 period, when anticipation of Proposition 13 could be expected to increase residuals, the results of the Mann–Whitney test indicate that there were significantly higher residuals on tax-allocation bonds relative to the control group. These significant differences also persisted during the remainder of 1978. For California general obligation bonds, however, the results of the Mann–Whitney test indicate that there were no statistically significant differences in residuals with the control group during 1978.

The fact that California bonds generally carried risk premiums equal to or lower than rates established on other tax-exempt bonds in 1977 suggests that the passage of Proposition 13 was not anticipated prior to 1978. This is not surprising since the chronology of

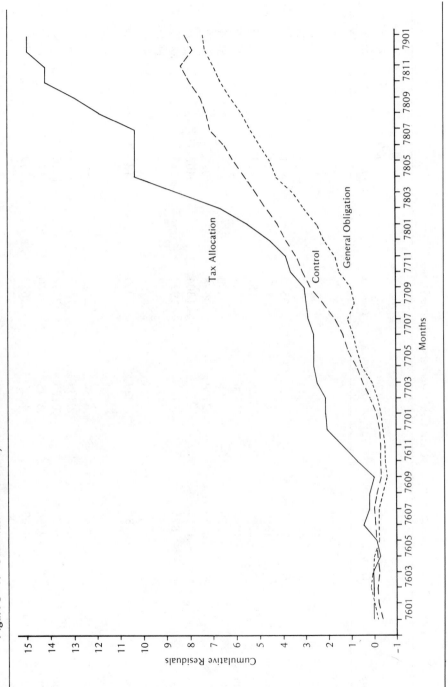

Figure 5-1. Cumulative Residuals, 1976-79.

Table 5-2. Mean Residual Breakdown: California versus Pacific States.

Date	California General Obligation	California Tax-Allocation	Control	California General Obligation - Control	California Tax-Allocation - Control
1976					
January	-.1728	...	-.3841	.2113	...
February	.1614	.0340	.1729	-.0115	-.1389
March	.1511	...	.0570	.0941	...
April	-.1360	...	-.1148	-.0212	...
May	-.0566	-.3158	.1157	-.1723	-.4315
June	-.1947	.1586	.0347	-.2294	.1239
July	.0579	.5468	.0450	.0129	.5121
August	-.0377	-.2609	.0698	-.1076	-.3307
September	-.1711	...	-.1304	-.0407	...
October	-.1875	-.1917	-.1990	.0115	.0073
November	.1157	.7471	.0623	.0534	.6848
December	...	.6725	-.0205	...	.6930
Year	-.0184	.1289	.0000	-.0184	.1289
1977					
January	.0941	.6454	.0388	.0553	.6066
February	.0837	.0889	.1332	-.0495	-.0443
March	.1473	-.0195	.2589	-.1116	-.2784
April	.2298	.3775	.3440	-.1142	.0335
May	.4362	.1595	.2623	.1739	-.1028
June	.2200	...	.3575	-.1375	...

July	.1470	-.0056	.2291	-.0821	-.2347
August	.2528	.2335	.3427	-.0899	-.1092
September	-.3200	.0941	.5098	-.8298	-.4157
October	.1718	.0872	.5726	-.4008	-.4854
November	.5510	.5936	.3749	.1761	.4175
December	.1642	.2124	.2776	-.1134	-.0652
Year	.2627	.2166	.2971	-.0344	-.0805
_1978_					
January	.4705	.6646	.4348	.0357	.2298
February	.3165	.9583	.3665	-.0500	.5918
March	.5410	1.1510	.4888	.0522	.6622
April	.4968	1.8006	.4670	.0298	1.3336
May	.7095	1.8721	.4618	.2477	1.4103
June	.2929	...	.4792	-.1863	...
July	.4665	...	.4036	.0629	...
August	.4156	...	.6188	-.2032	...
September	.3212	1.4821	.1496	.1716	1.3325
October	.4927	1.1055	.2309	.2618	.8746
November	.4212	1.3160	.4797	-.0585	.8363
December	.2927	...	.3503	-.0576	...
Year	.4810	1.4248	.4349	.0461	.9899
_1979_					
January	.3580	.7734	.5062	-.1482	.2672
February	.1101	...	.3544	-.2443	...
March	.2203	...	.4273	-.2070	...

Table 5-3. Results of Mann-Whitney U Test on Comparison of Monthly Mean Residuals; Selected Six-Month Periods.

Period of Test	Control versus California General Obligation	Control versus California Tax-Allocation
January-June 1977	Not significant[a]	Not significant
July-December 1977	Significantly lower	Significantly lower
January-June 1978	Not significant	Significantly higher
July-December 1978	Not significant	Significantly higher

a. Tests were conducted at the 0.05 significance level.

public announcement dates of Proposition 13 did not begin until December 1977. The significant dates are as follows:

- December 6, 1977. Petitions are begun to be circulated to place Proposition 13 on the state ballot.
- December 30, 1977. Proposition 13 qualifies for the ballot.
- April 13, 1978. Moody's refuses to provide bond ratings on any new property tax-supported bonds.
- June 6, 1978. Proposition 13 passed.
- July 1, 1978. Effective date of Proposition 13.

The fact that California general obligation bonds did not experience significant differences in average residuals relative to bonds from other Western states also conforms to expectations. The credit quality of these bonds was not directly affected by Proposition 13.

On the other hand, the fact that average residuals for tax-allocation bonds did increase significantly from the control group in 1978 is consistent with expectations. These bonds did suffer a marked decrease in credit standing.

SUMMARY AND CONCLUSIONS

This study has investigated the response of the California bond market to the passage of Proposition 13 using an analogue to the residual analysis done in the stock market. The regression results indicate that the interest rate model is well behaved and produces econometrically sound results.

The residual analysis indicates that the passage of Proposition 13 was an informational event that was not fully anticipated. The bond market in the Western states appears to have been experiencing generally higher risk premiums during 1977 and 1978. After controlling for the overall market changes, however, the response of the California bond market is consistent with the semistrong form of the efficient market hypothesis.

NOTES TO CHAPTER 5

1. Industrial development bonds are sold by tax-exempt issuers, but the proceeds of the issue are used by taxable issuers. The net interest cost (NIC) of these bonds may not be a function of the characteristics of the tax-exempt issuer. The final sample consisted of 127 California and 154 Western states issuers in 1976. In the 1977–79 period the final sample had 320 issues from California and 565 from all Western states.

2. The market model is stated generally as follows:

$$R_{j,t} = \alpha + \beta R_{mt} + \tilde{u} \; ,$$

where

$R_{j,t}$ = the return on security j in period t;

R_{mt} = the return on the market in period t;

$\tilde{u}$ = the error term.

3. The internal rate of return is referred to as the true interest cost (TIC). The net interest cost is computed as follows:

$$\text{NIC} = \frac{\sum\limits_{n=s}^{m} n \, A_n \, C_n - P}{\sum\limits_{n=s}^{m} n \, A_n} \; ,$$

where

C_n = the coupon rate of bonds maturing in n periods;

A_n = the total par value of bonds maturing in n periods;

n = number of years to maturity;

s = the number of years to first maturity;

m = the number of years to last maturity;

p = the bid premium (– discount) over the par value of the issue.

REFERENCES

Fama, Eugene F. 1970. "Efficient Capital Markets: A Review of Theory and Empirical Work." *Journal of Finance* (May): 383-417.

Fama, Eugene F.; Lawrence Fischer; Michael Jensen; and Richard Roll. 1969. "The Adjustment of Stock Prices to New Information." *International Economics Review* (February): 1-21.

Fisher, Lawrence. 1959. "Determinants of Risk Premiums on Corporate Bonds." *Journal of Political Economy* (June): 217-37.

Fraser, Donald R., and R. Malcolm Richards. 1977. Note, "Further Evidence on the Informational Value of Bond-Rating Changes." *Quarterly Review of Economics and Business* (Autumn): 73-78.

Grier, Paul, and Steven Katz. 1976. "The Differential Effects of Bond Rating Changes among Industrial and Public Utility Bonds by Maturity." *Journal of Business* (April): 226-39.

Grossman, Stanford J., and Joseph E. Stiglitz. 1976. "Information and Competitive Price Systems." *American Economic Review* (May): 246-53.

Hastie, Larry K. 1972. "Determinants of Municipal Bond Yields." *Journal of Financial and Quantitative Analysis* (June): 1729-48.

Hendershott, Patric H., and David S. Kidwell. 1978. "The Impact of Relative Security Supplies: A Test with Data from a Regional Tax-Exempt Bond Market." *Journal of Money, Credit and Banking* (August): 337-47.

Hettenhouse, George W., and William L. Sartoris. 1976. "An Analysis of the Informational Value of Bond-Rating Changes." *Quarterly Review of Economics and Business* (Summer): 65-78.

Hopewell, Michael H., and George G. Kaufman. 1974. "Costs to Issuers of Using NIC in Competitive Bond Sales." *Daily Bond Buyer* (June 24).

_____. 1973. "Bond Price Volatility and Term to Maturity: A General Respecification." *American Economic Review* (September): 749-53.

Katz, Steven. 1974. "The Price Adjustment Process of Bonds to Rating Reclassifications: A Test of Bond Market Efficiency." *Journal of Finance* (May): 551-59.

Kessel, Reuben. 1971. "A Study of the Effects of Competition in the Tax-Exempt Bond Market." *Journal of Political Economy* (July-August): 706-38.

Kidwell, David S. 1975. "Call Provisions and Their Effect on Municipal Bond Issues." *Governmental Finance* (August): 28-32.

Petersen, J. 1978. "Jarvis-Gann: What It Is and What It Means." *The Daily Bond Buyer* (June 19): 1.

Pinches, George E., and J. Singleton. 1978. "The Adjustment of Stock Prices to Bond Rating Changes." *Journal of Finance* (March): 29-44.

Standard and Poor's. 1979. *Fixed Income Investor* (January 13).

Tanner, J. Ernest. 1975. "The Determinants of Interest Cost on New Municipal Bonds: A Reevaluation." *Journal of Business* (January): 74–80.

Weinstein, Mark I. 1977. "The Effect of a Rating Change Announcement on Bond Price." *Journal of Financial Economics* 5: 329–50.

Wilbur, Robert Wyatt. 1977. "Corporate Bond Rating Changes: A Test of Bond Market Efficiency." Unpublished dissertation, 1977.

6 CALIFORNIA BONDS AFTER PROPOSITION 13

Jack H. Beebe

Proposition 13 has revamped the structure of public finance in California. Aside from the highly visible effects of a $7 billion reduction in property taxes and a $4 1/2 billion transfer of funds from the state to local governments in its first year, it also has resulted in a large redistribution of wealth among local governments and special districts and has severely restricted the flexibility of municipal tax structures.

In a less visible sphere, the constitutional amendment also has had dramatic effects on the market for California state and local government debt. For example, Proposition 13's tax-rate ceiling has been considered tantamount to removal of local government's legal authorization to issue "new" general obligation debt—debt for which voter approval was not obtained prior to July 1, 1978. (General obligation debt authorized earlier is still being issued, however.) With that avenue closed, local governments and other entities will have to finance construction through current revenues, state assistance, or debt other than general obligation bonds.

Because of the amendment, new tax-allocation bonds issued by redevelopment agencies will be extremely difficult to float and the

The author thanks Pat Weber for his valuable statistical and computer assistance. This is an updated and revised version of a paper that appeared in the Federal Reserve Bank of San Francisco *Economic Review* (Winter 1979) and the *National Tax Journal* (June 1979).

majority of existing tax-allocation issues will be exposed to default. The effect on new debt may well have been intended in the amendment. However, when asked why he did not protect existing debt of redevelopment agencies in drafting the amendment, Proposition 13 co-sponsor Howard Jarvis replied, "I never even gave a thought to it." (*Business Week* 1978: 57).

California has an initiative process by which voters can petition to place constitutional amendments directly on the state ballot. Since the early 1970s California property values and hence tax assessments have soared. After repeated attempts to enact property tax relief in the state legislature, tax protestors began to circulate tax-limitation petitions, with most of them uniting behind a 1977 proposal developed by Howard Jarvis and Paul Gann that called for a dramatic decrease in (and a permanent restriction on) property taxes. By December 29, 1977, the Jarvis–Gann amendment has gained the needed signatures to qualify as Proposition 13 on the June 1978 state primary ballot. On June 6, the measure passed by an overwhelming two–to–one majority; it took effect on July 1, 1978.

By restricting revenue sources, Proposition 13 not only decreased the expected future income stream of local governments and special districts in California but also greatly restricted and largely removed the flexibility of these entities in controlling their current incomes (tax receipts). It also restricted increases in the state's taxing powers, thereby blocking large increases in state taxes as an alternative source of government revenue. Since such restrictions should affect the ability of municipalities to service and retire debt, Proposition 13's passage may have adversely affected both the cost of new issues and the value of existing California municipal debt.

Proposition 13 has affected the various kinds of municipal debt to different degrees. For example, tax-allocation debt secured solely by restricted property tax revenues has been severely affected. Moreover, while new general obligation bonds are effectively prohibited, existing general obligation debt has been unaffected. Other kinds of debt have fallen somewhere between these extremes. It is concluded that restrictions on the size of government, if property structured, need not have dramatic effects on the cost or value of government debt. However, if such restrictions are applied only to certain sources of revenue, they may have large unintended side effects.

This study examines what happened to new-issue interest costs for different categories of California municipal bonds from the time

Proposition 13 was placed on the ballot at the end of 1977 through March 31, 1979. Because data rarely exist for secondary-market yields, the interest cost for new issues is used here to represent the yield on existing debt. In this manner, the study also provides estimates of the effects of Proposition 13 on the value of outstanding debt. In the first section, Proposition 13 is described and hypotheses are presented concerning its effects on each category of state and local bond. In the second section, an econometric model is developed to explain statistically the interest cost of new issues. The model is estimated for each category of local bond, and an estimate is obtained for the overall effect of Proposition 13 as well as for the individual effects of changes in bond ratings and other explanatory factors. In the third section, inferences are drawn regarding the adverse effects on the value of outstanding California municipal debt. In the final section the summary and conclusions are presented.

HYPOTHESIZED EFFECTS

Factors that affect default risk vary widely for municipal bonds, depending principally on each bond's security—that is, the legal and economic constraints affecting the cash flow available for debt service and retirement. At one extreme, a pure revenue bond is secured solely by the revenue generated from the financed project, such as a parking lot. For such a bond, the cash flow of the project, and hence the security of the bond, is completely independent of the cash flow of the issuing municipality. Thus, the risk of the bond depends solely on the risk of the project, and not on the general condition of the government. At the other extreme, a general obligation bond is secured by the general cash flow of the issuing government and thus is not tied to a specific project or revenue source. Thus, risk of a general obligation bond depends on the solvency of the issuing government.

There are many variations of municipal bonds. In analyzing the risk of a particular bond, one looks first at the legal provisions for the bond's repayment and second at the economic prospects involved. Since Proposition 13 reduces revenues from property taxes and generally attempts to restrict tax increases at the state and local levels, it should affect debt whose security is limited principally to property tax revenue. It might also affect debt whose security depends on the overall cash flow of the state and local governments. For these reasons, one needs to consider the legal provisions of Proposition 13, and then its possible consequences for various kinds of municipal debt.[1]

PROPOSITION 13

Proposition 13 "rolls back" current taxes—both tax rates and assessed values—on all property to 1 percent of 1975–76 market value.[2] Tax rates must then be held at the 1 percent ceiling, while assessed market values may rise no more than the annual percentage increase in the consumer price index or 2 percent per year, whichever is less. However, properties sold, traded, or newly constructed after 1975–76 may be reassessed at current market values.

Proposition 13 also attempts to prevent other taxes from rising to offset the lost property tax revenues. First, it requires that state tax increases be passed by a two-thirds vote of all members (not just those voting) of both houses of the legislature. Second, it states that property taxes cannot be raised beyond the above limits (even by voter approval), and that other local tax increases must gain the approval of two-thirds of all "qualified electors"[3] in the affected municipality.

Proposition 13 specifically exempts tax increases needed to service *prior voter-approved debt*: "The limitation . . . shall not apply to ad valorem taxes or special assessments to pay interest and redemption charges on any indebtedness approved by the voters prior to the time this section becomes effective." For this reason, payments on debt approved by voters prior to the effective date of Proposition 13 (July 1, 1978) are not subject to the specific tax constraints placed on property. But payments on all new debts approved after that date, and on all prior debt not voter-approved, would be constrained by the tax-limitation provisions of the amendment.

From its introduction until the June 6 election, Proposition 13's effects on the cost of municipal debt were a function of the probability of passage. Throughout much of the preelection period, poll results indicated probable passage. However, the landslide victory was not apparent until the last several weeks before the election, when voters rallied behind the strong message that Proposition 13 carried to all levels of government (Table 6–1).

Table 6-1. Poll Results through the Preelection Period.

Proposition 13	Feb. 11-23	March 27– April 3	May 1-8	May 29-31	June 6 Election Results
Yes	20%	27%	42%	57%	65%
No	10	25	39	34	35
Undecided/ unaware	70	48	19	9	. . .

Sources: Field Institute surveys as reported in the *San Francisco Chronicle*, June 2, 1978. Election results as reported in the *California Journal* July 1978.

EFFECTS ON TYPES OF DEBT

Proposition 13's effects on the municipal bond market depend very much on the security of each type of bond as is seen below.[4] To aid the reader, Table 6-2 provides a summary of the hypothesized effects for the various types of bonds.[5]

General Obligation Bonds
(State and Local)

Also known as "full faith and credit" general obligation bonds, are normally issued by state or local governments only with prior voter approval. Debt service for such bonds may be paid out of any available revenue source, with the issuing authority pledging its full faith and credit to meet such payments.

Despite the emergence of Proposition 13 and the reduction of the large surplus in the state budget, the State of California is still rated triple A (AAA by Standard and Poor's (S&P), and Aaa by Moody's), largely because of the state government's fiscal conservatism and a rapidly growing tax base. Proposition 13 conceivably might have jeopardized the state's strong credit rating, for several reasons: 1) A decrease of the state surplus and an increase in state expenditures was required to assist local governments. 2) Increases in state tax rates henceforth will require two-thirds favorable vote of both houses of the legislature. 3) State debt might be increased to finance public works projects that otherwise would have been financed by

Table 6-2. Hypothesized Effects of Proposition 13 on California Municipal Debt.

Bond Type	Effect
State general obligation	Aaa rating would be jeopardized at least in transition period. Longer-term effect depends on whether expenditures are reduced sufficiently.
Local general obligation	Existing[a] debt not affected because of its exemption from revenue ceiling. New debt severely affected unless authorized under a non-*ad valorem* special tax.
State and local revenue	No effect on new or existing "pure" revenue bonds, which constitute the majority of revenue bonds. Small negative effect on hybrid bonds with tax revenue as backup security.
Local tax-allocation	Severe negative impact on new and existing debt due to restrictions on property tax assessments and rates.
Local Lease-Purchase	Negative effect on non-voter-approved existing debt and on new debt because of local government's increased difficulty in meeting lease payments. Extent of effect highly variable depending on whether facility is "essential" and whether it would generate sufficient revenue to sustain debt service if local government failed to meet lease payments.

a. "Existing" debt comprises bonds that were approved prior to July 1, 1978; "new" debt comprises issues approved July 1 and thereafter.

local general obligation issues. And 4) analysts may have believed that Proposition 13 would have a depressing effect on the state economy.

Over the near term, it is possible that Proposition 13 would have an adverse effect on the safety of state general obligation bonds. Although a two-thirds vote of the legislature would permit additional taxes to pay off debt, such use of revenues would represent one of many demands for funds. Over the longer term, the effect on state debt would depend largely on how the state elects to run its fiscal operation in response to the needs of local government on the one hand and to pressures from voters for fiscal conservatism on the other.

Because Proposition 13 singles out *ad valorem* (property) taxes, local general obligation debt would be affected differently from state general obligation debt. For "existing" voter-approved bonds (those that received voter approval prior to July 1, 1978, regardless of when they were actually issued), debt service would be exempted from the one percent tax rate ceiling imposed on *ad valorem* taxes. Thus, property tax overrides could be employed without special voter approval to meet the payments on existing voter-approved debt, and such debt should not be affected by the amendment. (In fact, because of its relative scarcity, some analysts have suggested that such secure debt would command a premium price and thus a lower yield.)

Payments on "new" general obligation debt (that approved by voters July 1 or thereafter) would have to be paid from available revenues as constrained by Proposition 13. However, by law general obligation bonds must be secured by "unlimited" taxing authority. Traditionally, the power of local governments to tax has been interpreted as the power to increase property tax levies, their discretionary source of income. For this reason, Proposition 13's tax rate ceiling has been considered tantamount to removal of local government's legal authorization to issue "new" general obligation debt. Thus, we should see an end to new local government general obligation financing.[6]

Revenue Bonds (State and Local)

Revenue bonds are normally issued to finance revenue-producing facilities, and user fees are generally pledged to pay the debt service. They may be issued by municipalities or special districts (such as sewer or hospital districts). The repayment of "pure" revenue bonds does not depend on the operating budget of the municipality.[7] Thus, Proposition 13 would presumably have no effect on either state or local "pure" revenue bonds.

In some cases, municipalities pledge general (property) tax revenues as backup security in the event that user fees prove inadequate to cover the debt service. In these cases, Proposition 13 would jeopardize the quality of the backup security. Furthermore, revenue bonds are now sometimes used to finance the cost of self-insurance plans such as workers' compensation and medical malpractice insurance. Not being tied to a revenue-producing facility, these bonds must be secured by the available revenues of the municipality involved. Despite such exceptions, revenue bonds normally are secured by the revenues of the facility rather than by property taxes or general tax revenues of the municipality. Thus, for revenue bonds in the aggregate, Proposition 13 should have little or no effect on interest cost.

Tax-Allocation Bonds

Tax-allocation bonds are used extensively to finance redevelopment projects in California and several other states. They are financed and secured primarily by the "tax-increment" revenues on a specific redevelopment project. In many cases, government loans and grants, as well as fees from facilities such as parking garages, provide additional revenue to the project.

Under tax-increment financing, property values prior to the project are "fixed" in the year during which the project is approved. Property-tax revenues generated by the fixed base year assessed value are allocated to existing tax bodies such as a city and county. Then, additional tax revenues from the increase in assessed value over the fixed base year level—the tax-increment revenues—are allocated to the redevelopment agency. They are used to pay off debt of the agency and to provide internal funds for further project expansion. Redevelopment agencies have commonly used long-term debt to finance improvements that are sold at less than cost. The tax-increment revenues are then used to pay off the debt, and in this manner, they indirectly provide for a subsidy on improvements.

Because it lowers assessed values and property-tax rates, Proposition 13 seriously affects the revenue base for tax-allocation bonds.[8] And because of the heavy debt service and limited sources of revenue of many redevelopment districts, with a few exceptions where the redevelopment district has little debt and considerable non–property tax income, such a severe restriction of property tax revenue could easily result in default in many cases. Increased default risk should result in an increase in interest cost for new issues and a decline in the market value of outstanding bonds. If severe enough, new issues should cease to exist because of ceilings on interest rates placed on these bonds by law. By state law, tax-allocation debt is subject to a coupon ceiling rate of 8 percent and a maximum discount of 95 percent. The empirical section will show that this limitation appeared to be binding in many instances.

Lease-Purchase Bonds

These bonds, also called lease-revenue or lease-rental bonds, are issued by a public, private, or nonprofit lease-back corporation (special district), which uses the proceeds to construct some facility that is then leased to a municipal government. The municipal government (lessee) makes rental payments to the corporation (lessor) sufficient to pay debt service on the bonds and operating expenses of the corporation. In general, such obligations are not voter-approved, and the municipality normally promises to provide for rental payments out of its operating budget.

Lease-purchase bonds are sometimes revenue-supported to the extent that the facility's revenues provide for the debt service, while municipal rental payments provide backup security. As with revenue bonds, Proposition 13's impact depends largely on the ability of the project, such as a parking lot, to be self-supporting in the event that the municipality reneges on its lease contract. However, many lease-purchase bonds are supported solely by lease payments from the municipality's operating budget. These will be negatively affected to the degree that the municipality's financial condition deteriorates and taxpayers regard the facility to be a nonessential service. Thus, the safety of lease-purchase bonds might decline somewhat under Proposition 13, because the municipalities might lack flexibility to meet payments within their budgets and taxpayers might regard continued lease payments as a nonessential expenditure.

EMPIRICAL EVIDENCE

The previous discussion suggests that Proposition 13 should have affected the interest cost of some types of new issues as the election results grew more certain. The effects can be measured by an examination of data on new issues of local municipal debt in California sold between January 1, 1977, and March 31, 1979,[9] and specifically by an analysis of the average yield spread between new California issues and Moody's Aaa new-issue index. Time is divided into three subperiods: all of 1977 (pre-Proposition 13); January 1-June 6, 1978 (the period of Proposition 13's increasingly likely victory); and June 7, 1978-March 31, 1979 (post-Proposition 13).

State Debt

Although new issues of California state debt are infrequent, there were a sufficient number over the sample period to give a rough approximation of the interest cost relative to the Moody's Aaa municipal bond rate (Table 6-3). Initially, the interest cost of state general obligation bonds was well below the yield of the Moody's index, averaging 37 basis points lower in 1977. After the election, this spread narrowed to 11 basis points. The Kruskal–Wallis test[10] leads to the conclusion that the differences in the three average yield spreads for general obligation bonds are statistically significant at the 10 percent level. Thus, we can conclude that there has been some increase in the cost of state general obligation debt that is probably attributable to the fiscal effect of Proposition 13.

There are insufficient data to test an hypothesis for state revenue bonds. However, there appears to have been a shift toward use of revenue-bond financing, a trend that one would predict in the aftermath of Proposition 13.

Table 6-3. The Effect on State–Government Issues, Spread between California and National New-Issue Rates, January 1977 to March 1979.[a]

	January 1977– December 1977	January 1978– June 6, 1978	June 6, 1978 on
General obligation			
Issues	7	3	4
Basis points	-37	-25	-11
Revenue[b]			
Issues	0	1	11
Basic points	. . .	3	75[c]

a. Spreads were calculated by subtracting the Moody's Aaa municipal bond index for the given week from the individual issue rate. All issues were then given equal weight in the averages.

b. Because state revenue and state-authority lease-purchase bonds are often sold through negotiation and interest costs are not reported, data in this category do not reflect the total number of new issues.

c. Some upward trend throughout the period. The three issues in 1979 had an average spread of 147 basis points over the Moody's index.

Sources: Daily Bond Buyer and Moody's *Municipal and Government Manual.*

Local Debt

Over the first half of 1978, and possibly beginning as early as December 1977, interest spreads increased for tax-allocation, lease-purchase, and possibly for revenue bonds (Figure 6-1). By the time of the election, the interest cost on tax-allocation bonds reached almost 300 basis points above the Moody's Aaa rate, compared with an average of 90 basis points in 1977. Moreover, as of March 31, 1979, there had been only one new tax-allocation issue after the election.

INTEREST-COST MODEL

Table 6-3 and Figure 6-1 give informative, albeit simplistic, pictures of Proposition 13's effect on the cost of California debt. Given the few numbers of state issues, detailed statistical analysis is impossible. However, local issues are sufficiently numerous to permit more rigorous methods of analysis. In this section, statistical models are used to obtain refined measures of the amendment's effect on each kind of bond. In the process, it will be possible to quantify the extent to which Proposition-13 related increases in new-issue interest cost have been associated with changes in bond ratings, number of bids per issue, and other factors that normally help to explain the interest cost.

According to earlier statistical studies, the most important factors explaining the interest cost of new issues of a given category of bond are the average level of municipal-bond yields nationwide and factors specific to new issues such as quality rating, size of issue, number of competitive bids, and type of placement—that is, competitive bidding, negotiated sale, or private placement. A regression relating all of these variables to new-issue interest cost explains a significant portion of the variation in interest cost from issue to issue. (See in particular Hendershott and Kidwell (1978), Kessel (1971), Kidwell (1977), Tanner (1975)).

Variables are omitted from this analysis, as they are in other empirical analyses. Differences in coupon patterns would affect the interest differential, as would the whole term structure of interest rates, because coupons are expected to provide future reinvestment

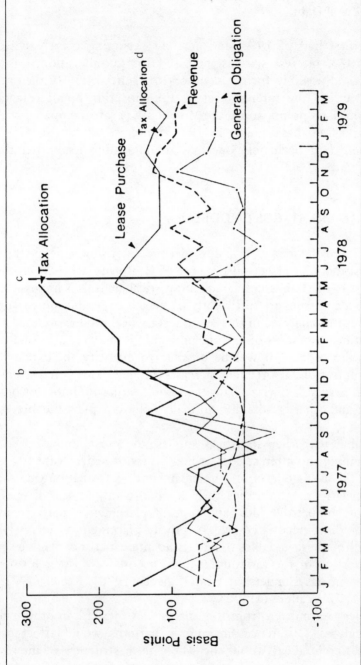

Figure 6-1. The Effect on Local Government Issues Spread between California and National New-Issue Rates[a] January 1977–March 1979.

a. Spreads were calculated by subtracting the Moody's Aaa municipal bond index for the given week from the rate on individual issues. All issues were then given equal weight in the monthly figures.

b. Date at which Proposition 13 was placed on the ballot.

c. Date at which Proposition 13 passed.

d. The only issue between June 6, 1978, and March 31, 1979.

income at rates implied by the whole term structure. Tax effects should also be included, even for municipal bonds, because capital gains/losses have tax effects. Also, probability functions for default and call should be included. The state of the art and limitations of the data preclude much headway in including these variables.

Theoretically, the effects of Proposition 13 may have been transmitted through two distinct channels. First, the amendment may have influenced ratings, bids, and other characteristics, thereby leading to a rise in interest cost. Second, it may also have directly increased the interest cost of new issues without necessarily changing these other characteristics. These alternative channels can be sorted out by fitting different models to the data. The alternative models developed in this section will enable us to distinguish between the different possible channels of influence.

For a typical period, such as the pre–Proposition 13 period, a model of the following specification can be used to explain the interest cost for new issues of California bonds:

$$\text{NIC} = a + b_1 \text{TERMST} + d_1 \text{DTERMST} + d_2 \text{Aaa} + d_3 \text{Aa} + d_4 \text{A} + d_5 \text{B} +$$
$$b_2 \text{LSIZE} + b_3 \text{LBIDS} + d_6 \text{NEGOT} \quad , \quad (6\text{-}1)$$

where

NIC	=	net interest cost (interest rate) for the new issue;
TERMST	=	variable reflecting the nationwide interest rate for bonds of high quality and comparable maturity (explanation follows);
DTERMST	=	dummy variable used when the average maturity of the new issue is unknown (explanation follows);
Aaa	=	zero-one dummy variable equal to one for Moody's Aaa (S&P AAA) rating;[11]
Aa	=	zero-one dummy variable equal to one for Moody's Aa (S&P AA) rating;
A	=	zero-one dummy variable equal to one for Moody's A (S&P A) rating;
B	=	zero-one dummy variable equal to one for Moody's Baa to B (S&P BAA to B) rating (no bonds were rated below B; nonrated bonds are the omitted class);
LSIZE	=	natural logarithm of the size of the total serial issue in thousands of dollars;
LBIDS	=	natural logarithm of the number of bids received in competitive bidding;

NEGOT   = dummy variable equal to zero for competitive bidding and equal to one for negotiated sale or private placement.

The dependent variable is net interest cost. In the municipal bond market, bonds are almost always sold to underwriters in a package known as a serial issue. A serial issue has many bonds with different coupons and maturities, and for the package an average maturity and net interest cost (average interest rate) are calculated. Average maturity is a simple weighted average of the maturities of the individual bonds in the issue. Net interest cost is a weighted average of coupon yields of the different bonds in the issue without regard to when the coupons are paid. Thus, future coupons are implicitly discounted at a zero rate of interest, and coupons in the first year are given the same weight as those in the last year. If the coupons imply rates on the par value bonds that differ markedly from the rates in the reoffer yields or in the municipal bond term structure, then net interest cost can differ markedly from the true economic interest cost. In California, constraints placed on the underwriters by the municipalities keep the coupon yields fairly well in line with the term structure. Thus, net interest cost used in this study is a fairly close approximation to true interest cost. For a full discussion, see Hopewell and Kaufman (1978, 1976, 1974) and Mendelowitz and Rockoff (1976).

The variable TERMST represents the national interest rate on a typical municipal bond of high quality and comparable maturity during the week that the new issue is sold. For the jth new issue, the value of TERMST can be calculated according to the following formula:

$$\text{TERMST}_j = i_{1t} + (i_{30t} - i_{1t}) \frac{\ln \text{MAT}_j}{\ln 30} , \qquad (6-2)$$

where

i_{1t} = yield on Salomon Brothers index for prime one-year general obligation municipal bonds furing the week that the jth issue is sold;

i_{30t} = yield on Salomon Brothers index for prime general obligation municipal bonds of 30-year maturity;

MAT_j = average maturity of the jth issue.[12]

This specification of interest cost captures the desirable logarithmic shape of a term-structure model. In particular, it not only allows the entire term structure to shift up and down but also allows the term structure to twist as short- and long-term rates change relative to one another.[13] $TERMST_j$ is then a single interest rate taken from the term structure for week t and maturity MAT_j. A hypothesis on the coefficient b_1 of TERMST is that $b_1 = 1$, so that NIC rises and falls with TERMST.[14] For some serial issues in the following analysis, TERMST cannot be used because it requires information on average maturity, which is not available from published sources. To compensate for this, the regression sets TERMST equal to i_{1t} and adds another variable DTERMST, equal to $(i_{30t} - i_{1t})$.

When average maturity is know, DTERMST is zero. When average maturity is not known, TERMST is set equal to i_{1t} and DTERMST is set equal to $(i_{30t} - i_{1t})$. The coefficient of DTERMST, d_1, is

$$d_1 = b_1 \times \frac{\overline{ln \ MAT}}{ln \ 30} \ , \quad\quad (6\text{-}3)$$

where $\overline{ln \ MAT}$ is an estimate of the average of the log average maturities for the missing data. Using $\overline{ln \ MAT}$ for the data with known values and b_1 from the regression, one can calculate a hypothesized value for d_1. The hypothesis would merely test whether or not the average maturity of the data with missing values was the same as that for data with known maturities.

The following hypotheses suggest how the other variables would affect interest cost. The rating variables measure the increase in interest cost over that of a comparable nonrated bond. The higher the quality rating, the lower the expected interest cost. Thus, the rating coefficients should have negative signs, although it is not clear that a rating of B would carry a lower interest cost than no rating. The effect of issue size is ambiguous. Bond traders state that both very small and very large issues pay a premium—small issues because of a tendency for underwriters to bid high due to the small potential payoff from obtaining detailed information, and large issues because of "supply effects," that is, the difficulty of reselling a large number of bonds in large serial issues in a short span of time. It is normally hypothesized that the number of bids reflects the degree of competition in underwriting and the importance of imperfect information (Kessel 1971). Interest cost should be higher the fewer the bids under competitive bidding and should be higher still under negotiated sale or private placement.

Adding Time Shifts

Aside from Proposition 13's effects on ratings and other variables, it probably also has had a significant effect on interest cost distinct from that felt through the other variables. It is reasonable to hypothesize that as the amendment's prospects became increasingly strong with the approach of the election (Table 6-1), its effect on interest cost would have increased. Then, the certainty after June 6 should have had a constant effect.

Given data limitations, it is best to hypothesize a linear trend for the preelection 1978 months. In addition, a linear trend for 1977 and an intercept shift for the first week in January 1978 are introduced to test whether or not the shift in 1977 was zero as hypothesized and whether there was any intercept shift in 1978. The full model with structural time shift now becomes as follows (see Figure 6-2):

$$NIC = a + b_1 TERMST + d_1 DTERMST + d_2 AAA + d_3 Aa + d_4 A + d_5 B +$$
$$b_2 LSIZE + b_3 LBIDS + d_6 NEGOT + b_4 WEEK77 + d_7 DJAN78 +$$
$$b_5 WEEK78 + d_8 DJUN78 \quad , \quad (6-4)$$

where

> WEEK77 = linear time trend for the weeks in 1977;
> DJAN78 = intercept shift dummy, dated January 1, 1978 (week 53);
> WEEK78 = linear time trend for the period January 1–June 6, 1978 (weeks 53–74);
> DJUN78 = intercept shift dummy, dated June 6, 1978 (week 75).

The hypothesized signs for the effects on each type of bond are as follows:

	General Obligation	Revenue	Tax-Allocation	Lease-Purchase
WEEK77	0	0	0	0
DJAN78	0	0	0	0
WEEK78	0	0	+	+
DJUN78	0	0	+	+

Figure 6-2. Model for Structural Shift in Interest Cost.

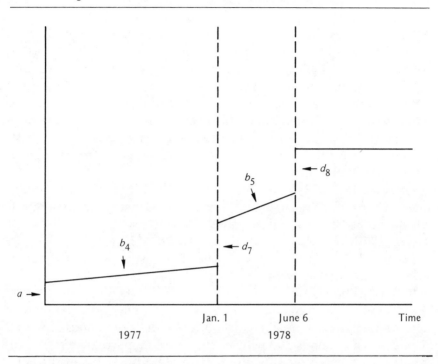

Jan. 1   June 6   Time

1977   1978

Proposition 13 states that general obligation bonds approved after its implementation (July 1) would be subject to property tax ceilings. However, the bonds issued after July 1 were all approved prior to July 1 (one as early as 1973). Thus, the hypothesized effect is zero.

Because ratings and other issue descriptors might have been affected by Proposition 13, Eq. (6-4) should also be estimated with right-hand variables that are not subject to possible endogeneity. For this purpose, the following model serves as an alternate measure of Proposition 13's effects:

$$\text{NIC} = a + b_1 \text{TERMST} + d_1 \text{DTERMST} + b_4 \text{WEEK77} + d_7 \text{DJAN78} +$$
$$b_5 \text{WEEK78} + d_8 \text{DJUN78} . \qquad (6-5)$$

This equation would attribute entirely to Proposition 13 those changes in 1978 net interest cost that are not related to changes in open market rates. Equation (6-5) would esentially estimate the time shifts apparent in Figure 6-1.

Changes in Issue Descriptors

Although ratings, size of issue, number of bids, and type of offering cannot be considered exogenous to Proposition 13 on a priori grounds, in fact, significant shifts in values were found ex post only for tax-allocation bonds. Between 1977 and 1978, there were no significant shifts in ratings for general obligation, revenue, and lease-purchase bonds, but there were shifts for tax-allocation bonds significant at the 5 percent level. The Chi-square test was used to test whether or not the 1977 and 1978 distributions came from the same underlying population.

On April 11, 1978, Moody's suspended its ratings on all previously rated California tax-allocation bonds (64 outstanding issues, of which 31 had been rated A and 33 Baa or Baa-1). (*Los Angeles Times* 1978, *Moody's Bond Survey* 1978:1339–41). During the same week, Standard and Poor's said that, in the event of Proposition 13's passage, it would assess the impact on existing ratings of all California bonds.

On June 8, Standard and Poor's suspended ratings on all but voter-approved, full faith and credit general obligation bonds, insured bonds, revenue bonds 100 percent enterprise supported, prerefunded bonds fully secured by U.S. government obligations, and institutionally supported revenue bonds. In all, ratings on 248 existing lease-purchase, tax-allocation, special assessment, and hybrid-revenue issues were suspended "due to lack of sufficient information regarding the action to be taken by the various levels of California government in response to the passage of the Jarvis–Gann initiative" (Standard and Poor's release, June 8, 1978). Some ratings have since been restored, and the only postelection tax-allocation issue up to March 31, 1979, was rated BBB by Standard and Poor's and A by Moody's.

There was also a significant shift to fewer bids for tax-allocation bonds but no significant changes for other categories. As the June 6 election approached, tax-allocation issues generally received only one bid, and during the six weeks immediately prior to that date, several issues received no bids and were retracted. Between June 6, 1978, and March 31, 1979, only one tax-allocation bond had been issued.

General Obligation Bonds

Although no Proposition 13 effects were hypothesized for existing general obligation bonds, the results in Table 6-4 suggest that there might have been a slight impact prior to the June election. (Figure 6-1 suggests the same result, with some increase in rates in the month of May.) Equation (6-4) in Table 6-4 shows a significant downward shift in interest cost in January 1978 of 38 basis points, and significant increase of 1.9 basis points per week until the June election when there was another significant downward shift of 32 basis points. When ratings and other descriptors are excluded (Eq. (6-5)), the time effects and the t-statistics are larger. However, the net effect of the 54 basis point decline in January and the 3.8 basis point rise per week thereafter was still only 30 basis points by the time of the election,[15] when there was a decline of 30 basis points. These effects may have been the result of a rush to issue general obligation debt just prior to the election (volume was heavy), but they appear to have been small and short-lived. There has been no clear postelection effect on prior voter-approved general obligation issues. However, general obligation debt approved by voters after June 30, 1978, has not been issued. The general obligation bonds in the sample either were approved prior to July 1, 1978, or were one-year tax anticipation notes that did not require specific voter approval.

Revenue Bonds

As hypothesized, there were no significant time shift effects for revenue bonds. However, there was an upward shift of 62 basis points in Eq. (6-5) at the time of the June 6 election that was almost significant. Detailed examination of the residuals and of the underlying data suggests that the market may have been distinguishing "pure" revenue bonds from those of a hybrid nature (as discussed earlier), and that higher rates on some hybrid bonds in the sample may have resulted in some postelection upward shift in rates. Redevelopment districts began to issue mortgage-backed revenue bonds after the election, whereas none were issued prior to the election. (Tax-allocation debt was issued instead.) These bonds have had net interest costs somewhat higher than the average for postelection revenue bonds.

Table 6-4. Regressions for Net Interest Cost of Various Types of Bonds.

	General Obligation		Revenue		Tax-Allocation		Lease-Purchase	
	Eq. (6-4)	Eq. (6-5)	Eq. (6-4)	Eq. (6-5)	Eq. (6-4)	Eq. (6-5)	Eq. (6-4)	Eq. (6-5)
CONSTANT	.39 (.82)	1.08 (2.22)[a]	1.41 (2.42)[a]	1.24 (1.75)[a]	7.24 (6.97)[a]	7.23 (8.32)[a]	2.86 (2.17)[a]	2.21 (1.45)
TERMST	1.10 (1.14)	.91 (-.93)	.92 (-.72)	.91 (-.67)	-.05 (-5.34)[a,b]	-.25 (-6.70)[a,b]	.84 (-.58)	.65 (-1.17)
DTERMST[c]	.80 (.07)	.76 (.08)	.67 (.12)	.74 (.14)	-.03 (.17)	-.14 (.19)	.76 (.24)	.85 (.25)
Aaa	-.66 (-4.34)[a]	...	-.93 (-3.19)[a]	...	...[d]	...	-.96 (-3.19)[a]	...
Aa	-.54 (-3.32)[a]	...	-.48 (-2.82)[a]	...	...[d]	...	-.92 (-3.56)[a]	...
A	-.48 (-5.56)	...	-.14 (-1.07)	...	-.87 (-3.99)[a]	...	-.55 (-2.81)[a]	...
Baa-B	-.03 (-.25)	...	-.04 (-.24)	...	-.45 (-2.30)[a]	...	-.19 (-.95)	...
LSIZE	.032 (1.29)	...	.027 (.91)	...	.050 (.46)	...	-.058 (-.80)	...
LBIDS	-.14 (-2.86)[a]	...	-.32 (-4.13)[a]	...	-.54 (-3.37)[a]	...	-.36 (-2.25)[a]	...

NEGOT	...[d]	...	.12 (.71)	...	...[d]	...	.08 (.25)	...
WEEK77	-.001 (-.19)	.000 (.05)	-.006 (-1.20)	-.009 (-1.49)	-.007 (-1.21)	-.002 (-.27)	.004 (.79)	.007 (1.25)
DJAN78	-.38 (-2.19)[a]	-.54 (-2.68)[a]	.01 (.03)	.29 (.85)	-.35 (-1.09)	-.04 (-.09)	-.36 (-1.49)	-.59 (-1.91)[a]
WEEK78	.019 (1.80)[a]	.038 (3.15)[a]	.008 (.39)	-.009 (-.32)	.108 (5.68)[a]	.130 (6.15)[a]	.034 (1.71)[a]	.077 (3.55)[a]
DJUN78	-.32 (-2.55)[a]	-.30 (-2.01)[a]	.20 (.65)	.62 (1.56)	-.59[e] (-1.00)[e]	-1.39[e] (-2.00)[a]	-.09 (-.33)	-.51 (-1.54)
$\bar{R}$-Squared	.61	.44	.78	.63	.80	.68	.74	.58
Standard error	.42	.50	.34	.45	.53	.66	.37	.48
Number of observations								
Total	186	186	74	74	74	74	67	67
Jan.-June 6, 1978	48	48	11	11	34	34	16	16
June 7-March 1979	52	52	32	32	1	1	10	10

a. Significant at the 5 percent level for one-tailed test. Numbers in parentheses are t-statistics against a null hypothesis of zero except for the coefficient of TERMST, for which the null hypothesis is one.

b. t-statistics for TERMST against $H_0:0$ are -.27 and -1.32, respectively.

c. For DTERMST, the figure in parenthesis is the standard error.

d. Insufficient data for estimation.

e. Estimate based on only one observation.

Tax-Allocation Bonds

The time shifts for tax-allocation bonds are large and highly significant. Interest costs rose at a rate of 10.8 to 13.0 basis points per week over the early 1978 period. They were 203 to 282 basis points higher by the week of the election as a result of the amendment. There was also a rush to issue tax-allocation bonds in the preelection months, and volume was very heavy. This volume almost certainly contributed to the high cost of tax-allocation debt in this period. However, since the heavy supply of such bonds was undoubtedly an effect of Proposition 13, a separate supply effect has not (and cannot) be determined.

Because of the unexpected negative coefficient on the term-structure variable TERMST, the time shift may be slightly overstated.[16] Adjusting for the contradictory term structure relation, it is reasonable to conclude that the effect on tax-allocation bonds was at least 200 basis points by the time of election. Indeed, this figure may be highly conservative, because several issues were retracted when unsold prior to the election, and only one new issue, that of a financially sound redevelopment project, had come to market by March 31, 1979.

An issue-by-issue study by Costa (1978) predicted that unless some sort of assistance were given to redevelopment agencies, debt for perhaps a majority of projects would face eventual default. Much of the debt issued in early 1978 falls into this category. Emergency loans from a state revolving fund were made available in late 1978, and in April 1979, California Senate Bill 55 was passed allowing for continued loans and special property tax assessments within redevelopment projects. These factors, together with some subsequent upward adjustments in 1975-76 tax assessments, have since greatly lessened the prospects of default.

Lease-Purchase Bonds

As hypothesized, lease-purchase bonds were also adversely affected by Proposition 13. In Eq. (6-4), the time shift accounted for an increase of 39-75 basis points in interest cost by the time of the election, depending on whether or not the insignificant dummy for January 1978 is included. In Eq. (6-5), the preelection shift amounted to 110 basis points (with a subsequent decline of 51 basis points). Since the election, there have been only ten lease–purchase issues, and net interest costs have declined somewhat from their peak in May 1978 (see Figure 6-1). Overall, the rate on lease–purchase bonds was affected by roughly 50 to 75 basis points.

Channels of Effects

The effects of Proposition 13 can be quantified further by applying the estimates of Eq. (6-4) in Table 6-4 through the various channels that account for the change in net interest cost between 1977 and the "postelection" period. (Because of lack of sufficient data, issues dated May 1, 1978, and thereafter are used to represent the postelection period for tax-allocation bonds.) Table 6-5 decomposes the shifts in net interest cost for each bond category into those related to changes in right-hand variables. It does not tell us which channels are statistically significant, but indicates how much of the change in net

Table 6-5. Shift in Mean of Dependent Variable Identifiable with Changes in Right-hand Variables between 1977 and Postelection[a] Period (*expressed in basis points*).

	General Obligation	Revenue	Tax-Allocation	Lease-Purchase
Net interest cost change in means	49	97	229	119
Right-hand variables				
Term structure	65	55	-10	68
Time shift	-30	20	172	39
Ratings	8	12	30	8
Other descriptors	6	10	37[b]	4

a. For general obligation, revenue, and lease–purchase bonds, the postelection period is used (all issues are after June 6, 1978). Because there was only one issue of tax-allocation bonds in the postelection period, all issues after May 1, 1978, were used as the postelection period.

b. Larger issue size accounts for -3 basis points and fewer bids per issue for 40.

Source: Calculated using estimates for Eq. (6-5) in Table 6-4 and means of right-hand variables for the two subperiods. In order for the components to sum to totals, both significant and insignificant variables were included.

interest cost was channeled through the 1978 time-shift parameters and how much was channeled through changes in ratings and other descriptors.

The change in net interest cost for general obligation bonds, which is only 49 basis points, can be related primarily to term-structure variables. The change for revenue bonds is greater (97 basis points), but only 42 basis points are identifiable with the time shift, ratings, and other descriptors. The rise in interest cost for tax-allocation bonds (229 basis points) is more than explained by the combined 239 basis-point effect of the time shift, ratings, and number of bids. Of the 119-point rise for lease–purchase bonds, 51 basis points are related to the time shift, ratings, and number of bids. Altogether, changes in ratings accounted for only a small portion of the increase in net interest cost for those bonds significantly affected. The only sizable effects were felt in the market for tax-allocation bonds. Clearly, the relation between ratings and risk premia is highly imperfect.

IMPLICATIONS FOR THE VALUE OF OUTSTANDING DEBT

Inferences regarding Proposition 13's impact on the value of existing state and local debt ideally should be derived from secondary-market yield data for actively traded issues. However, such data are not available, so that inferences are drawn here from the effect on new-issue yield cost. Most existing California debt is in the form of general obligation and revenue bonds (Table 6–6). On the basis of the findings in the empirical section, we can presume that Proposition 13 has had no effect on the $7.3 billion of existing local general obligation bonds, perhaps some effect on certain hybrid bonds within the $5.5 billion of revenue bonds, and a definite effect on the $845 million of tax-allocation and $2.2 billion of lease–purchase bonds.

To estimate the effect on the present value of outstanding debt, one can calculate the impact of the rise in new-issue interest cost on the present value of a bond of comparable maturity. For tax-allocation bonds in May 1978 and thereafter, average interest cost was 8.45 percent and at least 200 basis points of the rise was due to Proposition 13. For lease–purchase bonds, the average postelection rate was 6.97 percent with at least 50 basis points resulting from Proposition 13.

Table 6-6. California State and Local Debt Outstanding
(*$ millions*).[a]

	General Obligation	Revenue	Tax- Allocation	Lease- Purchase	Other
City	$1,097	$2,757	$ 0	$ 0	$ 593[b]
County	109	8	0	0	148[b]
School district	2,235	253	0	n.a.	2,103[c]
Special district	3,852	2,519	845	2,163[d]	1,106[e]
Total local	$7,293	$5,537	$845	$2,163	$3,950
State	$5,589	$1,148	0	n.a.	n.a.

a. Figures for local debt are as of the fiscal year ending June 30, 1977. Figures for state debt are as of December 31, 1977.

b. Mostly special assessment and improvement district debt.

c. Loans from the state and public school building funds.

d. Lease arrangements with cities account for $826 and counties $1,143.

e. $566 related to construction financed by the state and U.S. government, $11 in time warrants, and $529 in "other long-term indebtedness."

Sources: Staff of the Assembly Committees on Local Government and Revenue and Taxation 1978: 347; Legislative Analyst 1978; annual reports of the California State Controller on financial transactions concerning cities, counties, and school districts 1976-77; and Costa 1978.

For these two categories of bonds, average maturities (the averages of the average maturities of the serial issues) ranged from twelve to fifteen years. If we assume fourteen-year bonds with equal payments at the end of each year, the Proposition 13 reductions in present value are 23 percent and 6 percent for tax-allocation and lease-purchase bonds, respectively. (The effect on present value of an individual bond would differ from these figures, depending on the maturity of the bond and the probability function by expected default.) If we apply these figures to the outstanding debt shown in Table 6-6, bonds values are reduced by $195 million for tax-allocation bonds and $130 million for lease-purchase bonds. It should be stressed, however, that subsequent legislation to assist redevelopment agencies in meeting debt service commitments made *prior* to enactment of Proposition 13 will reduce the risk premium on existing debt. Also, the average effect on lease-purchase bonds and on some kinds of local revenue bonds appears to have diminished somewhat since the large effects immediately following the election.

SUMMARY AND CONCLUSIONS

Proposition 13 resulted in a $7-billion, or roughly 60 percent, reduction in local-government property taxes. Not only has the amendment diminished the expected income stream of local governments and special districts, but it has also practically eliminated these entities' discretionary control of their receipts. Thus, local governments and special districts are constrained in both the level and flexibility of receipts, while the state has shouldered much of the burden of filling the gap between receipts and expenditures. This study has shown the resulting effects on the cost of new debt for the state, local governments, and special districts and has pointed out roughly the implications for the value of existing debt.

Proposition 13 has apparently increased the cost of California's general obligation bonds by roughly 25 basis points and may have induced the state to issue (higher yielding) revenue bonds in place of some general obligation debt. The amendment has had diverse effects on the cost of local debt. It appears to have had no significant effect on local general obligation bonds approved prior to July 1, 1978, except for perhaps some minor impact on new issues sold just prior to the election. Newly approved general obligation debt has ceased. The interest cost effect apparently has been nil for "pure" revenue bonds but possibly significant for hybrid-revenue bonds. Moreover, there has been an adverse effect of at least 50 basis points on lease-purchase bonds, with the temporary effect at the time of the election greater than this figure. Tax-allocation issues initially suffered an increase in risk premium over 200 basis points, and there is little indication that this premium would have declined without legislative assistance to redevelopment agencies. New general obligation bonds of local governments and special districts and tax-allocation bonds of redevelopment agencies thus appear to have been the principal debt-market casualties of Proposition 13, although subsequent legislation has rectified much of the problem afflicting tax-allocation debt.

The findings of this study imply that restrictions on the size of government, if properly structured, need not increase the cost of new debt nor decrease the value of existing debt to any significant extent. Funds needed to pay off all existing debt could be exempted from revenue ceilings (as was voter-approved debt under Proposition 13), thereby protecting existing debt. Alternatively, restrictions could be placed on government expenditures rather than revenues, in order to protect both existing and new debt. In this vein, debt for long-term capital projects could simply be exempted from the revenue or expenditure ceilings on the proviso that all such debt receive two-thirds voter approval (as required for general obligation debt). Moreover, voters and government officials may wish to consider such alternatives in structuring ways to restrict government. In the meantime, investors in municipal bonds should keep a wary eye on what the voters are saying.

NOTES TO CHAPTER 6

1. On the ballot of June 6, 1978, there were actually two competing tax-reduction alternatives—Propositions 13 and 8. Defeat of Proposition 13 and passage of Proposition 8 would have put in force a legislative act known as the Behr bill. This author previously hypothesized the effects of both Proposition 13 and the Behr bill on California municipal debt. In all cases, hypothesized effects were directionally the same for the two measures, although those of the Behr bill were much weaker. Because of the eventual passage of Proposition 13, discussion of the Behr bill has been omitted here.

2. State budget analysts originally estimated that this would mean an initial $7 billion, or 57 percent, reduction in California property taxes—one-third attributable to owner-occupied homes and the rest to rental, non-residential, and personal properties, as well as inventories. The $7 billion reduction has turned out to be an overstatement, because of subsequent upward reassessments of market values for the 1975–76 year.

3. The meaning of the term *qualified electors* has yet to be determined in the courts. It is not known whether it will be interpreted as those voting or as those qualified to vote.

4. This section draws heavily from the legislative analyst (California Legislature 1978), California Assembly Staff report (1978) and Friedlander (1978 a and b).

5. Local assessment bonds have been excluded from the discussion. There should be no effect on *1911 Act* assessment bonds (for which private property provides backup security) and minor effects on *1915 Act* assessment bonds (for which municipal revenues provide backup security). My analysis of 1915 Act bonds (not reported here) has found some adverse effect on this debt.

6. In the opinion of the legislative analyst (California Legislature 1978: 338) it would be possible for the *state* legislature to authorize a new category of

non-*ad valorem* "special tax" for the purpose of financing capital expenditures. In this instance local governments could issue, with a two-thirds approval of "qualified electors," general obligation bonds to be repaid from the special tax that would fall outside the revenue limitation of Proposition 13.

7. Although not legally obligated, local governments often have subsidized pure revenue bonds in order to avoid default, since such action would strengthen the government's ability to float future issues. Because of this fact, pure revenue bonds could be affected by Proposition 13.

8. Property that changes hands or is newly constructed after 1975–76 would be assessed at current market value. An unresolved question is whether the fixed base year assessed value for a project approved after 1975–76 would be rolled back as well. If so, Proposition 13 would lower the base year assessed value, which would reduce revenue to the local taxing bodies and increase tax-increment revenues. By itself, this effect would strengthen tax-allocation bonds, although it would surely be outweighed by the negative effects of the proposition's constraints.

9. Secondary-market yield data for municipal bonds are too scanty for statistical analysis. New-issue data for January 1, 1977, through March 31, 1978, were obtained through the Public Securities Association in New York City and the Municipal Finance Study Group at the State University of New York at Albany. They are derived principally from the *Bond Buyer New Issue Worksheets* and the *Daily Bond Buyer*. Data after March 31, 1978, were taken directly from the *Daily Bond Buyer*. Issues that did not report net interest cost were deleted. These were usually negotiated or private-placement issues.

10. The Kruskal–Wallis test is a nonparametric test on the rankings to test whether or not the rankings within a sample are drawn at random from the population of rankings. The null hypothesis was rejected at the 10 percent level.

11. A single rating was used for each bond. Either Moody's or Standard and Poor's was used if only one of the two organizations rated the bond. If both did and there was a discrepancy, Moody's rating was used.

12. It is necessary that $MAT_j \geq 1$, which holds for the sample presented here.

13. The specification grew out of a use of term structure in a paper by Hendershott and Kidwell (1978). Their specification was different, as it was designed to pick up a different effect of term structure on NIC.

14. The risk differential is assumed to be independent of the level of rates. This assumption is commonly accepted, although there may be some reason to believe that the risk premium is positively related to rates. For this argument, see Kessel's development of Hicks' theory (1971: 724, 731).

15. The figure of 30 basis points is calculated using the coefficients in Table 6–4 and allowing for the fact that WEEK78 had a duration of 22 weeks: $3.8 \times 22 - 54 = 30$.

16. The coefficient on TERMST should be approximately equal to one. This result holds for the other three categories of bonds. However, for all regressions run on tax-allocation bonds, the coefficient was zero or slightly negative. This result occurred even for Eq. (6-1) fitted to 1977 data.

REFERENCES

California Legislature, Joint Budget Committee, Legislative Analyst, *An Analysis of Proposition 13, The Jarvis-Gann Property Tax Initiative*, Sacramento, no. 78-11, May 1978.

California Assembly Staff of the Committees on Local Government and Revenue and Taxation. 1978. *The Impact of Proposition 13 on Local Government Programs and Services.* Sacramento, May.

Costa, Alan. 1978. "Report on the Status of Redevelopment Agency Bonds and Notes as of June 30, 1978." Mimeo, California Assembly Office of Research. August 18.

Friedlander, George D. 1978. "The Jarvis-Gann Initiative, the 'Behr Bill' and the Investment Climate for California Municipal Securities." Smith Barney, Harris Upham, April 4.

_____. 1978. "The Jarvis-Gann Initiative, A Taxpayer Revolt in California: Implications for Municipal Bonds." Smith Barney, Harris Upham, February 3.

Hendershott, Patric H., and David S. Kidwell. 1978. "The Impact of Relative Security Supplies." *Journal of Money, Credit, and Banking* (August).

Hopewell, Michael H., and George G. Kaufman. 1978. "The Incidence of Excess Interest Costs Paid by Municipalities in the Competitive Sale of Bonds." *Journal of Monetary Economics* (April).

_____. 1976. "The Municipal Bond Auction: Reply." *National Tax Journal* (March).

_____. 1974. "Costs to Municipalities of Selling Bonds by NIC." *National Tax Journal* (December).

Kessel, Reuben A. 1971. "A Study of the Effects of Competition in the Tax-Exempt Bond Market." *Journal of Political Economy* 79.

Los Angeles Times. 1978. (April 12).

Mendelowitz, Allan I., and Hugh Rockoff. 1976. "The Municipal Bond Auction: An Alternative View." *National Tax Journal* (March).

Moody's Bond Survey. 1978. 70, no. 16 (April 13): 1339-41.

Tanner, J. Ernest. 1975. "The Determinants of Interest Cost on New Municipal Bonds: A Reevaluation." *Journal of Business* (January).

COMMENT – *James N. Tattersall*

Chapters 4–6 have demonstrated clearly that a significant increase in the cost of credit and an impairment in the availability of credit for California local governments was an important and apparently unintended side effect of Proposition 13. The chapters agree on the types of debt issues that were most affected and that the most serious effect has been impaired ability to issue new general obligation bonds.

I infer from Chapter 6, especially from Table 6–6, that in the absence of corrective action, California local governments' capacity to issue new debt would be reduced by about half.

As a result of the attention being devoted to this problem, however, some corrective action has been taken by the legislature, and further steps are being contemplated. An article by James S. Saffran in *Western City* (February 1979) outlines an eight-point legislative program developed by the Securities Industries Association, including a proposed constitutional amendment that would exempt legally issued debt from the 1 percent limitation on property tax.

Such an incremental approach to correcting the deficiencies of Proposition 13 may be all that is politically feasible at present, but it would still leave California state and local finance with many serious problems: impairment of local government *current* expenditures, the shift of power to the state level, and unequal assessment of identical properties.

There are two aspects of Chapter 4 that should receive comment. Professor Thomas hypothesizes that a shift of local revenue sources to more volatile tax bases—from property taxes to sales and income taxes—will increase the riskiness and therefore the cost of local government debt. That this is really an important part of the problem created by Proposition 13 is debatable. At any rate the hypothesis needs to be supported by an effort at empirical verification.

In a different context, public finance experts have frequently advocated lessened local dependence on property taxes, and a broadening of local government tax bases. The dangerous reduction in sales and income tax revenues that some associate with recessions seems to be a phenomenon associated with 1930's Great Depression conditions, not with our more recent "inflationary recessions," when such revenues have held up well. Furthermore it appears that an important factor leading to voter support for Proposition 13 was the high volatility of California *property* tax revenues in the later 1970s.

Professor Thomas argues early in her chapter that "all fiscal limitations will have some impact on credit availability," and in the last section reviews a number of limitation measures adopted in other states. What is missing is a more systematic association of the different types of revenue and expenditure limitations with their hypothesized effect on municipal credit. Personally, I am inclined to agree with Jack Beebe's conclusion that "restrictions on the size of government, if properly structured, need not have dramatic effects on the cost or value of government debt" (p. 136).

From my own survey of tax and expenditure limitation measures proposed in various states, my conclusion is that California's Proposition 13 is so much more restrictive than the limitations adopted in most other states that it is a qualitatively different animal. Mr. Beebe refers to "Proposition 13, and similar measures that are now sweeping the country . . . " My own perception is that very few of these limitation and tax relief measures are really similar to Proposition 13. Proposition 13 may have swept Idaho and Nevada, but that was hardly a coast-to-coast tidal wave.

Even the Idaho and Nevada Proposition 13 prototypes differ from the California model in that Idaho's measure was statutory rather than constitutional, and the Nevada measure requires a 1980 revote. The other November 1978 ballot measures that would have come closest to Proposition 13's severely restrictive effect on local debt and expenditures (in Michigan, Oregon, Colorado, and Nebraska) were defeated by the voters.

The uniqueness of the California situation is worth emphasizing. Proposition 13 is important because California is one-tenth of the nation, not because the rest of the nation is adopting this type of rate limitation measure. Voters and legislators in other states are generally adopting more moderate approaches to limiting the size of government. Some programs are "comprehensive" tax reform measures with income tax indexation as one important aspect.

A comparison with the neighboring state of Oregon may be interesting. A virtual copy of Proposition 13 (except that the proposed rate limit was 1½ percent) was placed on the November 1978 Oregon state ballot by initiative petition. Both this measure and an alternative hastily constructed in a special legislative session were defeated by the voters. Part of the explanation for the different voter response in Oregon may be the following. 1) Oregon had enacted substantial property tax reform earlier in the 1970s, including the nation's most extensive homeowner–renter circuit breaker program, and a significant increase in state financial support of local schools. 2) In contrast to California, increases in assessed values of property in Oregon usually cannot be transformed into increases in property taxes without a popular vote, because Oregon has a constitutional property tax *levy* limitation (which allows only a 6 percent annual levy growth without a popular vote). 3) Per capita governmental expenditures in Oregon were lower than in California.

Thus reprieved, the 1979 Oregon legislative assembly went on to enact a "comprehensive" $705 million tax reduction program for the 1979–81 biennium. It is a complex measure, but explicitly rejects the rate limitation type of approach that has been so troublesome in California. A newly adopted state expenditure limitation explicitly excludes debt service from the limitation.

A major feature of this 1979 legislation provides a generous state rebate of 30 percent of residential property tax up to a maximum of $800. The legislation contains a rather mild effort to restrain the growth of local government property tax levies. The 30 percent state rebate is applicable to local levies adjusted for population growth and inflation. Levy growth in excess of that amount must be separately approved by local voters, and must be paid entirely by local property owners.

The Oregon property tax relief system may need incremental adjustment from time to time. Overall, it may prove too great a strain on the state government's revenue sources. It should prove more enduring than the present California system, however.

I do not think Californians will find Proposition 13 viable for the longer run. The state has an enormous reservoir of intellectual talent that I suspect will find a way, either incrementally or by substituting a new program, to develop a more viable state and local finance system.

COMMENT — *Alan S. Costa*

The major finding of Jack Beebe in Chapter 6 is that "restrictions on the size of government, if properly structured, need not have dramatic effects on the cost or value of government debt" (p. 136). The implication that Proposition 13 was not properly structured, in that it clearly exposes certain types of debt instruments to default, although accurate, should have added that the most important consequence of Proposition 13, insofar as the cost of future debt is concerned, is that it makes it impossible for local government to issue general-obligation bonds. Hence, local governments will be forced to finance additions to and replacement of their existing capital stock using less efficient and more costly debt instruments. Beebe introduces but does not develop this point.

Of specific issues raised by Beebe, first consider his suggestion that "the majority of existing tax-allocation issues will be exposed to default." Although it is true that a significant number of the 120 currently outstanding redevelopment agency tax-allocation issues will experience exposure to default, my research suggests that no defaults will actually occur. There are four reasons why this should be true:

1. The property tax revenues of redevelopment agencies did not fall by as much as was anticipated.

2. Many city governments have indicated that they will not permit such defaults to occur.

3. Legislation permitting the creation of special assessment districts within redevelopment project areas has recently been enacted.

4. The state has created a Local Agency Indebtedness Fund to assist local agencies through periods of cash flow problems.

Not only will existing tax-allocation bond issues survive their current trial, but also the redevelopment process will continue, albeit at a reduced level and using a wider spectrum of financing mechanisms. Since the passage of Proposition 13, six tax-allocation bond issues have been marketed at average net interest costs of 7.07 percent, unweighted. This represents a return to a level of interest costs that prevailed before Proposition 13 qualified for the June 1978 ballot.

Second, consider Beebe's suggestion that Proposition 13 has blocked large increases in state taxes as an alternative source of governmental revenue (presumably state-imposed taxes to be used for local government purposes). The apparent reference is to Proposition 13's requirement that increased tax rates be approved by two-thirds of each house of the legislature. Inflation, however, continues to increase state tax revenues. State sales tax collections will increase by 14 percent for fiscal 1978–79 over fiscal 1977–78 and revenues from taxes on personal income, and bank and corporation profits will experience similar inflation induced increases. Thus, the state will continue to possess the capacity to bail out local government.

Third, as suggested, it is clear that it is no longer legally possible to authorize local government general obligation bond issues in California because of the loss of local government's power to pledge their full faith and credit as security; that is, they cannot levy taxes to service such bonds. By eliminating general obligation bond issues as revenue source, Proposition 13 has created a profound problem in financing local government capital expenditures. Although the magnitude of this problem is not generally appreciated at present, in time it will become apparent as existing capital facilities prove to be inadequate to meet the demand for the services such facilities provide. No actual or potential substitute exists that will permit local government to finance tax-supported capital improvements as efficiently as general obligation bonds. For example, local government revenue bonds may be used to finance capital outlay. However, the net interest costs of revenue bonds are greater than general obligation bonds, other things equal.

Last, let us consider the specification of Beebe's model. A variable for prefunded payments on principal and interest should have been specifically included. Among the bond issues sold after Proposition 13 qualified for the June 1978 ballot, some provided that a sizable portion of the proceeds from the sale would be held by the fiscal agent for payment on subsequent years' debt service. For example, the Merced tax-allocation bond issue of May 1978 (par value $8.5 million) set aside $2.0 for bond reserve and funded interest. Did such prefunding of principal and interest payments have a statistically significant effect on net interest costs? An additional suggestion would be to include a respecification of the model to account for the unprecedented number of tax-allocation bond issues marketed in the first five months of 1978. Of the 158 tax-allocation bond issues marketed in California since 1956 (aggregate original par value $1,104,000,000) 33 were marketed in the first five months of 1978 (aggregate par value $328,000,000). Could this frenetic activity have shifted the supply curve of California tax-exempt bonds outward sufficiently to raise the net interest cost on tax-allocation bonds over this period?

7 TAX AND EXPENDITURE LIMITATIONS
Projecting Their Impact on Big City Finances

John E. Petersen

Tax and expenditure limitations have recently become the object of popular discussion, political action, and academic investigation. The situation on all fronts is in flux, but early returns indicate that Proposition 13 and its alternatives for achieving less and, presumably, less costly government have taken hold and already are working changes throughout the public sector.[1]

Formal constraints or taxes and spending are not new to the state and local governments, although the newer variants appear to be more comprehensive (and harder to evade) than the traditional ceilings, which typically aimed at tax rates rather than at the dollar levels of tax levies and spending. Beyond that generalization, however, the new wave of fiscal constraints comes in a dizzying array of designs. Whatever the commonality of objectives, the technical details of their design promise to greatly condition their impact. Furthermore, as the evolving California experience demonstrates, the ultimate impacts of a constraint at either the state or the local level can be muted or amplified within the web of intergovernmental financial and political relations (see the essays in Mushkin 1979).

Nowhere will the impact of tax and expenditure limitations on local government be of greater consequence (or more complex in their analysis) than in the nation's major cities. The finances of the cities already the target of much speculation and concern, the impending imposition of limits on taxes and spending further heightens the need to replace general speculation with specific analysis.[2] There are many barriers to making even summary projections of city finances, as are discussed subsequently. Even when we can project over time the fiscal condition of a particular city with some confidence, there is no guarantee (in view of data difficulties) that fiscal comparisons among cities are justified. Nonetheless there is merit in developing a methodology to organize the analytical problem and to illustrate, at least, how one might go about converting specific policy actions into dollar outcomes.

This chapter is intended to provide insights into how the financial condition and operations of the government of major cities might be influenced by the application of tax and expenditure constraints. For the purposes of this book, this means examining the relationship found in the cities' accounting identity—the relationships among sources of the revenues, expenditures and changes in assets and liabilities—and how they would change under the impact of various caps on taxes and outlays.

Clearly, such fiscal outcomes may be major or minor, of short-term duration or chronic, depending on the particulars of the limitation employed. Thus, a complete rendering of potential effects would have to envision a broad range of possibilities. As a start, I chose to focus only on governments' general accounts, examining how they have been changing through time and then illustrating how they might react to tightly defined circumstances in the future. The limitation types posited are a flexible cap on state aid that gears city receipts to increases in prices and population, an absolute cap on property tax revenues, and the double whammy of enforcing both types of revenue limitations. On the city expenditure side, increases are tied generally to changes in population and prices. This could constitute another type of constraint, although the immediate purpose is to describe a baseline case of budgetary behavior that resembles a "constant-service" notion of spending objectives. The analytical technique used is to calculate various financing gaps for the largest forty-five cities caused by differential rates of growth in revenues and expenditures and then to examine how such gaps might be financed or otherwise closed. The method and basic data were originally developed in Petersen and Rafuse (1979).

The basic data set for the analysis is derived from the U.S. Bureau of the Census. These data have many limitations and, thus, the projections made using them should be taken as illustrative. Nevertheless, they can, after numerous adjustments as discussed in the appendix to this chapter, be used for our general purposes. Prior to explaining methodology and performing analysis, a brief review of major trends in big city finances will help set the scene.

RECENT PATTERNS IN BIG CITY FINANCE

The largest forty-five cities have seen their budgets grow under the impacts of inflation and an increasingly rich array of services delivered to the public. Many, however, have had to contend with declining populations and with residents' personal incomes that have been growing more slowly than those of the nation at large.

Table 7-1 documents on a per capita basis the trend in outlays and receipts of the largest forty-five cities, using unweighted averages and showing annual rates of growth in the individual items. Between 1967 and 1977, the latest year for which complete information is readily available, the per capita general expenditures and general revenues of the cities grew at an average annual rate of approximately 12 percent.[3]

City current outlays rose much more rapidly than capital outlays. Revenue in the form of intergovernmental payments grew at more than three times the rate of revenues collected from the cities' own sources. Also, the largest forty-five cities during the decade saw their per capita general government (nonutility) long-term debt rise at a fairly modest annual rate of 7.2 percent, actually declining in real terms.[4]

Perhaps the most important development in the finances of the largest forty-five cities has not been the rate of growth in expenditures, but rather the revolution in the way the cities have been financing them. Panel B of Table 7-1 shows the changing composition of the major sources of revenue, giving the percentage breakdown among the various sources.

The largest forty-five cities saw their reliance on revenues raised from local sources drop from 74 percent in 1967 to approximately 58 percent by 1977. The largest decline came in the property tax, whose proportionate share fell from 36 to 23 percent of total general revenues during the decade.

The slack was picked up by the growth in intergovernmental payments, with the most impressive growth in federal aid. In 1967, fed-

Table 7-1.   Trends in Expenditures and Receipts for the 45 Largest U.S. Cities, 1967-77.

A. Selected Financial Items Per Capita Amounts and Rates of Growth, Comparisons with the Overall State and Local Sector.[a]

	1967	1977	Annual Rate of Growth, %
General expenditures	$184.06	$550.64	11.6
Current outlays	141.99	449.27	12.2
Capital outlays	42.07	101.40	9.2
General Revenues	179.63	578.97	12.4
Own-source revenues	133.44	244.89	6.3
Intergovernmental payments	46.19	334.08	21.9
Gross city debt outstanding	351.57	655.49	6.4
General government long-term debt outstanding	226.61	455.95	7.2

B. Percentage Composition of General Revenues

	1967	1977
Total General Revenues	100.0%	100.0%
Own-source revenue	74.3	57.7
Property tax	36.2	22.7
Other taxes	24.9	23.2
Charges and fees	13.2	11.8
Intergovernmental revenue	25.7	42.3
State	18.6	19.3
Federal	4.7	21.1
Other localities	2.4	1.9

a. Unweighted average of city per capita amounts.

Sources: U.S. Bureau of the Census, City Government Finances data. Adjustments have been made by the author to reflect current-year estimates of city population.

eral aid payments represented 4.7 percent of total general revenues; 10 years later, its share was more than 21 percent. The most interesting conclusion, aside from any speculation on the necessity and desirability of such growth in intergovernmental payments, is that the fiscal fortunes of cities have become intertwined progressively with those of the states, and to a great extent, the federal government.[5]

STRUCTURE OF CITY FUNDS

Most cities are required to balance the budget although the practical meaning of this is difficult to ascertain in many cases. Generally, over the long haul, it means that receipts and outlays must balance out over the course of time. Receipts can be on the current account (taxes, fees, charges) or on the capital account (debt proceeds). Likewise, expenditures are typically partitioned into those for current operating and capital purposes. Normally, differences in any period between total receipts and outlays can be reflected in changes in various fund balances, which, after sundry adjustments, can be translated into changes in cash and investment holdings.

Unfortunately, cities do not define and account for their financial activities in the same way; thus, one cannot be sure that receipts for general purposes and expenditures made for general purposes are tabulated on the same accounting basis or encompass the same underlying activities.[6] Nonetheless, the following accounting identity, barring fiscal chicanery or gross reporting error, must ultimately be observed:

$$\text{Sources of funds} \quad = \quad \text{Uses of funds} \quad .$$

This identity, when restricted to general-purpose government translates into:

$$\text{General revenue} \quad = \quad \text{General expenditure} \; +$$
$$\text{Change in general fund balances} \quad .$$

Going a step further, we have the following relations:

$$\text{General revenue} \quad = \quad \text{Own-source revenue} \; +$$
$$\text{Intergovernmental revenue} \quad .$$

$$\text{General expenditure} \quad = \quad \text{Current outlays} \; +$$
$$\text{Capital outlays} \quad .$$

$$\text{Change in financial balances} \quad = \quad \text{Net change in debt} \; +$$
$$\text{Change in cash and investments} \quad .$$

These identities abstract from numerous complications but allow a focus on the broad aggregates. Clearly, if a city continues to take in more general revenue than it spends, it is either building up its cash and security holdings and/or reducing its indebtedness. However, the foregoing simplification of accounts abstracts from a major problem, which is the availability of major components of revenue and expenditure and changes in the fund balances. For example, most city accounts include a variety of funds with restrictions placed on the particular revenues that can finance them or expenditures for which they can be used.[7]

The effects of varying economic situations and policy decisions among the cities on the underlying components may be examined in the preceding accounting framework. Specifically, we will focus on the overall general expenditures, including the capital outlay component.[8] Capital outlays are of special interest because of their greater volatility and because they are often financed on the capital account by borrowing or by specially targeted grants.

Turning to revenues, of primary importance is the distinction between revenues raised locally by a city ("own revenues") and the intergovernmental grants it receives from the federal government and from the states. Within the own-revenue category there are two major categories by source: property taxes and all other locally raised taxes and types of current receipts (charges and fees).

By summing up forecasts of expenditures and current revenues, one gets an inkling of the financing gap that needs to be closed through use of assets, the increasing of debt, reducing expenditures, or by increasing revenues. Because of the many alternative ways in which a gap can be closed, the initial projection of such a gap should not be taken as a sign of strength or weakness. Of at least equal importance in making such a judgment are 1) the magnitude of the gap in relation to the overall size of the budget and 2) if the gap is negative, the evident ease through which it might be closed by increasing the outstanding indebtedness or by an increase in own revenues.

PROJECTION METHODS

The approach used here can be summarized as follows: Total general expenditures by cities are determined by population and the level of prices. City-raised revenues are determined by total personal income. Intergovernmental revenues are determined by federal and state policies.

The difference between projected total general revenues and expenditures, a financing gap, is first calculated. This gives an initial magnitude of adjustments that would be necessary to bring them into balance. Since the expenditure component contains some objects that would be appropriately the object of borrowing (capital outlays), the next step is to adjust the gap to be financed by permitting borrowing as a source of funds. Thus, the implied level of change in indebtedness that is needed to bring balance between sources and uses is estimated and its credibility examined. As a final item, the increase in current own-source revenues is examined to see how large an increase would be needed to fill the gap. Numerous simplifying assumptions are needed to make the analysis possible given the limited number of observations and data gaps. A more detailed description of the projection methods used appears in the appendix.

Figure 7-1 provides a rough idea of how economic and policy variables interact with the city fiscal variables. The basic accounting identity is influenced by demographic and economic variables; specifically, the state and local price deflator, city personal income, and, implicitly, credit conditions that can modify borrowing costs and availability. On the policy side, intergovernmental aid is determined by state and federal policies. Also, own revenues are affected by state or locally imposed tax lids, and expenditures may be restricted by expenditure limitations.

Finally, changes in debt can be affected by investors' perceptions of credit quality and the ratings assigned by the credit rating agencies.

Within the framework just given, three alternative cases of city revenue limitations are examined; a limitation on state assistance received by the city (the result of limitation-induced stringency at the state level), a limitation on local property tax revenues, and a combination of the two limitations—the double whammy case.

On the expenditure side, there is also a constraint of sorts posited, which is that expenditures rise only to keep pace with inflation and changes in population. The properties of these alternative scenarios are discussed in detail in the next section. This case is a rough approximation of the recent spending limitation, the Gann initiative (Proposition 4), adopted in 1978 in California.

FORECASTING CITY FINANCES IN 1982

As is detailed in the appendix of this chapter, all of the city financial models are driven by two key national economic assumptions, the rates of growth in personal income and in prices. As a basis for

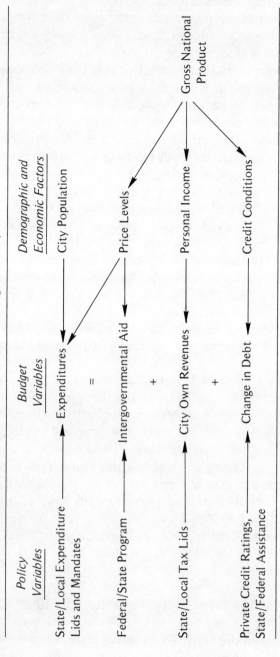

Figure 7-1.   Paths by Which Variables Influence Budget Identity.

explaining budgeting behavior, it is assumed that personal income grows by 9.3 percent per year and that the state and local deflator grows by 7.7 percent per year (the same as the personal income deflator) between 1977 and 1982.

For the set of forty-five cities, it is assumed that total general expenditures remain on a constant-service basis where growth in the total is only sufficient to keep real per capita expenditures at a constant level between 1977 and 1982, the latter being the forecasted year. Regarding city revenues, three different possibilities are explored:

In *Case A* city own revenues are assumed to be determined by the sensitivity of individual revenue sources to changes in personal income. Otherwise, the revenue system (rates, bases, and types of sources) is assumed to be unchanged. Per capita state aid in real terms is assumed, however, to grow at the same historical rate as observed for the period 1967 to 1972. (In those cases where there has been negative growth in real per capita terms, or where the city is projected to lose population, total state aid is assumed to remain at the 1977 level in real terms.) Federal aid is assumed to remain at 1978 real total levels by city except that two federal countercyclical programs—Local Public Works (LPW) and Anti–Recessionary Fiscal Assistance (ARFA)—are terminated. Thus, total federal aid grows only at a pace to keep up with inflation *after* subtraction of the two programs. Furthermore, federal aid is not affected by changes in city population.

Case B follows the same economic and city expenditure assumptions as Case A. However, on the revenue side, state aid to city governments does not grow at historical rates of growth in real terms but only at a rate sufficient to maintain real per capita levels observed in 1977. Thus aid is affected only by changes in prices and city population, except for cities projected to lose population, where the total 1977 real level is maintained.

This case is somewhat consistent with the large number of state-level expenditure limits that essentially constrain further state expenditure to growth in state income and similar caps on the revenue side that seek to confine state revenues to that amount sufficient to keep up with inflation. It does not take into consideration, however, as do many such limits, the real growth increment in state income. Federal aid, frozen at the 1978 real total as noted, is the same as in Case A.

Case C represents the double whammy, where both the state is subject to a restrictive limit and the local government has imposed upon it a "Proposition 13" constraint that limits the total revenues from the property tax to the actual, current-dollar yield in 1977 for each city. Although extreme, this scenario can serve as a crude approximation of what occurred in California in 1978 with the adoption of Proposition 13. The assumptions regarding the economy, expenditures, and federal aid remain the same and, as specified, state aid is limited to maintaining the real 1977 levels.

Certain observations are in order before examining the results of these hypothetical behavior patterns upon city finances. First, maintaining local expenditures at real per capita levels (or real total levels, where cities lose population) reflects an assumption that maintaining current services will be a budget goal rather than any expansion in city services. Aside from the constraints on own revenues, this expenditure target in itself appears both conservative and realistic. Population growth has greatly slowed nationwide, school enrollments are declining, and public goods carry increasingly high price tags. Local government employment seems to be stable, if not declining. In the absence of new spending initiatives and new federal or state stimulants, a "holding-your-own" expenditure plan in the face of 8 percent inflation seems most realistic. (For recent evidence see Puryear and Ross 1979.)

Case B says the preceding situation pertains not only at the local level, but also at the state level. In other words, state governments aim at a preservation of current (1977) real level of assistance to local governments, easing up only enough to allow such aid to keep pace with inflation (and to reflect increases in population in those cities where that occurs). Clearly, the impact of such a state policy on city governments will depend on the degree of reliance of the city on state assistance. Where state aid is important, the possibility for negative budgetary gaps is enhanced. Conversely, where the city's financial structure is self-contained, the impact of slower growth in state aid should be minimal.

Case C represents a blend of constraints at the state and city level. At the local level the constraint is selective, the property tax is capped off in terms of total nominal receipts to 1977 levels. This revenue effect is combined with the more restrained growth in state aids to the city contained in Case B. Cities that are reliant both upon high level state assistance and the property tax are particularly vulnerable. As noted previously, in 1977 cities derived on average only 41 percent of their own-source revenues from the property tax. This last assumed case may be unduly harsh on those jurisdictions that rely on that local revenue source, but does illustrate the application of the local fiscal meat cleaver approach.[9]

Initial Results: Financing Gaps

Tables 7-2 and 7-3 present the first round of results for the forty-five cities. Table 7-2 gives in Column 1 the projected amount of general expenditures in 1982 (the baseline projection for all cases as explained earlier). Column 2 gives the projected dollar total of general revenues under Case A, whereby the existing revenue structure grinds away, unmolested in response to changing personal incomes. Column 3 represents the positive (or negative) gap between expenditure and Case A revenues. Column 4 gives the gap in Case B (state aid in real per capita terms remains constant at 1977 levels). The incremental impact of this on the gap can be easily computed by subtracting the Case B gap from Case A's gap. For example, in the case of Phoenix it would be $13.8 million, as that city moves from a positive difference of revenues exceeding expenditures in Case A by $10.9 million, to a negative difference under Case B of $2.9 million.

Finally, Column 5 of Table 7-2 gives the gap in dollar terms of Case C where lids exist at both the state and local level, on total property tax receipts in the latter instance. Again the net impact of the local property tax lid can be easily computed by subtracting the gap in Case C from that in Case B. In the case of Los Angeles, for example, Case C results in a negative gap of $101.0 million. Its total impact is to reduce the otherwise positive gap of $85.4 million by $23 million because of the fall in state aid growth (85.4 − 62.4) and by $163.4 million (62.4 −(−) 101.1) attributable to the property tax lid.

More useful in analysis of the relative impact on a city's fisc under the various cases is to view the gap as a percentage of total expenditures. Thus, Table 7-3 presents the results of Table 7-2, showing the gaps as percentages of the total expenditures projected for 1982. The cities with largest negative gaps as a percentage of expenditures are Cleveland (18%), Honolulu (18%), San Antonio (13%), and Fort Worth (12%).[10] The cities in Case A with the largest excess of rev-

Table 7-2. Total General Expenditures, Revenues, and Financing Gaps as Projected for 1982 for 45 Largest Cities (*$ millions*).

City	General Expenditures	General Revenue	Size of Gap		
			Case A	Case B	Case C
Phoenix	397.0	407.9	10.9	(2.9)	(31.7)
Long Beach	261.0	247.5	(13.5)	(17.6)	(33.9)
Los Angeles	1,699.8	1,825.4	85.4	62.4	(101.0)
Oakland	264.0	243.7	(20.3)	(23.7)	(36.3)
San Diego	336.7	422.7	86.0	79.1	42.2
San Francisco	1,161.2	1,163.2	2.0	(65.2)	(145.6)
San Jose	347.9	336.6	(11.3)	(16.2)	(50.6)
Denver	547.9	588.8	40.9	22.0	(12.6)
Jacksonville	437.4	435.2	(2.2)	(35.6)	(87.3)
Miami	197.3	210.1	12.8	12.8	(17.5)
Atlanta	322.4	380.6	58.2	44.0	22.8
Honolulu	544.8	457.6	(96.9)	(96.9)	(223.3)
Chicago	1,803.4	1,745.3	(37.1)	(95.5)	(190.5)
Indianapolis	531.2	571.2	40.0	(13.4)	(109.7)
Louisville	242.2	236.4	(5.8)	(7.3)	(13.3)
New Orleans	361.2	378.1	16.9	14.5	(2.8)
Baltimore	1,632.5	1,720.3	87.8	(140.6)	(212.6)
Boston	1,162.9	1,065.7	(97.2)	(97.2)	(235.8)
Detroit	1,186.6	1,357.6	171.0	100.5	53.6
Minneapolis	308.2	273.2	(35.0)	(57.6)	(73.8)
Kansas City	363.8	384.1	20.3	16.7	0.4
St. Louis	413.5	426.8	13.3	4.2	(3.0)
Omaha	179.4	181.6	2.2	(6.7)	(30.3)
Newark	423.9	607.9	184.0	88.8	61.1
Buffalo	532.9	509.2	(23.7)	(72.8)	(96.0)
New York	19,502.0	22,535.0	3,033.0	1,654.8	32.6
Cincinnati	675.0	689.7	14.7	(35.0)	(43.3)
Cleveland	462.0	378.6	(83.6)	(84.2)	(92.9)
Columbus	254.8	277.3	22.5	22.5	15.1
Toledo	215.6	202.8	(12.8)	(12.8)	(17.7)
Oklahoma City	232.8	209.2	(23.6)	(25.1)	(42.5)
Tulsa	200.6	178.1	(22.5)	(25.5)	(35.1)
Portland	205.5	232.7	27.2	25.6	(7.0)
Philadelphia	1,739.7	1,893.7	154.0	84.0	23.4
Pittsburgh	233.0	254.4	21.4	10.1	.8
Memphis	530.3	485.7	(44.5)	(49.2)	(88.5)

Table 7-2. continued

City	General Expenditures	General Revenue	Size of Gap		
			Case A	Case B	Case C
Nashville–Davidson	482.6	468.9	(14.0)	(14.0)	(82.3)
Dallas	389.9	421.8	31.9	30.4	(30.5)
El Paso	114.0	143.4	29.4	29.4	13.1
Fort Worth	173.8	153.0	(20.8)	(23.1)	(40.5)
Houston	639.5	712.1	72.6	67.9	(54.0)
San Antonio	300.6	262.2	(38.4)	(40.9)	(72.6)
Norfolk	317.2	347.8	30.6	(.9)	(20.5)
Seattle	356.6	372.4	15.8	12.8	(.2)
Milwaukee	372.4	386.8	14.4	14.4	12.9

enues over expenditures are Newark (43% of total expenditures), El Paso (26%), San Diego (26%), and Atlanta (18%).

The cities with projected positive gaps may do the following: increase expenditures, reduce current revenues, decrease outstanding debt, or build up financial assets.

A negative gap, which indicates that total projected expenditures will exceed total current revenues, leaves cities the options to reduce expenditure, increase the yield of the current revenue system, increase outstanding debt, or draw down financial assets.

For the forty-five cities, the Case A scenario results in twenty-eight having positive gaps (revenues greater than expenditures) and seventeen having negative gaps. Reference to Table 7-4 shows that this result would be a favorable result for the cities as a group compared to historical performance. In fiscal year 1967, thirty-two cities had negative gaps; five years later, the number had reduced to twenty-seven and, by 1977, only twenty-three experienced negative gaps. Thus the baseline projection embodied in Case A shows a continuation of the positive trend.[11]

The Case B scenario moves an additional five cities into the negative gap category, creating a total of twenty-four cities with negative gaps. Relative major declines are experience by Oakland (total revenues drop by 17% of expenditures), Baltimore (16%), Newark (22%), Indianapolis (10%), and Norfolk (10%).

Table 7-3. Financing Gaps for 1982 as a Percentage of Projected Expenditures.

City	Case A	Case B	Case C
Phoenix	2.7	(.7)	(7.9)
Long Beach	(5.2)	(6.7)	(13.0)
Los Angeles	5.0	3.6	(5.9)
Oakland	7.7	(9.0)	(13.7)
San Diego	25.5	23.5	12.5
San Francisco	0.0	(5.6)	(12.5)
San Jose	(3.2)	(4.7)	(14.5)
Denver	7.5	4.0	(2.3)
Jacksonville	(0.1)	(8.1)	(20.0)
Miami	6.5	6.5	(8.9)
Atlanta	18.1	13.6	7.1
Honolulu	(17.8)	(17.8)	(40.2)
Chicago	(2.1)	(5.3)	(10.6)
Indianapolis	7.5	(2.5)	(20.6)
Louisville	(2.4)	(3.0)	(5.5)
New Orleans	4.7	4.0	(0.1)
Baltimore	5.4	(8.6)	(13.0)
Boston	(8.4)	(8.4)	(20.3)
Detroit	14.4	8.5	4.5
Minneapolis	(11.4)	(16.5)	(23.9)
Kansas City	5.6	4.6	0.0
St. Louis	3.2	0.1	(0.1)
Omaha	1.2	(3.7)	(16.9)
Newark	43.4	20.9	14.4
Buffalo	(4.4)	(13.7)	(18.0)
New York	15.5	8.5	0.0
Cincinnati	2.2	(5.2)	(6.4)
Cleveland	(18.1)	(18.2)	(20.1)
Columbus	8.8	8.8	6.3
Toledo	(5.9)	(5.9)	(8.2)
Oklahoma City	(10.1)	(10.8)	(18.3)
Tulsa	(11.2)	(12.7)	(17.5)
Portland	13.2	12.5	(3.4)
Philadelphia	8.9	4.8	1.3
Pittsburgh	9.2	4.3	0.0
Memphis	(8.4)	(9.2)	(16.7)
Nashville-Davidson	(2.9)	(2.9)	(17.0)
Dallas	8.2	7.7	(8.9)

Table 7-3. continued

City	Case A	Case B	Case C
El Paso	25.7	25.7	11.5
Fort Worth	(12.0)	(13.3)	(23.3)
Houston	11.4	10.6	(8.4)
San Antonio	(12.8)	(13.6)	(24.1)
Norfolk	9.6	0.0	(6.5)
Seattle	4.4	3.6	0.1
Milwaukee	3.9	3.9	(3.5)
Negative gap	17	24	34
Positive gap	28	21	11

Case C, with both a slowdown in state aid and a property tax cap, moves thirty-four of the forty-five cities into a negative gap situation.

Financing the Gap on the Capital Account

To refine the foregoing analysis one must consider what is occurring on the cities' capital accounts in terms of borrowing, the retirement of debt, and possible changes in asset holdings. To the extent that a city is borrowing more than it needs to meet current retirements of debt, this net borrowing is adding to the sources available to finance that shortfalls between expenditures and available current revenues.

In this exercise, we are dealing with intermediate to longer term concepts of financing gaps (taking 1982 as a typical even though specific year). Thus, two important simplifying assumptions are made regarding the closing of the financing gap:

1. The stock of financial assets is not a significant user or supplier of funds for any of the cities.
2. Net changes in short-term borrowing are not a significant source or use of funds.[12]

Thus, we will look only at changes in the general long-term debt accounts. To project the funds available from borrowing in 1982,

Table 7-4. Historic Financing Gaps for 1967, 1972, and 1977 as a Percentage of Projected Expenditures.

City	1967	1972	1977
Phoenix	-3.4	-12.0	-6.9
Long Beach	14.3	3.8	-11.0
Los Angeles	-4.2	-9.5	1.7
Oakland	2.6	.4	5.8
San Diego	-15.0	-7.9	10.5
San Francisco	6.7	2.8	1.2
San Jose	2.0	1.1	1.8
Denver	-2.7	2.5	-2.1
Jacksonville	-33.8	-25.2	-6.5
Miami	.1	-6.7	-16.8
Atlanta	-15.3	-17.4	-3.9
Honolulu	4.6	6.3	-7.9
Chicago	-3.1	-12.0	-1.5
Indianapolis	-13.9	-7.4	-.1
Louisville	14.6	12.0	1.6
New Orleans	-12.5	5.5	1.3
Baltimore	3.1	-6.5	-4.1
Boston	-14.4	-8.3	5.8
Detroit	-10.4	-.0	9.3
Minneapolis	-11.5	-15.5	-16.5
Kansas City	-6.2	-21.1	5.0
St. Louis	-3.5	-.5	3.0
Omaha	-1.8	1.6	3.2
Newark	-14.0	-2.1	9.6
Buffalo	-1.7	-3.2	10.1
New York	2.6	-8.3	6.2
Cincinnati	.8	5.3	2.5
Cleveland	5.5	-.8	-10.2
Columbus	-31.6	3.9	-3.4
Toledo	-7.1	.4	-11.9
Oklahoma City	-1.5	-19.2	6.2
Tulsa	-22.2	.4	-3.5
Portland, Oregon	-12.5	11.8	2.3
Philadelphia	2.8	-7.7	.8
Pittsburgh	-4.2	17.1	-6.2
Memphis	-13.9	-18.6	-4.5
Nashville-Davidson	-21.7	4.8	-10.6
Dallas	-11.6	-14.2	3.2

Table 7-4. continued

City	1967	1972	1977
El Paso	-11.3	-4.0	5.6
Fort Worth	-9.2	-37.6	-5.3
Houston	-19.5	-3.1	-1.1
San Antonio	-14.2	24.3	-15.7
Norfolk	-4.8	-9.4	-.7
Seattle	.4	-15.1	5.6
Milwaukee	-.4	2.8	-1.7
Negative gap	32	27	23
Positive gap	13	18	22

one must assume a target level of borrowing to conform with what might be reasonable expected (and accepted) by the credit market. This volume of borrowing can then be compared to the borrowing that would be needed to cover the financing gap and to meet bond retirements.

To perform this part of the analysis a target level of outstanding debt for 1982 is specified and then the average annual *net* borrowing allowable each year to move from the level of outstanding debt in long-term 1977 to the target level of 1982 is calculated.[13] If the target annual level of borrowing is adequate to close the gap, there would appear to be less of a problem. By the same token, if the gap is positive (revenues exceed expenditures), we can infer the city has fewer borrowing needs. Or, conversely, it has an opportunity to reduce current revenues, increase expenditures, or build up its financial asset holdings.

As a baseline case, it is assumed that the cities attempt to keep the level of real long-term debt per capita at the same level as in 1977. This means that the target level of indebtedness in current dollar terms will grow only to reflect population changes and price levels, a posited behavior pattern that is consistent with the expenditure assumptions made here.

Table 7-5 displays in the first column the amount of annual *net* borrowing consistent with meeting the 1982 target level of outstanding debt, stated as a percentage of city expenditures in that year.

Table 7-5. Budget Financing Gap after Adjustment for Target Net Borrowing as a Percentage of Projected Total General Expenditures in 1982.

City	Target Borrowing as a Percentage of Total Expenditures	Adjusted Gap Case A	Case B	Case C
Phoenix	7.0	9.7	6.7	-0.9
Long Beach	4.3	-0.9	-2.4	-8.7
Los Angeles	3.5	8.5	-.1	-2.4
Oakland	4.7	12.4	-4.3	-9.0
San Diego	4.2	29.6	27.4	16.7
San Francisco	3.3	3.3	-2.3	-9.2
San Jose	5.4	2.2	.7	-9.1
Denver	4.3	12.8	8.3	1.7
Jacksonville	9.5	9.4	1.4	-11.5
Miami	6.6	13.1	13.1	-2.4
Atlanta	13.0	31.1	26.6	20.1
Honolulu	5.3	-12.2	-12.2	-34.9
Chicago	4.1	2.0	-1.2	-6.5
Indianapolis	7.7	15.2	5.2	-12.9
Louisville	5.0	3.6	2.0	-.5
New Orleans	6.3	11.0	10.3	6.2
Baltimore	2.2	7.6	-6.4	-11.8
Boston	3.2	-5.2	-5.2	-17.1
Detroit	3.0	17.4	11.5	7.5
Minneapolis	4.0	-7.4	-12.5	-19.9
Kansas City	7.5	13.1	12.1	7.5
St. Louis	16.7	19.9	16.8	16.6
Omaha	7.3	8.5	3.6	-9.6
Newark	2.7	46.1	23.6	17.1
Buffalo	2.4	-2.0	-11.3	-15.6
New York	5.0	20.5	13.5	5.0
Cincinnati	2.1	4.3	-3.1	-4.3
Cleveland	3.4	-14.7	-14.0	-16.7
Columbus	6.3	15.1	14.7	12.6
Toledo	3.1	-2.8	-3.2	-4.9
Oklahoma City	12.8	2.7	2.0	-5.5
Tulsa	11.7	-0.5	-1.0	-5.8
Portland	1.5	14.7	14.0	-1.9
Philadelphia	5.5	14.4	10.3	6.8
Pittsburgh	3.1	12.3	7.4	3.1

Table 7-5. continued

City	Target Borrowing as a Percentage of Total Expenditures	Adjusted Gap		
		Case A	Case B	Case C
Memphis	7.0	-1.4	-2.2	-9.7
Nashville-Davidson	4.1	1.2	1.2	-12.9
Dallas	11.2	19.4	18.9	2.3
El Paso	4.1	29.8	29.8	15.6
Fort Worth	8.0	-4.0	-5.3	-15.3
Houston	9.9	21.3	20.5	1.5
San Antonio	5.6	-7.2	-8.0	-18.5
Norfolk	5.5	14.4	5.5	-1.0
Seattle	3.3	7.7	6.9	3.3
Milwaukee	4.4	8.3	8.3	.9
Negative Gaps	. . .	11	17	28
Positive Gaps	. . .	34	28	17

This represents an additional source of funds from the capital account and it can be used to reduce the size of a negative gross gap or, of course, to increase the size of positive gaps. Columns 2, 3, and 4 show the financing gaps for Cases A, B, and C after having been adjusted for the additional sources available from borrowing, also expressed as a percentage of 1982 expenditures.

Taking into consideration the use of borrowed funds reduces the number of negative financing gaps in Case A from 17 to only 11. In Case B, the negative gaps drop from 23 to 17.

Case C, assuming the cap on real per capita state aid and the imposition of a restrictive property tax lid, continues to generate many more negative gaps, even after adjustment for net borrowing possibilities. There are twenty-eight negative gaps. However, many of the remaining negative gaps are relatively small (eight are less than 5 percent of total 1982 expenditures).

The preceding analysis provides us with insights into the use of borrowing in bringing balance between total sources and uses of funds. But it is important to keep in mind some of the simplifications that have been made. First, units that *already* had large per capita amounts of debt outstanding are implicitly assumed to be in a better position to use borrowed funds to close the gross gap. This is because their target debt capacity will grow more in absolute terms than units that had a relatively small debt outstanding in 1977. This, in turn, derives from the assumption that cities will be inclined to keep real debt per capita constant.[14] Second, units that have much debt outstanding (and that will have the greatest growth in net borrowing as a funds source under our two assumptions) have two potentially major drawbacks in calling upon future net new borrowings as a source of funds:

1. High debt outstanding implies high retirement of debt in the future. These are a fixed claim that in the first instance drain cash from current revenues. A credit crisis might confound a city's ability to borrow enough even to cover retirements—not to mention covering the current financing gap.

2. As noted, long-term borrowing must usually be coupled with capital outlays to be financed. Even though we consider the funds under the budget constraint as largely fungible among capital and current uses, there is an upper bound of gross long-term borrowing that is set by the desired or feasible level of capital expenditures to be financed by that source.

Gap Financing Options

A final refinement is to examine in what ways cities with negative financing gaps might bring the sources and uses into balance in 1982. Here, we focus only on Case C, the double whammy case. Table 7–6 lists those ten cities that continued to experience negative financing gaps of greater than 10 percent even after adjustment for funds from a level of net borrowing consistent with the previously discussed assumptions. The columns of that table give various alternatives of how the gap might be closed. Column 1 gives the dollar size of the adjusted gap. Column 2 shows the reduction required in total expenditures to bring about a balance between receipts and outlays. Correspondingly, since the property tax is inflexible, Column 3 gives the percentage by which own revenues other than the property tax would have to be increased to cover the gap. Column 4 illustrates by

Table 7-6. Dollar Amounts of Large Adjusted Gaps and Percentage Change in Selected Financial Items Needed to Close Gaps in 1982, Based on Case C Projection.

City	(1) Adjusted Financing Gap, $ Millions	(2) Reduction in Total Spending, %	(3) Increase in Nonproperty Revenue, %	(4) Increase in Gross Borrowing, %
Jacksonville	$50.3	-11.5	28	137
Honolulu	$190.1	-34.9	164	386
Baltimore	$192.6	-11.8	70	269
Boston	$198.7	-17.1	161	257
Minneapolis	$36.7	-19.9	70	132
Buffalo	$83.1	-15.6	178	285
Cleveland	$77.2	-16.7	46	204
Nashville–Davidson	$62.3	-12.9	38	164
Fort Worth	$26.6	-15.3	39	98
San Antonio	$55.6	-18.5	54	181

what percentage gross borrowing would need to be increased consistent with the net borrowing needed to close the gap.

Focusing on the cut in expenditures, it is important to bear in mind the particular relation between capital outlays and borrowing. If capital outlays were to be cut drastically, it would be difficult to borrow "against" them for purposes of closing the total budget gap. It should be remembered that the gap shown in Table 7-6 has already been reduced, assuming the addition of net new borrowing consistent with the target debt outstanding assumption. Such borrowing must be of sufficient volume to offset retirement payments and to contribute to closing the total gap and must also be directed toward nominally paying for real capital goods. This puts a bottom limit on capital spending, at least for planning purposes, equal to retirement and the net increase in debt. Such a limit is flexible through time; but over any sustained period of time, it would be difficult to borrow more than was planned to be spent on capital items (also, it would most likely be illegal). However, such behavior might provide some interim relief during an adjustment period.

Table 7-6 illustrates the large percentage increases needed in non-property-tax current revenues as compared to reductions in expenditures. This results from the fact that many cities are both fairly highly "levered" in terms of current receipts flowing from intergovernmental payments aid and reliance on the property tax. The trade-offs reflect the different fiscal structures of the cities. For example, both Fort Worth and Buffalo face adjusted negative gaps equal to about 15 percent of their projected 1982 expenditures. But for Buffalo, the options are a 178 percent increase in non-property-tax revenues or a 285 percent increase in annual borrowing, as opposed to 39 percent and 98 percent, respectively, in the case of Fort Worth.

The increase in annual borrowing levels varies greatly in magnitude, depending on the size of the gap and the traditional dependency of debt financing. Of course, the percentage increases in net borrowing over the target level (not shown) would be of much greater percentage magnitudes and typically about twice as great. Increases of this size need not be overly serious in any given year. But neither should they persist over a period of time.

The feasibility and costliness of financing the gap by borrowing will depend on city's existing debt load and creditworthiness (typically, as embodied in its credit rating). In the latter regard, the ten cities do not start on an equal footing. As rated by Moody's and in ascending order of credit quality, Cleveland (in default) carries a very low bond rating (Caa) and Boston and Buffalo are low rated (Baa); Baltimore and Jacksonville are rated A; Honolulu, Nashville–Davidson, Fort Worth, San Antonio are rated Aa; and only Minneapolis carries the highest rating of Aaa.

More sophisticated analysis would require looking at the adjustments in terms of the underlying economic conditions of the cities and, in particular, the burden of resulting revenues and debt changes in relationship to personal income (see Petersen and Rafuse 1979).

It should be noted that the assumptions used regarding the growth in expenditures and debt mean that, for almost all the cities, own revenues and debt as a percentage of personal income would decline between 1977 and 1982. For cities with small gaps to close and projected strong growth in personal income, merely keeping the debt or revenues at approximately the same percentage of personal income as in 1977 would help close the gap. But, as has been noted, severe constraints on local revenue sources by type—such as the property tax—can greatly abbreviate the list of options left to city revenue collectors.

CONCLUSION

The foregoing analysis has demonstrated a method for examining the impacts of three types of fiscal limitations in city finances: a cap on total local property tax levies, a cap on real per capita state aid, and a freeze on real per capita outlays per capita. The impacts of these constraints on overall budget balance were examined in a model of city finances, employing explicit assumptions about economic and population trends through 1982. Under the assumed conditions, constraining expenditures in real per capita terms (while leaving the revenue systems unmolested) led to a preponderance of positive (budget surplus) projections and a general improvement of city fiscal condition. Institution of a freeze on real state aid to cities led to a larger number of negative gaps, but still not a large number by historical standards. However, the imposition of a cap on property tax receipts had generally strong impacts, especially when combined with the slowdown in state assistance, leading to negative financing gaps in three-quarters of the cities (despite the latter holding their outlays to constant levels in real per capita terms).

Large negative gaps—where expenditures exceed revenues—were analyzed to see by what adjustments these gaps might be closed. Net long-term borrowing proved capable of reducing the negative gaps, using fairly conservative assumptions about growth in outstanding debt. In those cases where large gaps might continue, their closure by' increasing local non–property tax revenues and greater long-term borrowing were examined. Of the ten cities with the largest projected gaps, Honolulu (because of the sheer size of the gap) and Boston, Buffalo, and Cleveland (because of their poor credit ratings) appear to face the largest adjustment problems under the assumed conditions.

APPENDIX: PROJECTION METHODS

This appendix provides a summary description of the methods used to develop the projections of the finances of the forty-five major cities. This appendix and much of the methodological discussion is drawn substantially from the 1979 paper by myself and Robert W. Rafuse.

General Expenditures

Twenty-five of the cities are projected to realize increasing populations between 1977 and 1982. It is assumed that total, per capita general expenditures in these cities in 1982 will be the same as in 1977 in real terms. The projections of total general expenditures in current dollars, therefore, are derived by multiplying 1977 real, per capita outlays by our estimates of population in 1982 and inflating to current dollars using a projection of the implicit price deflator for state and local government purchases of goods and services.

Twenty of the cities in the sample are projected to experience declining populations during the 1977–82 period. In those cases, *total* general expenditures at 1972 prices will be the same in these cities in 1982 as they were in 1977. The projections adjust the 1977 data to 1982 prices using an estimate of the implicit price deflator mentioned previously.

Capital outlays in all forty-five cities are assumed to account for the same percentage of total general expenditures in 1982 as they did on average in 1967, 1972, and 1977.

City Retirement Fund Contributions

Cities may finance their public employee retirement systems in a variety of ways. Unfortunately, how they choose to do so affects the general expenditure levels as reported by the U.S. Bureau of the Census. Payments made by cities into their own retirement system are not included in the census definition of general expenditures, but rather are treated as a form of intragovernmental transactions. Contributions paid into funds not administered by the city, however, such as a state-administered fund, are treated as expenditures. The census treatment is therefore asymmetrical since such contributions, no matter what the level of administration, represent a drain on city resources and the funds held by city-administered plans are restricted either in the legal or practical sense to the payment of benefits to retirees and are not available for their purposes. In recognition of this fact, it is therefore necessary to treat contributions to cities' own retirement systems (which fortunately are shown as a separate line item) as an expenditure and to add them to the reported general government expenditure figure. In this way, comparability can be achieved among the various cities, irrespective of their particular pension financing techniques.

Utility Finances

In addition to the general government activities, cities may also carry on a variety of utility enterprise activities. Generally these activities, while part of a cities' financial structure, are viewed as autonomous and largely self-sustaining, their being supported by user charges and fees that are restricted to that purpose. However, city-owned utilities can as a practical matter be either the recipients or sources of subsidies from or to the cities' general fund. These subsidies can either be direct, such as an explicit appropriation to cover a utility loss, or indirect, such as the utility absorbing more than its fair share of certain city costs when it receives services from the city.

Differences in accounting practices make impractical adjustments for the claims or contributions of utilities in this exercise. The omission of the interaction between the utility and city general government finances, however, is not too consequential in most cases.[15]

Implicit Price Deflator

The implicit price deflator for state and local government purchases of goods and services in 1982 used in this study is estimated to grow at the same rate as the GNP deflator. In 1978, the state-local deflator was 160.4 (1972 = 100) and the GNP deflator was 152.09. It is assumed that both deflators will rise at 7.9 percent per year through 1982. Thus the state–local deflator used in this study is 214.8 for 1982.

Population

The projections of the populations of the forty-five cities are based upon the historical trend in each city. The 1982 populations of forty of the cities are derived from the trend implicit in the data for 1960, 1970, 1972, 1973, 1975, 1976, and interpolated/extrapolated estimates for 1967, 1972, and 1977. In five cases (New Orleans, Portland, Memphis, Nashville–Davidson, and Dallas) the 1982 projection is based on the observed rate of increase between 1973 and 1976.

Personal Income

Estimates of national per capita income in 1982 are calculated using a projection of the total population of the United States in that year (226,387,000). This projection is derived from the Census-II series, assuming that the rate of growth shown in published data for 1980-85 will be that experienced during the 1980-82 period.

Estimates of per capita personal income in each of the forty-five cities are developed on the basis of regressions of city and U.S. data for 1959, 1969, 1972, 1974, and 1975. The city data are on a Census Bureau money income basis, but it is not believed that the differences between this and the BEA concept present only serious problems.

Total personal (or money) income in each of the cities is calculated by multiplying the per capita estimates by actual and projected city populations in each of the relevant years.

City Own Revenues

The revenues of each city from its own sources are projected separately by major source using a priori estimates of the income elasticity of each source. These elasticities refer to the yield responsiveness to changes in income on the assumption that tax rates and other characteristics of each source remain constant. Thus the revenue projections assume that no discretionary actions are taken by the cities to increase the yields of their revenue sources as they actually existed in 1977.

In fact, of course, nearly all—if not all—of the cities increased rates, changed bases, and adopted new sources between 1967 and 1977. These actions have resulted in rates of increase in actual yields of the major revenue sources that imply "gross" income elasticities that are considerably higher than the constant-structure elasticities used in the projections. The actual elasticities used in the projections appear in the first column of Table A-1, the gross elasticities implicit in the actual record, 1967-77, appear in the second column (weighted by actual yield in 1977).

For the property tax, the low elasticity (0.7) was used for those that were declining in population (annual rate of population loss, −0.05 percent or more); the middle elasticity (1.0) was used for cit-

Table 7-A1. Income Elasticities of the 45 Major Cities, 1967-77.

	Projected	Gross
Property tax	0.7, 1.0, 1.2	1.13 (1.01[a])
General sales and gross receipts	1.1	1.36 (1.34[a])
Income taxes	1.5	2.12[b] (1.46[c])
Current charges	0.9	1.69 (1.61[a])
All other	0.8	1.68 (1.56[a])

a. Excluding New York City.

b. Weighted average, 1967–77 elasticity.

c. Weighted average, calculated using lowest elasticity for each city for 1967-72 and 1972-77, but omitting Pittsburgh, which appears to have cut its rate drastically during period.

ies with stable population (between +0.05 and −0.05 percent); and the high elasticity (1.2) was used for those cities with growing population (over +0.05 percent per year). The elasticities were based on unweighted averages of the elasticity of changes in fair market property value to changes in personal income.

State Aid

Nearly all of the cities realized large increases in aid from their respective state governments during the 1967–77 period. The projection methods used assumed, first, that the trend would continue and, second, that real state aid per capita would remain constant through 1982 at the level actually achieved in 1977. The 1977 data are adjusted for population changes and price increases as discussed previously for general expenditures.

Federal Aid

As is well known, federal grants-in-aid to cities have increased at extraordinary rates since the early 1970s. The projections developed in this study are based on a breakdown of federal grants to each of the cities in 1978 (federal fiscal year) prepared by the Advisory Commission on Intergovernmental Relations (general revenue sharing is the only break available in the annual census reports).

The projections assume that no payments will be made in 1982 under the LPW and ARFA programs. All other federal grants are assumed to remain constant at the real levels of total payments in federal fiscal year 1978. Current price projections are therefore derived by adjustment using the state and local implicit price deflator.

Payments from Localities

This is usually a small item that rounds out intergovernmental receipts. In all cases it is assumed to remain constant at 1977 levels in real per capita terms, only changing to reflect population and price level changes. Thus, this variable is sensitive to the price deflator assumptions related to GNP forecasts.

NOTES TO CHAPTER 7

1. For a recent summary of the tax and expenditure movement see Pascal 1979.

2. Research into city finances has blossomed since the near collapse of New York City in 1975. For a recent survey of efforts see Dearborn 1978.

3. General expenditures are those expenditures carried out by the city government for purposes defined by the U.S. Bureau of the Census as being of a general governmental nature. The principal exclusions are expenditures by what the Census Bureau defines as local utility functions, namely water supply, gas, electric, and transit utilities. The expenditure figures, and revenue figures, do not reflect expenditures, and revenues, made by independent entities such as counties, special districts, and school districts that are local government jurisdictions under separate political control. It is always necessary to remember when dealing with city government revenues and expenditures that only part of the supply of public services and, consequently, revenues are being counted, since many services are rendered and taxes and fees collected by jurisdictions other than the city in a given geographic area.

4. Between 1967 and 1977, the implicit price deflator for state and local purchase of goods and services rose from 72.5 and 148.5, an annual rate of inflation equal to 7.4 percent. As a result, real per capita expenditures and revenues (adjusted for the rate of price increase) rose at a rate of approximately 4.5 percent.

5. It is important to note, before passing on to other topics, that using 1977 as a terminal year misses the sizable growth in federal assistance that occurred in fiscal 1978. As is discussed later, preliminary estimates of the 1978 data indicate a dramatic reliance of cities—even during recent relatively good times—on federal aid.

6. Generally accepted accounting principles for governments do exist for cities but they are often not observed and they do not lend themselves to analysis of the financial condition of the government as an economic and financial entity.

7. Capital expenditures, for example, are frequently financed by borrowing and grant funds that are restricted to use for that purpose. On the other hand, borrowing may be undertaken for a variety of purposes other than to finance general capital outlays (for example, to acquire assets such as home mortgages, the city thereby acting as a financial intermediary). Furthermore, the current expenditure and debt figures may not reflect the building up on nonsecurity liabilities, such as unfunded pension fund obligations.

8. In addition, city contributions to the city-administered pension funds are also added to the current outlays as is explained in the appendix to this chapter. Possible transfers between the utility accounts and the general accounts have not been adjusted for, as is also explained in the appendix.

9. However, the emphasis on the property tax is not misplaced. Judging by the history and progress of the tax cutting movement, that tax presents particular problems in terms of public visibility and susceptibility to change. Other major local revenue sources — the sales and income taxes — appear either reasonably safe from public scorn or difficult to change at the local level in terms of rate and base. But for a majority of cities, it is the property tax that is locally assessed and collected, and where the rate is set as a final legislative act to balance revenues and expenditures. And clearly, it is the local property tax that has been the subject of greatest public ill-will. See Advisory Commission on Intergovernmental Relations 1979.

10. The absence of New York City from this list might be questioned. There are two major reasons for its absence: First, the method used presumes consistency in the financial data reported (a virtue not found in that city's reports during the early 1970s). Second, the use of 1977 as the terminal data point for projections did catch the city in a favorable fiscal trend (especially when coupled with large state aid payments and an assumption of constancy real per capita expenditures). Of course, things may go wrong. For an exhaustive treatment of recent progress future pitfalls, see Brecker and Horton 1979.

11. This result comports well with the earlier observation that there is less use of debt and the fact that a growing proportion of capital spending is being financed by federal assistance.

12. Short-term borrowing may act as an interim substitute for long-term borrowing (bond anticipation notes) and in that capacity changes in short-term debt are subsumed under our long-term debt discussions.

13. An alternative would be to calculate explicitly the gross borrowing required to meet retirements and to meet the target level of debt.

14. There is another problem with this interpretation. That is, governments that have borrowed sparingly in the past most likely have underutilized debt capacity that can be called upon to close a gross gap without ill effects on their creditworthiness. This possibility is further explored later.

15. The Bureau of the Census arbitrarily defines local utilities to include water, gas, electric, liquor stores, and urban transit, even though these utilities may not be enterprise activities in the strict sense of the word. On the question of the impact of their financial operations on general government finances see Clark 1977:65–69.

REFERENCES

Advisory Commission on Intergovernmental Relations. 1979. *Changing Public Attitudes on Governments and Taxes.* Washington, D.C.

Brecker, Charles, and Raymond Horton. 1979. *Setting Municipal Priorities, 1980.* New York: Universe Books.

Clark, Terry Nichols. 1977. "Financial Management of American Cities: Funds Flow Indicators." *Journal of Accounting Research* 15 (supplement): 65–69.

Mushkin, Selma. ed. 1979. *Proposition 13 and Its Consequences for Public Management.* Council for Social Research, Washington, D.C.

Pascal, Anthony, et al. 1979. *Fiscal Containment of Local and State Government.* RAND Corporation. September.

Petersen, John, and Robert Rafuse. 1979. "Big City Finances: Will Closing Budget Gaps Cause Financial Strain?" Unpublished paper.

Puryear, David, and John Ross. 1979. "Tax and Expenditure Limitations: The Fiscal Context." *National Tax Journal* (June, supplement): 23–35.

COMMENT — *Bruce Wallin*

In recent congressional debates on raising the debt ceiling limit, political scientist and Senator Daniel Patrick Moynihan suggested that economic projections be accepted "at the general intellectual level of witchcraft." John Petersen's chapter presents us with the interesting case where the witchcraft or methodology appears valid, but it produces what many would view as counterintuitive results.

As for the assumptions on which the projections are based, there are a few basically supportive observations. The "constant-service" basis for predicting local expenditure growth is very realistic. First, local expenditures from own funds have been declining as a percentage of GNP since 1975. Second, and reenforcing this trend, is the fact that more and more local authorities are having their fiscal discretion limited by state action; sixteen states took action to impose some kind of restraint on local property tax authorities in 1979, while six states imposed spending limitations on their local governmental units.

This emphasis on *local* restrictions is one of the paradoxes of the tax revolt, since a recent poll by the Advisory Commission on Intergovernmental Relations found for the first time local government to be the level of government providing citizens the most for their money. In any case, no great expansion of local expenditure responsibilities seems likely.

The three local revenue cases set out by Petersen also present a realistic range of options. All three cases assume federal aid to local governments to be held basically constant at a 1978 real level. Although some congressmen have warned that a drive to balance the federal budget could result in disproportionate cuts in federal aid to state and local governments (one of the largest discretionary items in the budget), a constant real level would appear neither too optimistic nor too pessimistic.

As for state aid to local governments, the assumption used in cases B and C predicting continued state aid at 1977 real levels seems the most reasonable. First, it is unlikely that state aid to local governments will grow as rapidly as it did from 1967 to 1972 (Case A), when it grew 92.9 percent. State expenditures overall were growing at a tremendous clip during this period, up 85.9 percent compared with a 47.1 percent increase in the economy, a growth that some analysts believe helped produce the tax revolt. Second, whereas some states have reacted to taxpayer unrest by more closely scrutinizing their expenditures, others have taken more concrete action by imposing spending limits on themselves, holding, for example, expenditure growth to the percentage increase in economic growth. Before Proposition 13, four such lids were in place; now there are sixteen. A slowdown in state expenditure growth suggests a stable budget composition, including the intergovernmental aid component.

It is worth noting two scenarios that could produce a shift in state aid to local governments. Pressure for fiscal restraint at the federal level combined with the relatively strong fiscal positions of most state governments has brought the state portion of general revenue sharing to the brink of extinction. Any slowdown in federal aid flows to state governments could conceivably result in a reduced ability of the state to support local activities. California's experience under Proposition 13 provides a different qualifier. That state's bailing out of local governments could lead one to predict increased state aid to local governments when tight taxing or spending lids are in place at the local level.[1]

In terms of improving the analysis, I would offer two suggestions. As for expenditures, disaggregating local budgets would be wise, in particular separating capital improvement and pension items from operating expenses and making separate projections in these areas. The condition of local capital stock and local pension programs varies widely among cities and could qualify the comparisons made in the paper. It could be expected, for example, that future capital improvement requirements of older cities in the Northeast and Midwest will be greater than those of the younger Sun Belt cities.

As for revenues, although the elasticities used are standard and quite acceptable, there is one suggestion that would not represent too difficult an undertaking. Given the importance of the property tax in local finance and the recently unstable relation between income and property values, it would be useful to adjust the revenue projections by looking at recent tax base growth, taking particular note of the added strength of those jurisdictions where the property tax base has expanded rapidly through new construction.

Some final observations are concerned with the somewhat counterintuitive findings of the study. The Case A projections produce some surprising results. Cities projected to have a surplus for 1982 include Newark (at the top of the list), Atlanta, New York, Detroit, Pittsburgh, and Philadelphia. My fear is that policy makers might use this evidence to argue that less aid to these cities is in order.

These results most likely are due to the relatively recent expenditure restraint exercised by these cities. Newark, for example, has been restricted by a state-imposed limit on spending; New York's restraint was a prerequisite for federal aid. A fairly standard means of achieving such restraint is through the deferral of capital improvements. Thus projecting capital expenditures at the same percentage of total expenditures that they were in 1967, 1972, and 1977 is probably unrealistic and produces "surpluses" that might not appear. A recent HUD-sponsored study, "Capital Stock Condition in Twenty-Eight Cities," found 90 percent of Newark's streets in fair or poor shape, and estimated that it would cost $200 million, or $600 per person, to repair them. The study also noted that 45 percent of Detroit's bridge mileage is substandard, and listed both Philadelphia and Pittsburgh as having serious water and sewage system problems.

Another favorite area of local expenditure deferral is that of pension obligations. An Urban Institute study warned that if the federal government tightened its funding standards for state and local governments to match those of the private sector, several cities would face large, immediate jumps in employer contributions, which would have to be funded from general tax revenues. Philadelphia, Pittsburgh, and Atlanta were mentioned as being among those in the worst pension fund situation. Again, I suggest that these expenditure items be disaggregated and separate projections made taking account of such evidence.

As a final qualifier, it should be noted that a recessionary economy has different impacts on different cities. Some localities have historically proven to be more cyclical in nature than others. Older cities, with heavy reliance on the durable goods industry, would suffer disproportionately should the economy slump. The projections under Case A do not, of course, account for this.

In sum, the comments here have sought to support the Petersen methodology, offer some ideas as to further analysis, and most importantly to underscore the fact that the projected fiscal positions of the cities studied should not be considered set in stone. The surpluses projected for 1982 for some cities could, for the reasons discussed here, prove illusory. Nonetheless the Petersen chapter provides extremely valuable insights into the differing effects of various limitations on local governments.

NOTE

1. This also means that the projections for California cities are less strong than others, since the model uses state aid in 1977.

8 THE IMPACT OF PROPOSITION 13 PROPERTY TAX REDUCTIONS
A Theoretical Note

Robert H. Edelstein

California's Proposition 13 reflects a substantial dissatisfaction with the levels of governmental expenditures, the types of public services being provided and their cost to taxpayers, and a strong desire for governmental fiscal reform. Without reviewing the particulars, it is fair to say that the proponents of Proposition 13 claim that reducing tax revenues and associated government expenditures would not necessarily reduce public services and that it might instead merely decrease the fat in government. They also claim, on the other hand, that property tax reductions through capitalization effects would tend to enhance real estate values, thereby augmenting the wealth and economic welfare of Californians. (See, for example, Church (1974) and Richman (1967)). The opponents counter that this analysis is politically naive because, if tax revenues were effectively reduced, expenditures and public services also would be curtailed and, through the capitalization effects, real estate values would be reduced. Furthermore, the opponents argue that governments facing reductions of property tax revenues would substitute alternative taxes and fees to regain lost sources of funds. In that case, Proposi-

The financial support for this research paper was provided by the Federal Home Loan Bank of San Francisco. The author happily acknowledges this fact; however, this does not imply that the Federal Home Loan Bank of San Francisco is either responsible for or agrees with the analysis and conclusions of this paper. The author assumes full responsibility for the contents of this paper.

tion 13 might create undesired and uncertain redistributional effects, depending upon who bears the fiscal burdens of new taxes and fees, without decreasing the overall fiscal yields to governments.

The objective of this chapter is to demonstrate analytically that, even if one were to grant the proponents of Proposition 13 their key assumptions, their conclusions are not inevitable and are likely to be untrue. The opponents' arguments similarly will be undercut by this reasoning. The overall impacts of Proposition 13 on property values and incidence of tax reductions are far from clear and are likely to require a deep understanding of general equilibrium economics. (See Aaron (1975) and Mieszkowski (1972)).

THE MODEL

To do the analysis it is necessary to abstract from the real world with a simplified economic model. Consider an area that is a closed economy, with fixed quantities of real estate (resources) R and fixed supply of labor (population).[1] One other factor input exists: K, the quantity of produced non-real estate capital. It is assumed that there exists a well-behaved aggregate production function[2] for real income Y:

$$Y = F(K, L, R) \quad . \tag{8-1}$$

With fixed L and R, there exists a stable equilibrium value for K corresponding to each tax rate on real estate, t.[3] Under our assumption of a closed economy, the level and rate of savings S depend upon the interest rate, which is a function of the marginal productivity of produced capital (F_K) and the income level Y.

$$S = S(F_K, Y) \quad . \tag{8-2}$$

Since this model has one good, consumption and non-real estate capital goods are identically priced at $1 per unit (the numeraire) and the price of real estate is set at P. It is assumed, also, that the wage rate paid labor is equal to its marginal product $W = F_L$. In the aggregate, total savings must be equal to the sum of the values of assets purchased with savings.

$$S(F_K, Y) = K + PR \quad . \tag{8-3}$$

In equilibrium, the after-tax rates of return on real estate and produced non-real estate capital must be equalized. Assuming non-real estate capital is not taxed, equilibrium implies the following equation:

$$F_K = \frac{(1-t)F_R}{P} \, . \tag{8-4}$$

Using (8-4) and (8-3), one can derive (8-5).

$$S(F_K, Y) - K - \frac{(1-t)F_R R}{F_K} = 0 \, . \tag{8-5}$$

Equation (8-5) is an equilibrium condition and implies that the supply of savings equals the purchases of capital assets.[4] Noting that the demand for non-real estate capital is equal to savings minus the value of real estate, then the excess demand for non-real estate capital in equilibrium must be zero. Also, this equilibrium is a function of the tax rate and the level of non-real estate capital because R and L are assumed to be fixed.

Finally, the stability condition for equilibrium is that the derivative of the excess demand for non-real estate capital, with respect to non-real estate capital, must be negative.

It is also the assumption of proponents of Proposition 13 that the public sector's activity is *not* adversely affected (or changed) by the reduction of property tax rates. Essentially, this argument means that the utility of households is unaffected by governmental expenditures activity before and after the tax rate change. Furthermore, for the assumed one-output-good economy, the possibility of tax effects on the composition of supply and demand is eliminated.

TAX EFFECTS ON THE OPTIMAL CAPITAL STOCK

A change in the tax rate t on real estate will engender an increase in the equilibrium capital stock for non-real estate capital. Total differentiation of Eq. (8-5) will yield (8-6).

$$\frac{dK}{dt} = \frac{-RF_R}{F_K\left(\dfrac{\partial E}{\partial K} - 1\right)} \, , \tag{8-6}$$

where

$$E = S(F_K, Y) - \frac{(1-t) F_R \cdot R}{F_K} \tag{8-7}$$

is the excess demand for non-real estate capital and $\partial E / \partial K < 1$ is the stability condition. Hence, $dK/dt \geq 0$. That is, a decrease in the property tax (real estate tax) will reduce the level of non-real estate capital.

As a result of the reduction in non-real estate capital, if real estate and labor inputs are given as fixed, real wages (F_L) are lowered, *gross* returns to real estate F_R are raised, with higher rates of return received by owners of non-real estate capital (F_R).

In essence, there will be an induced decrease in the size of the non-real estate capital stock. This induced change may create a shifting of *more than 100 percent* of the real estate tax; that is, the *net* (after tax) return to real estate may *fall* with the fall in the property tax rate.

$$\frac{d((1-t) F_R)}{dt} = -F_R + (1-t) F_{RK} \frac{dK}{dt} \quad . \tag{8-8}$$

Using Eqs. (8-7) and (8-8), the net return on real estate will be found to be

$$\frac{d((1-t) F_R)}{dt} = -F_R - \frac{(1-t) F_{RK} \cdot F_R \cdot R}{F_K \left(\frac{\partial E}{\partial K} - 1 \right)} \quad . \tag{8-9}$$

Equation (8-9) will be greater than zero if and only if condition (8-10) holds,

$$\frac{(1-t) F_{RK} \cdot R}{F_K} > \left(1 - \frac{\partial E}{\partial K} \right) \quad . \tag{8-10}$$

The left-hand side of condition (8-10) is the elasticity of the marginal product of non-real estate capital with respect to real estate multiplied by $(1-t)$. The smaller the value of the elasticity of substitution between non-real estate capital and real estate, the higher will be the value of the left-hand side of condition (8-10). The right-hand side of condition (8-10) is bounded by the open interval (0, 1).

Therefore, it is not clear a priori that in fact the *net* returns to real estate may rise as a result of real estate tax rate reductions; it seems plausible under likely circumstances that *net* returns to real estate *will fall*.

TAX EFFECTS ON THE PRICE OF REAL ESTATE

It should be noted that even if *net* real estate returns were to rise, however, the *value* of real estate may fall if the marginal product of non-real estate capital (F_K) falls proportionately more. In such a case, the current owners of real estate lose from the real estate tax reduction because they presumably are concerned with their real estate "wealth."

$$\frac{dP}{dt} = \frac{-F_R}{F_K} + (1-t) \frac{d\left(\frac{F_R}{F_K}\right)}{dK} \cdot \frac{dK}{dt} . \qquad (8\text{-}11)$$

If R is fixed, then

$$\frac{d\left(\frac{F_R}{F_K}\right)}{dK} = \frac{F_R}{K \cdot F_K \cdot \sigma} , \qquad (8\text{-}12)$$

where σ is the elasticity of substitution between real estate and non-real estate capital. Hence, $dP/dt > 0$ will be true if and only if

$$\frac{P \cdot R}{K \sigma} > \left(1 - \frac{\partial E}{\partial K}\right) . \qquad (8\text{-}13)$$

The inequality in condition (8-13) is likely to be true; therefore, a decrease in the property tax rate may very well decrease property values.

The conclusion that property values may fall seems to deny common logic. A decrease in the real estate property values at first glance implies that, for a given level of savings, more non-real estate accumulation would occur. With more non-real estate capital accumulation vis-à-vis the original tax rate situation, there would be a rise in the marginal product of real estate and a lower interest rate (that is, F_K would fall). This appears to yield a contradiction because it implies a rise in the price for real estate. However, this reasoning neglects the possibility that a lower price for real estate is consistent with less accumulation of non-real estate capital if the rate of overall savings decreases sufficiently with an increase in interest rates. That is, a sufficient decrease in savings can reduce the stock of non-real estate capital, even with a lower value for real estate.

CONCLUSION

The traditional view of tax incidence suggests that a reduction in real estate property tax rates will be shifted only by increasing the supply of real estate, for if the level of real estate is relatively fixed, the original static general equilibrium gross prices continue to persist in the economy. (Of course, a tax change may affect the net prices.) However, it is argued that, since the prices of all other goods and services are unchanged, real estate will reap the entire benefits of the tax reduction, which will result in increased property values because of tax capitalization effects. The error of this analysis is that it neglects that a tax reduction on one factor, even a relatively fixed factor, may affect the supply of other factors. Hence, the tax may have an impact upon general equilibrium valuations for the economy. This, in turn, may affect and shift the benefits of the tax reduction across factors.

APPENDIX

In the foregoing analysis it is assumed that the quantity of real estate inputs is fixed. In fact, though the total land inputs available for real estate activity may be considered ultimately fixed, nonland (capital-improvement) inputs for real estate may be variable. Hence, the production function may be written as Eq. (8-A1) instead of Eq. (8-1) in the text;

$$Y = F(K, L, R) , \qquad (8\text{-}A1)$$

where

$R = R(N, G)$, the subproduction function for real estate inputs;

$N =$ nonland (real estate capital) inputs;

$G =$ land inputs, considered fixed.

The foregoing analysis can be performed in a similar fashion; clearly, the new outcome will depend upon, among other things, the rate at which non-real estate capital K can be substituted for real estate capital inputs N.

The crucial differences in the argument in the text occur when dK/dt is derived. (Compare (8-A2) with (8-6)):

$$\frac{dK}{dt} = \frac{-\dfrac{\partial E}{\partial R} \cdot \dfrac{\partial R}{\partial N} \cdot \dfrac{dN}{dt} - \dfrac{F_R \cdot R}{F_K}}{\left(\dfrac{\partial E}{\partial K} - 1\right)} \ . \tag{8-A2}$$

Equation (8-A2) will be positive under the plausible conditions that the numerator is negative.

Corresponding to Eq. (8-10), the following equation examines the property value effect of the tax change:

$$\frac{dP}{dt} = \frac{-F_R}{F_K} + (1-t)\frac{d\left(\dfrac{F_R}{F_K}\right)}{dK} \cdot \frac{dK}{dt} \ . \tag{8-A3}$$

Because $dR \neq 0$, then

$$\frac{d\left(\dfrac{F_R}{F_K}\right)}{dK} = \frac{F_R(1-\eta)}{KF_K \sigma} \ , \tag{8-A4}$$

where $\eta = dR/dK \cdot K/R$, the cross elasticity of supply between real estate and non-real estate capital.

If one assumes that $\eta < 1$ and $dK/dt > 0$ (from 8-A2), then it follows from the arguments that $dP/dt > 0$ if and only if condition (8-A5) holds.

$$\frac{P \cdot R(1-\eta)}{K \cdot \sigma}\left[\frac{\partial E}{\partial R} \cdot \frac{\partial R}{\partial N} \cdot \frac{dN}{dt} \cdot \frac{1}{P \cdot R(1-t)} + 1\right] > \left(1 - \frac{\partial E}{\partial K}\right) \ . \tag{8-A5}$$

Condition (8-A5) is the analog to condition (8-13) and on a priori grounds seems probable. Thus, even if real estate is not fixed and capital accumulation can be substituted and allocated between real estate and non-real estate activities, given the nature of the production process, it still seems likely that a decrease in property tax rates may reduce property values.

NOTES TO CHAPTER 8

1. Fixing the amount of real estate R is an analytic convenience, that can be relaxed without affecting the thrust of the paper. See the appendix to this chapter. It is convenient to fix the level of population, employment, and so forth in order not to confuse the influences of demographic and socioeconomic changes on the outcome.

2. The production function is assumed to be quasi-concave; in particular it is assumed that $F_i > 0$, $F_{ii} < 0$, and $F_{ij} > 0$ for all i and $i \neq j$.

3. The tax rate for real estate is assumed to be proportional to its gross or net income. In essence, it is reasonably subsumed that the actual and assessed value of a real estate parcel is a function (a multiple) of gross or net income.

4. The model has a one-period framework; hence, the flows and stocks of savings are identical and must be equal to the value of the stock of real assets.

REFERENCES

Aaron, Henry J. 1975. *Who Pays the Property Tax: A New View.* Washington, D.C.: The Brookings Institute.

Church, Albert M. 1974. "Capitalization of the Effective Property Tax Rate on Single Family Residences." *National Tax Journal* 27 (March): 113-22.

Mieszkowski, Peter M. 1972. "The Property Tax: An Excise Tax or a Profits Tax?" *Journal of Public Economics* 1 (April): 73-96.

Richman, Raymond L. 1967. "The Incidence of Urban Real Estate Taxes under Conditions of Static and Dynamic Equilibrium." *Land Economics* 43 (May): 172-80.

9 INFLATION, PROPOSITION 13 FEVER, AND SUGGESTED RELIEF

George G. Kaufman

Researchers have been unable to identify a single cause for the Proposition 13 fever that originated in California and has threatened to spread throughout the United States. Rather, they have attributed it to a number of causes, including dissatisfaction with government, dissatisfaction with the public school system, and dissatisfaction with taxes (see, for example, Levy 1979, Levy and Zamold 1979, Citrin 1979, and Citrin and Levy in this volume). Indeed, the underlying reason appears to be dissatisfaction in general. It is my theme in this chapter that at least a good part of this dissatisfaction has solid economic grounding and may be attributed to the acceleration in the overall inflation rate in recent years. Proposition 13 fever has two symptoms: First, it attempts to reduce residential property taxes; this symptom may spread to encompass reductions in other state and local taxes and spending as well. Second, it has often resulted in an attempt to impose rent controls. If permitted to go untreated, these symptoms can do lasting damage to the economy, in general, and housing, in particular. The obvious solution is to treat the cause: inflation. But a quick slowing in the inflation rate is unlikely. As an alternative I will make recommendations on how the symptoms may be treated in ways that are likely to minimize the magnitude of the undesirable consequences.

The economic, political, and social damage sown by accelerating inflation has only recently become obvious to economists and policy

makers in the United States. The long delay in recognizing the harmful effects may be attributed to four reasons: 1) For the economy
as a whole, reductions in income occur only when inflation rates
become volatile and are smaller and less evident than those stemming
from unemployment. 2) There are both winners and losers, and it
takes longer for the harm to the losers to become visible both to
themselves and to others because the losses are likely to be relatively
small to each individual in comparison to the larger and more evident
gains of the winners. 3) Only after some incubation, during which
the harmful economic effects have been building to a critical magnitude, do they break out and spread to the social and political structure; and 4) until recently it was generally believed by economists
and lay persons alike that a little inflation was a good thing; it was
thought to stimulate the rate of growth and reduced unemployment.
Thus, people were not searching for any harms and tended to dismiss
them when they were identified. Not until the mid-1970s did the
harmful effects of the acceleration in the inflation rate that had com-
menced a decade earlier become generally recognized.

Indeed, until recently inflation was viewed both in theory and in
practice as not a totally undesirable state of affairs. Not only was
there almost complete and blind faith in the Phillips curve, but a
"little" inflation was actually recommended by reputable economists
to accelerate growth both in the United States and abroad. And best
of all, there were no disadvantages. True, hyperinflations of the Ger-
man and Chinese types were not recommended, but neither were
they considered a possibility for the United States. A search of the
textbooks of that day substantiates my recollections.

Unfortunately, time and events have shown this optimism to be
not only naive and incorrect, but downright dangerous. Except for
ever briefer periods, faster inflation did not result in lower unemployment. The Friedman hypothesis that faster inflation leads to
greater uncertainty and higher rates of unemployment appears to
have become more accurate. Nor, on average, did countries experiencing faster inflation experience faster growth. But worst of all,
inflation produced undesirable side effects on the economy. The
changes in the rate of inflation were not equally anticipated by
each and every decision-making unit. As a result, real income was
redistributed.

Preliminary evidence suggests that the redistribution was pretty
much arbitrary, cutting across income, social, age, racial, and other
groups. It affected units differently depending on their contract

cycle, willingness to engage in protracted negotiations, and so on. In a completely closed economy, the redistribution would be a zero sum game. The aggregate gains to the winners would equal the aggregate losses to the losers. But perceptions appear to differ from reality, in part, because prices on products consumers buy rise more frequently and visibly during the year than household income, so that annual salary increases are either catch-up or quickly dissipated, more units view themselves harmed than benefited. In addition, because the gains cannot be attributed to superior economic contribution, they are viewed as arbitrary and unequitable. Thus, inflation breeds discontent and frustration. To make matters worse, economy is not closed; in the 1970s the biggest winners were foreign oil producers. Domestic aggregate and average income was reduced, intensifying the hurt.

The discontent and frustration are demonstrated in a number of ways. Disillusionment sets in with the government or establishment that condones these "injustices." The units actually harmed or perceived to be harmed consider themselves to be victims. They become readily receptive to proposals that promise relief at the expense of apparent gainers, almost regardless of the consequences. This explains the contagious nature and extraordinary virility of Proposition 13 fever.

The inflation of recent years has particularly affected residential real estate, but in conflicting directions. On the one hand, residential housing prices have increased faster than consumer prices ever since World War II. Between 1953 and 1978, residential housing prices increased at an average annual rate of 7.0 percent, while consumer prices increased only 3.6 percent. Since 1969, both housing and consumer prices have accelerated to 10.2 and 6.5 percent, respectively. Equally important, since 1969, real estate has become the major consumer inflation hedge, replacing equities. Between 1953 and 1969, the return on residential housing increased at an average annual rate of 7 percent, while stocks increased 9.8 percent. Since 1968, the rates have been 10.2 and 4.9 percent, respectively (Ibbotson and Fall 1979:89). This has both encouraged additional households to purchase residential housing and made housing a more important and visible part of wealth portfolios. Thus, inflation has made winners out of most homeowners.

On the other hand, inflation has increased the immediate burden of the property tax, as measured by the ratio of tax to income, even faster than home values. This has occurred because inflation increases real estate and other asset prices immediately but income only slowly through time. Property taxes are the product of the assessment tax rate and the assessed value. If the tax rate is unchanged, increases in assessed values proportional to increases in market values would increase annual tax amounts proportionately. Thus, the ratio of tax payments to income increases. Through time, however, *ceteris paribus*, the tax payments remain fixed and income increases so that the burden will decline. If house values and income rise by the same percentage, the average long-run tax burden will be the same as before the price rise. This problem is similar to the familiar tilt problem with fixed- and variable-rate mortgages.[1] The increased burden effect is clearly evident from California. Despite reductions in the effective tax rates, the ratio of residential property taxes on single-family dwellings as a percentage of personal income increased from 2 percent in 1969–70 to 2.6 percent in 1978–79 (Oakland 1979). At the same time, the tax became viewed as less equitable as its proportion of total property tax revenues increased from 35 to 44 percent. This occurred both because residential real estate increased faster in value than commercial real estate and because reforms enacted to equalize assessment rates lowered the rates on commercial property (Oakland 1979:22). At the time, California was among the most heavily taxed states and relied greatly on taxes visible to the public (Oakland 1979: 21–22; Levy 1979; Levy and Zamold 1979).

The property tax has another characteristic that makes opposition to it particularly susceptible to inflation. It is a tax on nonliquid wealth that must be paid from either current income or liquid wealth. Thus, it is a more difficult tax to pay than other taxes, which are either on income when received or on spending, which already requires liquidity. Because the return on residential housing is in the form of implicit rental value and does not produce cash, to pay the property tax from the property requires that nonliquid wealth must be transformed into liquid wealth or cash. But it is difficult to sell off a house foot by foot or room by room! The cash must be obtained from an alternative source not associated with the real estate. The cash flow problem becomes more extreme in periods when property values and taxes increase faster than current income, the primary source of liquidity. Many homeowners become wealth rich but income poor. This is particularly true for the elderly, whose income and liquidity tend already to be significantly below their previous levels and who are reluctant or unable to consume wealth in the form of their life-long residence.

As a result, hostility is greater toward the property tax than other taxes. Surveys in California showed that residents considered the property tax the least fair tax. Surprisingly, social security and sales taxes were viewed the fairest (Citrin 1979). This is likely to reflect the relatively low amounts of these taxes and the liquidity available when they are paid. The resentment against the property tax is particularly unfortunate because in actuality it is economically a rather good tax. Contrary to public belief, recent evidence suggests that it is, at minimum, proportional if not progressive (Aaron 1975: 45–46; Browning and Johnson 1979). Moreover, the distribution of wealth is far less even than that of income. Property taxes also have weaker disincentive effects, if any, and do not reduce aggregate welfare. Property taxes are reasonably efficient to monitor and collect. Last, these taxes provide a relatively stable revenue base not subject to major cyclical instability.

Because of its desirability, the property tax should be rescued from Proposition 13 fever. Any solution must deal with the cash flow tilt problem. The obvious solution is a sharp slowing in the rate of inflation. In the absence of such manna from heaven, the tilt can be leveled and the cash burden eased by partially or totally deferring tax payments until the residence is liquified at sale or the owner's death.[2] Revenues temporarily lost to the tax-collecting governmental unit may be offset by the sale of tax-exempt bonds secured by the market value of the residences. The only risk would be that, in time, the amount of the tax deferral and interest thereon would exceed the market value of the residence. This can occur over long periods of time, particularly if the rate of inflation slows significantly. To minimize this risk, a "circuit breaker" could be installed in the deferment program to limit the deferred amount plus interest to no more than, say, 70 percent of the assessed value of the residence at the time the tax is first deferred or 95 percent of the current assessed value, whichever is lower. As further protection, deferments to the elderly could be total, and deferments to others would be only partial. The deferred amount could be equal to the excess in the annual increase in tax assessment above the increase in consumer prices. It is evident that a large number of other details of such a program would need to be worked out before it becomes operational, but the plan appears feasible and is operational for elderly homeowners in a few states.

Inflation has caused Proposition 13 fever among renters as well as among homeowners. Proposition 13 promised reductions in rent. The rent problem is analogous to the property tax and mortgage tilt problem (Poole 1972:356-57). Because rent is the return on housing, increased property values cause dollar amounts of rent to increase faster immediately than household income, increasing the rent burden sharply. In later years, the burden will be lower as income increases faster, other things equal. The sharp jumps in values of rental properties in recent years have brought forth sharp increases in rent in some areas and cries for rent controls by those affected.[3] Both Los Angeles and San Francisco have adopted rent control ordinances. The solution to the rent burden problem is to smooth out the burden through time. This may be achieved by tying rent increases to the consumer price index (nationally or locally, before or after inclusion of rent). This will shift the financing burden from the renter to the owner but will not affect the latter's overall return over the long run. Landlords may reasonably be assumed to be better able to obtain any necessary financing, say to cover higher mortgage payments, than are renters. A number of communities that have adopted rent control ordinances have indexed rent increases to the CPI, but less than proportionately. This reduces the overall rent burden on the tenant but also reduces the long-term return to the owner and is likely to reduce investment in rental property. To avoid Proposition 13 fever from forcing such long-term undesirable solutions, it would be the better part of wisdom for landlords voluntarily to index their rents to the CPI proportionately.

CONCLUSIONS

The theme of this chapter has been that accelerating inflation produces particular problems for residential real estate, the popular reaction to which is likely to be "solutions" that will create undesirable social and economic consequences in the longer term. I have suggested tentative and preliminary economically sounder solutions. To avoid undesirable reductions in property taxes, partial or complete tax deferrals could be granted homeowners. The temporary revenues lost thereby to the tax collecting municipality would be recouped through the sale of tax-exempt bonds. The bonds would be collateralized by the market value of the homes on which the property tax is deferred. To avoid undesirable controls on rents, landlords can voluntarily agree to fully index their rents to the CPI. This would smooth out the rent burden to tenants without reducing the long-term average return to rental property owners.

NOTES TO CHAPTER 9

1. For a good analysis of the mortgage tilt problem see Kearl 1979. An earlier description of this problem appears in Poole 1972.
2. Such programs are in operation on a limited basis in a number of states (Aaron 1975:77).
3. On the whole, rent has increased more slowly than either home ownership costs or all consumer prices. This reflects landlord policy. At times rental properties are sold and new mortgages are obtained at higher interest rates, rents are likely to be increased to cover the monthly mortgage costs. Thus, the mortgage tilt problem is "passed-through" to renters.

REFERENCES

Aaron, Henry J. 1975. *Who Pays the Property Tax?* Washington, D.C.: The Brookings Institution.

Browning, Edgar K., and William R. Johnson. 1979. *The Distribution of the Tax Burden.* Washington, D.C.: The American Enterprise Institute.

Citrin, Jack. 1979. "Do People Want Something for Nothing?" *National Tax Journal* 32, no. 2 (June).

Ibbotson, Roger G., and Carol L. Fall. 1979. "The United States Market Wealth Portfolio." *Journal of Portfolio Management* (Fall).

Kearl, J.R. 1979. "Inflation, Mortgages, and Housing." *Journal of Political Economy* (October).

Levy, Frank. 1979. "On Understanding Proposition 13." *Public Interest* (Summer).

Levy, Frank, and Paul Zamold. 1979. "The Preconditions of Proposition 13." Unpublished paper, The Urban Institute, January.

Oakland, William H. 1979. "Proposition 13 and Financial Markets." Federal Reserve Bank of San Francisco. *Economic Review* (Winter): 7–24.

Poole, William. 1972. "Housing Finance Under Inflationary Conditions." In Board of Governors of the Federal Reserve System, *Ways to Moderate Fluctuations in Housing Construction.* Washington, D.C., pp. 355–76.

INDEX

ABOUT THE EDITORS

Kenneth T. Rosen is Associate Professor of Economic Analysis and Policy, and Chairman, Center for Real Estate and Urban Economics at the University of California, Berkeley. Previously, he was a professor at Princeton and Research Associate at Harvard University. He earned his Ph.D. in Economics with a specialization in Housing Finance from MIT. Professor Rosen's policy work includes authorship of the Young Families Housing Act, which earmarked tax exempt savings accounts for first-time buyers. In addition, he has testified on housing finance before both the U.S. Senate and the California Legislature. Published articles which he has authored concern the topics of the mortgage credit gap, the use of passthrough securities, the asset and liability structure of savings and loan associations, the optimal use of FHLMC and FNMA, alternative mortgages, and the demand for housing. His most recent book is *Seasonal Cycles in the Housing Market: Patterns, Costs, and Policies.* Professor Rosen is also on the board of editors for the journals *Land Economics, Housing Finance Review*, and *Journal of Urban and Real Estate Economics.*

George G. Kaufman is a John F. Smith Jr. Professor of Economics and Finance at Loyola University of Chicago. Professor Kaufman received his B.A. from Oberlin College (1954), M.A. from the University of Michigan (1955), and Ph.D. in economics from the University of Iowa (1962). He was a research fellow, economist and senior economist at the Federal Reserve Bank of Chicago from 1959 to 1970. From 1970 to 1980, he was the John B. Rogers Professor of Banking and Finance and Director of the Center for Capital Market Research in the College of Business Administration at the University of Oregon. He has been a visiting professor at the University of Southern California (1970), Stanford University (1975–76), and the University of California at Berkeley (1979) and a visiting scholar at the Federal Reserve Bank of San Francisco (1976) and the Office of the Comptroller of the Currency (1978). Professor Kaufman also served as Deputy to the Assistant Secretary for Economic Policy of the U.S. Treasury in 1976.

Professor Kaufman's teaching and research interests are in financial economics, institutions, and markets, and he has published extensively in the *American Economic Review, Journal of Finance, Journal of Financial and Quantitative Research* and other professional journals. Professor Kaufman is the author of *Money, the Financial System and the Economy* (third edition, Houghton–Mifflin, 1981) and *The U.S. Financial System: Money, Markets, and Institutions* (Prentice–Hall, 1980). He served on the board of directors of the American Finance Association (1977–80) and is past president (1974–75) of the Western Finance Association.

LIST OF CONTRIBUTORS

Frederick Balderston, University of California at Berkeley, School of Business Administration.

Jack H. Beebe, Director of Market Studies, Federal Reserve Bank of San Francisco.

Jack Citrin, University of California at Berkeley, Department of Political Science.

Alan S. Costa, Economic Analyst, National Foreign Assessment Center, Washington, D.C.

Robert Edelstein, University of Pennsylania, Wharton School.

Philip Fischer, State University of New York at Albany, School of Business.

Ronald Forbes, State University of New York at Albany, School of Business.

Alan Frankle, University of Tulsa, College of Business Administration.

I. Michael Heyman, Chancellor, University of California at Berkeley.

George G. Kaufman, Loyola University of Chicago, Department of Economics and Finance.

Frank Levy, Senior Research Associate, The Urban Institute.

William H. Oakland, Tulane University, Department of Economics.

John E. Petersen, Director, Government Finance Research Center, Municipal Finance Officers Association, Washington, D.C.

Kenneth T. Rosen, University of California at Berkeley, School of Business Administration.

Wallace Smith, University of California at Berkeley, School of Business Administration.

James N. Tattersall, University of Oregon, Department of Economics.

Ann R. Thomas, The University of Michigan, School of Business Administration.

Bruce Wallin, University of Wisconsin–Madison, Department of Political Science and Center for Public Policy and Administration, Advisory Committee on Intergovernmental Relations, Washington, D.C.

DATE DUE

		WITHDRAWN	

HIGHSMITH 45-102   PRINTED IN U.S.A.